STUDENTS LEAD THE LIBRARY:

The Importance of Student
Contributions to the Academic Library

Edited by
Sara Arnold-Garza
and Carissa Tomlinson

Association of College and Research Libraries
A division of the American Library Association
Chicago, Illinois 2017

The paper used in this publication meets the minimum requirements of American National Standard for Information Sciences–Permanence of Paper for Printed Library Materials, ANSI Z39.48-1992. ∞

Library of Congress Cataloging in Publication Control Number: 2016055675

Printed in the United States of America.

21 20 19 18 17 5 4 3 2 1

This book is dedicated to the A-LIST students at
Towson University's Cook Library who continue to lead our library
in a variety of new and exciting directions.

TABLE OF CONTENTS

Part 3: Students as Ambassadors

Part 4: Library as Client

Part 5: Student Groups as Library Leaders

Part 6: Students as Library Designers

INTRODUCTION
Setting the Context

AS ACADEMIC LIBRARIANS, we are driven by the belief that student scholars are at the heart of the academic library. Our libraries—collections, programs, and services—are meaningless without the students who use them, and they are our motivation to make our libraries welcoming places. We build our websites and other digital services to be apparent and useful to them. We improve our buildings, our marketing, our communication strategies, and our content to meet their needs. The library exists, at least in large part, for the students, but how do we know what they need?

Academic librarians have tried a variety of strategies to understand our students' needs. We often make educated guesses or try to use evidence, such as asking professors what they think students need. However, the best information comes from observing student behavior and asking them what they want. This book seeks to elevate the act of asking students what they need and want by not simply involving students, but instead putting them into a leadership role, where they will determine what gets improved and how. Only recently have libraries considered what impact we can have on our student employees and volunteers as well as our student patrons. Only recently have many libraries sought student leadership within the library as a means to improve services and facilities, and as a way to give new opportunities to our students and support institutional goals. This book is meant to provide practical examples of these new student roles and opportunities at libraries around the United States and Canada.

Defining "Students Lead"

For college students, getting a job in the library might seem like an easy way to earn money while studying. Typical student functions include checking books in and out, shelving, and answering basic questions.

These typical, task-oriented jobs usually require no leadership and very little problem solving. From the student perspective, these jobs might be easy, but are not very engaging. However, this role is changing at many academic libraries, and now student responsibilities might include such things as research assistance, outreach to other students, and even developing and leading events or other substantial library projects. Outside of direct student employment, libraries are also offering student leadership and experiential learning opportunities through student advisory boards, volunteer positions, and by acting as the client for class projects. These changes might be a product of short staffing or part of a new approach to reaching students and supporting their needs—most likely a combination of these factors. Whatever the motivation, many of these enhanced student roles and responsibilities have the fortunate benefit of aligning with higher education priorities. This alignment is especially important when institutions have increasing pressures from government, budgets, and parents to show value.

The chapters in this book illustrate that there are a variety of ways to involve students in driving and shaping library programs and services. They are adaptable and can meet student academic, social, emotional, and professional needs, among others. Despite this variety, in each case students are empowered through engaging roles to shape programs, services, and spaces to lead our libraries into the models of the future.

Setting the Theoretical Framework

Student contributions provide important feedback about what the library should do and how to do it, helping us better serve other students. Student contributions also provide students with leadership development opportunities, improve student engagement and learning, and help support campus goals. The benefits of these opportunities are rooted in a variety of higher education and library theories and priorities, such as those related to high-impact practices, user experience, and ACRL's Value of Academic Libraries initiative.[*] When students lead the library, our students and our libraries benefit, and by supporting the priorities and guiding theories of our profession and our institution, libraries show their value.

---

[*] Find more on the Value of Academic Libraries initiative here: http://www.acrl.ala.org/value/.

Benefits for Students

Students benefit personally and academically from this approach through leadership development, high levels of engagement, and peer learning opportunities.

Leadership Development

Leadership experience is emphasized as part of the college experience. Most administrators, educators, and students seem to assume the value of leadership experience is self-evident. However, scholars have explained and advocated leadership development theories in detail, arguing their benefits for interpersonal and community success. For example, leadership identity development[1] is a result of the influence of relationship development on student identity that matures over time to become more collaborative. The social change model of leadership development[2] identifies leadership through desirable individual qualities, but those qualities are developed through relational processes—experiences with others that develop self-understanding—and should lead to action for the greater good. Finally, the relational leadership model[3] emphasizes that leadership happens during interaction processes. Leaders must work in the context of a group and develop skills through relating in the group. These theories are exhibited throughout the book in practice. For example, Hoag and Sagmoen, Meyer and Torreano, and Bianco and O'Hatnick all discuss utilizing students in the hiring process for new student employees. Barnes tells us that the University of Nebraska-Lincoln Libraries delegates peer guide responsibilities specifically to develop leadership skills. The ambassadors group described by Gonzalez, Kearns, Martin, and Reed exhibits leadership development through their self-governance model.

Student Engagement

Academic libraries have an opportunity to support student engagement through enhanced employment and other student opportunities. Higher education literature often uses student engagement as an umbrella term that incorporates a variety of different curricular, co-curricular, and extracurricular learning and teaching theories and pedagogy that encourage student success. According to the National Survey of Student Engagement[4] (NSSE):

> Student engagement represents two critical features of
> collegiate quality. The first is the amount of time and ef-
> fort students put into their studies and other educational-
> ly purposeful activities. The second is how the institution
> deploys its resources and organizes the curriculum and
> other learning opportunities to get students to participate
> in activities that decades of research studies show are
> linked to student learning.

More simply, George Kuh, founding director of NSSE, defines it as "quality of effort and involvement in productive learning activities."[5] Recently, libraries have mapped their work to "high-impact practices," a student engagement and retention framework that grew out of NSSE's Engagement Indicators and Kuh's research.

So far, the discussion of student engagement in the academic library has focused on how the library can engage student library users, but the chapters in this book suggest additional opportunities for engaging our students through student employment and leadership roles. Pemberton, Wiegand, and Rhodes discuss a variety of library-based applied learning opportunities that are rooted in Kuh's high-impact practices. For example, in support of their university's Experiencing Transformative Education through Applied Learning initiative, their library has served as client to add real-world experience to class assignments, and also serves as a facility to showcase work.

Hoag and Sagmoen write about the leadership opportunities and increased responsibilities in their student employment program, which provide an integrated learning opportunity and a chance to build real-world skills while improving their job satisfaction and ownership in the library. McCartin, Brown and Feid discuss a variety of ways their College Cohort Program integrates high-impact practices for both student leaders and student participants.

Experiential Learning

Experiential learning is a concept that brings together the common foundations of previous learning theories. Kolb[6] proposed that learning is a process, dependent on resolving conflict by building on what is already known to create new learning, and happens by engaging and adapting to environment. Libraries have provided the environment for students to do this in other disciplines through research resources, but student leadership roles can provide a real-life lab for this new knowledge creation to happen for the benefit of both the students and the library. Bianco and O'Hatnick describe a peer educator program that emphasizes experiential learning through intentional reflection and growth—for the students themselves and as contributors to the student community. Leither illustrates the library-as-client model as a way for libraries to contribute to experiential learning opportunities. By working with architectural students in designing a library addition, students get to learn while receiving real-world experience as a part of their class.

Peer Learning

There are as many different ways to leverage peer learning in the library as there are reasons to do so. McCartin, Brown, and Feid indicate that the use of so-called College Leaders at NYU's College Cohort Program is meant to address the "affective domain,"* creating a comfortable and approachable learning environment for new students, and using the influence peers have on each other's learning and behavior. Similarly, Mawhinney and Zhao describe McGill University's Multilingual Services for Engineering Students peer support program, which turns the influence of peers toward helping the campuses large body of international and foreign language speaking students to learn about the library's resources and services.

Meyer and Torreano and Bianco and O'Hatnick both provide examples of peer learning through their student consultant programs, where students help each other with research, writing, or other needs. In these programs, not only are the student users benefiting from what they are learning, Boud also tells us that peer learning builds skills related to "working with others," improving "critical enquiry and reflection" capabilities, and the cementing of ideas and knowledge through "communication and articulation."[7]

Benefits for Libraries

Areas where academic libraries benefit from student leadership include participatory design processes, enhancement and transformation of the library's core functions, and addressing library value for stakeholders.

---

* For a succinct and thorough discussion of the concept of affective domain and relevant research, see pages 129–131 of Schroeder and Stern Cahoy's 2010 article titled "Valuing Information Literacy: Affective Learning and the ACRL Standards."

Participatory Design

Libraries employ many methods for getting feedback directly from users. For example, we focus on user-centered design in our websites and learning objects. Spinuzzi[8] provided a synthesis of the participatory design methodology for technical communications, and many from other domains, including libraries, have extended this concept to improve our virtual and physical services. These are often also labeled as user experience work. Notably, the anthropologist Foster[*] has demonstrated for academic libraries how they can place users of their spaces and services at the center of their planning and creation.

Daly, Chapman, and Crichlow highlight a variety of methods deployed from their Assessment and User Experience Department, which are meant to include student voices in their development and implementation, including nearly spontaneous conversations with students for feedback, more rigorous and lengthy surveys and interviews, and observation.

At Grand Valley State University, where students are the front face of library services, the customer service and experience of the library spaces are dependent on students, too. Meyer and Torreano acknowledge that the student User Experience Team is responsible for ensuring that when users come in contact with the library, they feel positive about the interaction.

Bianco and O'Hatnick argue that peer educator programs encourage libraries to design and deliver services that acknowledge the variety of student experiences and systemic inclusion/exclusion. They exemplify this by emphasizing to their peer educators the importance of acknowledging and valuing the many different ways their users learn and live, which may be quite different from their own.

Barnes acknowledges the benefit of employing peer guides as part of the library's User Experience and Student Success team to administer user surveys and gather feedback that will be used by the library to make decisions, like book purchases for the leisure collection.

With so many models to engage students, and a variety of user experience methods to consider, libraries are often hindered by indecision or overwhelmed by choice. Burhanna highlights an informal and easy method for including students in the design and experience decisions of the

---

[*] See the 2012 *Library Journal* interview with Fried Foster to get a brief introduction to her work.

library, by offering an incentive and a low-stakes opportunity to engage in conversation with students.

Transforming Core Functions

Libraries are often viewed as storehouses or gatekeepers—perspectives derived from core functions like providing research materials, and facilitating access to knowledge. Students who steer the core functions of libraries contribute to an evolving perspective of the library as a platform for learning and teaching.

Daly provides a prime example of expanding the core function of lending to the realm of electronic device chargers. Although the idea had been discussed at Duke University Library before, it was the student voice that convinced library administrators that it fit within their domain.

Another important and underrepresented aspect of many academic libraries is the work of special collections and archives. Todd-Diaz, Scribner, and Lewis acknowledge the underappreciated view of the Special Collections and Archives department on the Emporia State University campus. Lack of awareness had undermined the ability of the department to acquire new materials. By shifting a focus to students, who were both the leaders of the initiative and the target donors, the vision of preserving university history could be revived.

Library outreach and communication are vital to sustaining use of services and collections. Hines, Baglier, and Walker created student ambassador roles that could enhance the library's outreach efforts in two ways: ambassador ideas about what form outreach could take often brought new and innovative approaches; they also delivered library messages through a new, more relatable voice. Kohler's approach to library social media also takes advantage of the student voice, transforming the one-way announcement tendency of librarians to a fun, engaging student perspective on their social media platforms.

Value of Libraries

The increased pressure on libraries to show value to the university and its students led to the development of the Association of College and Research Libraries' (ACRL) Value of Academic Libraries Initiative, which pushes libraries to show their value to their institutions in a variety of ways, including impact on student enrollment, retention, graduation rates, job success, achievement, learning, and engagement[9]. These impacts directly result from student-led libraries, and we must share our programs and initiatives in order to show their value to our institutions. Several of the chapters in this book do so by directly aligning student leadership opportunities with established university goals or programs. For example, Glassman, Lee, Salomon, and Worsham explain how their student-led collection development program connected to named campus initiatives. For example, a health and wellness program was supported by a student-developed cookbook collection. Leither explains how working with architecture students to design a library addition directly supports the university's priority for "signature experiences" and sustainability. Pemberton, Wiegand, and Rhodes emphasize the library's role as partner and platform for moving applied learning initiatives forward on campus.

Conclusion

The chapters in this book provide some specific examples of students leading the library, which rely on the evidence provided for success of students and success of the library. Student success as a result of this approach is defined through leadership development, high levels of engagement, and peer learning opportunities. Library success comes in the form of participatory design processes, enhancement and transformation of the library's core functions, and addressing library value for stakeholders. The following chapters provide practical perspectives about implementing these kinds of initiatives so that readers can easily adopt and adapt to best fit their own needs and circumstances. They demonstrate that it can be done and how to avoid some of the mistakes or capitalize on the success of others. Learn from their experiences to try on your own.

Notes

1. Susan R. Komives, Felicia C. Mainella, Julie E. Owen, Susan D. Longerbeam, and Laura Osteen. 2005. "Developing a Leadership Identity: A Grounded Theory." *Journal of College Student Development* 46, no.6 (2005): 593. doi:10.1353/csd.2005.0061.
2. Helen S. Astin and Alexander W. Astin. 1996. *A Social Change Model of Leadership Development.*
3. Komives, Mainella, Owen, Longerbeam, and Osteen. "Developing a Leadership Identity," 593–611.

4. "High Impact Practices," NSSE: National Survey of Student Engagement, accessed November 1, 2015 http://nsse.indiana.edu/html/high_impact_practices.cfm.
5. Ibid., 6.
6. David A. Kolb. *Experiential Learning: Experience as the Source of Learning and Development* (Englewood Cliffs, N.J.: Prentice-Hall, 1984).
7. David Boud, Ruth Cohen, and Jane Sampson, *Peer Learning in Higher Education: Learning from & with Each Other* (London: Kogan Page, 2001), 8–9.
8. Spinuzzzi, Clay. "The Methodology of Participatory Design." *Technical Communication* 52, no. 2 (May 2005): 163–174.
9. Association of College and Research Libraries, "Value of Academic Libraries: A Comprehensive Research Review and Report," researched by Megan Oakleaf (Chicago: Association of College and Research Libraries, 2010).

Bibliography

Association of College and Research Libraries. "Value of Academic Libraries: A Comprehensive Research Review and Report," researched by Megan Oakleaf. Chicago: Association of College and Research Libraries, 2010.

Boud, David, Ruth Cohen, and Jane Sampson. *Peer Learning in Higher Education: Learning from & with Each Other*. London: Kogan Page, 2001.

Komives, Susan R. "Developing a Leadership Identity: A Grounded Theory." *Journal of College Student Development* no. 6 (2005): 593–611.

NSSE: National Survey of Student Engagement. "High Impact Practices." Last accessed July 1, 2016. http://nsse.indiana.edu/html/high_impact_practices.cfm.

Schroeder, Robert, and Ellysa Stern Cahoy. 2010. "Valuing Information Literacy: Affective Learning and the ACRL Standards." *portal: Libraries and The Academy* 10, no. 2: 127.

Schwartz, Meredith. "Seven Questions with Library Anthropologist Nancy Fried Foster." *Library Journal*, 2005. http://lj.libraryjournal.com/2012/12/academic-libraries/seven-questions-with-library-anthropologist-nancy-fried-foster/.

Spinuzzzi, Clay. 2005. "The Methodology of Participatory Design." *Technical Communication* 52, no. 2: 163–174.

Part 1

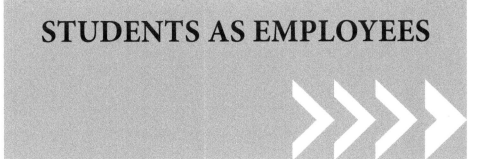

STUDENTS AS EMPLOYEES

CHAPTER 1*

LEADING, LEARNING, AND EARNING:

Creating a Meaningful Student Employment Program

Beth Hoag and Sarah Sagmoen

Introduction

Student employment is vital to the functioning of academic libraries. Students are charged with a wide range of day-to-day tasks and often staff service points as the front line for patrons. Student employment provides libraries with an economical way to achieve many daily functions while providing individual students the benefit of a paycheck and work experience. Additionally, on-campus student employment has been shown to increase persistence, academic achievement, and student engagement.[1] Despite this symbiotic relationship, student employees are often underutilized, and little focus has been directed to creating employment programs that intentionally maximize individual student growth, development, and learning.

This chapter outlines the creation of a student-centered employment program at the University of Illinois Springfield's (UIS) Brookens Library and provides practical strategies for application. UIS, a public liberal arts university, is one of three universities in the University of Illinois system. With an approximate enrollment of 5,000 students, UIS is a teaching-focused institution with strengths in online education and public affairs programs. While student employees have always served an important role at Brookens Library, the library has not always placed their development in front of the library's needs. Student employees were underutilized, lacked knowledge of general library operations and customer service, and had little sense of ownership in their positions.

In the summer of 2013, the library prioritized reinventing the program by creating an environment where students were able to learn and demonstrate leadership and teamwork skills. This reinvention has resulted in the achievement of numerous positive outcomes, both organizationally and for individual students. Since implementing this change, the library has witnessed increased ownership and efficiency in its student workforce. As students became responsible for more tasks, full-time staff were able to reallocate time to meet increasing demand for new services and special projects. Likewise, students reported higher levels of ownership and satisfaction in the workplace and demonstrated increased competence in information literacy, leadership, teamwork, and problem solving. Some student employees have linked their employment to their continued persistence and graduation, and others have translated the skills learned in the library to obtain full-time jobs.

Background and Rationale

The Brookens Library User Services department underwent a reorganization and change in leadership during the spring of 2013. As the new director of learning commons and user services, Sarah Sagmoen (co-author) began an informal audit of services, policies, and operations. The unit was feeling the strain of implementing additional services with a flat budget and decrease in staff. Initial observations also showed a lack of buy-in from student employees and underutilization of student employees by library staff.

Concurrently, Sagmoen had been leading the library's effort to forge a partnership with the Office of Student Life. The offices joined forces to produce student programs, enhance library operations, and work collaboratively on a number of initiatives. Sagmoen reached out to a former student affairs colleague and current PhD student in Higher Education Administration, Beth Hoag (co-author), to evaluate the student employment program. Hoag had a background in student affairs and 10 years of experience managing student employment programs.

Hoag came to Brookens in the summer of 2013 with the goal of evaluating the current student employment program and subsequently recommending changes based on student development and learning principles. The following were the initial goals of the program:

- Create a team environment where students are able to learn and demonstrate leadership and teamwork skills.
- Provide student employees the opportunity for advancement.
- Empower student employees to manage a broader range of library tasks and educate them on library mission and operations.
- Enhance student employees' customer service skills.
- Streamline current processes and procedures.

The User Services department employs a team of twenty to twenty-four student employees who are primarily undergraduates. When Hoag arrived, circulation student employees were assigned duties such as shelving and pulling materials, preparing materials for interlibrary loan and hold requests, and staffing the library's circulation desk. However, they only completed specific tasks within various workflows, with the steps considered more advanced to be completed by circulation supervisors. When staffing the library's circulation desk, student employees were limited to basic tasks such as checking materials in or out and answering directional questions. Patron interactions beyond these tasks required assistance from a circulation supervisor or librarian, often leaving the patron standing at the desk waiting. This resulted in circulations supervisors frequently being called to the desk, practically negating the purpose of employing students.

In the new employment model, students were given more responsibility and ownership of daily tasks. We implemented new hiring, training, and evaluation procedures and updated policies and procedures. Students became active members in guiding the direction of the department and identified ways to improve services, while linking their jobs to learning outcomes. During the fall of 2013, we expanded upon the redesign by creating two student manager positions. These students were responsible for assisting with new employee training, facilitating monthly staff meetings and serving as circulation managers.

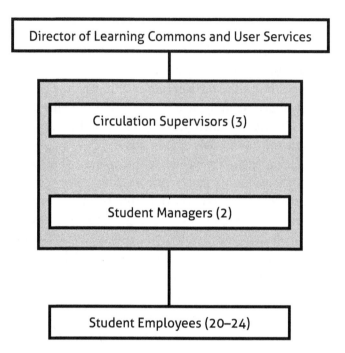

Figure 1.1. The newly created hierarchical structure of the User Services Department at Brookens Library.

Putting a Plan in Action

First Steps

To understand what changes needed to be made, we first conducted a thorough assessment of student employment policies, procedures, and practices. Hoag worked alongside student employees and assumed many managerial roles to get a grasp on day-to-day operations. This perspective allowed her to analyze workflow and identify areas where student employees could have a greater impact. As a non-librarian, she was able to bring a fresh set of eyes to common practices and procedures. Hoag had a background in student union management, which frequently relies on students to act as the sole evening facility supervisors. Her experience with students autonomously managing a wide breadth of operations challenged library staff to expand their understanding of student responsibilities.

During the planning stages, we worked to build buy-in across the library staff. Hoag met with User Services staff to learn more about their position and their perception of student employment. She shared potential ideas and received frequent feedback. The dean had been supportive of the initiative and the topic was discussed at staff meetings. In addition, Hoag met with all current student employees to gauge their understanding of the job and possible improvements.

Based on this feedback, we set forth to create a comprehensive student manual that clearly articulated policies and procedures. Each existing policy and procedure was first reviewed and revised to create clear employment expectations and to set up students for success. One of our primary goals was to enable students to independently complete a wider range of tasks and have the knowledge to provide exceptional customer service. Overall, our policies had been unclear, punitive, or non-existent. Additionally, students did not have a central resource they could consult for procedures (e.g., checking out books, emergency procedures, shelf reading procedure, and requesting time off). We designed a student employment manual that covered institutional employment policies and procedures, emergency procedures, and library policies and procedures. (See Figure 1.2). This process also allowed us to identify redundancies in our practices. For example, student employees were completing some tasks that were then re-done by library staff. Conducting an analysis of our procedures enabled us to eliminate this duplication of work, and free up more time for our library staff members.

INSTITUTIONAL EMPLOYMENT INFORMATION
☐ University Paperwork
☐ Pay Rates, Time Sheets and Pay Schedule
☐ Employee Rights and Responsibilities
☐ FERPA

EMERGENCY PROCEDURES
☐ General Evaluation Guidelines
☐ Fire, Tornado, Utility Failure
☐ Active Shooter, Bomb Threat
☐ Harassing Customers, Depressed/
   Suicidal Customers

LIBRARY EMPLOYMENT POLICIES AND EXPECTATIONS
☐ Coverage Procedures, Calling in for Illness
☐ Tardiness
☐ Dress Code/Uniforms
☐ Food, Drink, Electronic Devices
☐ Friends and Socializing
☐ Performance Reviews
☐ Disciplinary Procedures

LIBRARY POLICIES
☐ Overdue Fines
☐ Charges
☐ Hold Policies
☐ Alumni Borrowers
☐ Library Equipment Checkout

LIBRARY EMPLOYEE PROCEDURES
☐ Customer Service & Phone Tips
☐ Printing/Copying/Faxing
☐ Charging/Discharging/InterLibrary Loan
☐ Call Slips
☐ Rounds
☐ Shelf Reading

APPENDICES
☐ User Services Contact Info
☐ Frequently Used Numbers
☐ Extended Hours Checklist
☐ FAQ
☐ Performance Review Template

Figure 1.2. Employment manual outline.

Hiring

In order to implement our vision of a student-centered, team-based model for employment, we needed to modify the hiring process. We initially identified the primary skills and characteristics that would qualify a student for a position and determined six assessment areas for potential applicants: team-orientated, attention to detail, customer service, reliability, knowledge of campus resources, and strong communication skills. In the past, library knowledge and usage were a determining factor in the hiring process, but we eliminated this criterion. We noted that these skills could be taught and we wanted to create a diverse student team that included students less familiar with our programs and services, as we felt they could provide critical insight and recommendations.

Since the creation of the program, we have made it a continued priority to recruit a diverse pool of applicants. In order to achieve this, we have implemented a variety of outreach strategies such as tabling, new-student orientation, website ads, and soliciting recommendations from Student Life staff. Currently, a large component of our recruiting process occurs at the annual on-campus employment fair, which also allows us the opportunity to interact with applicants.

Next, we examined the job description and application. University policy requires all student employment postings and applications be funneled through Career Connect, an online career development portal accessible to all students. Students must upload a résumé and use the system to apply for both on- and off-campus positions. This process is standardized and offered little opportunity to tailor an initial application to our specific needs. Additionally, Brookens Library had consistently received a high number of applications for open positions and needed a more robust process to assess and select the best candidates.

We implemented an additional information form that was sent to candidates after applying through Career Connect. We asked specific questions about availability and overall interest in the position. One question listed our identified characteristics of a successful employee, and applicants were asked to choose their strongest characteristic from the pre-determined list and describe why they felt it was a strength. In order to move forward in our hiring process, candidates were required to complete the form by the deadline and correctly follow all instructions on the form. We continue to use the pre-screening process as a way to narrow our candidate pool.

Qualified applicants were invited for an interview. Interviews were scheduled sequentially and lasted approximately fifteen minutes in length. (See Figure 1.3 for list of sample interview questions.) Since the implementation of our new model, student managers assist with interview scheduling, question formation, and are actively involved in the interview process. Successful candidates are chosen by consensus (staff supervisor and student managers) and decisions are based on the pre-determined criteria with special emphasis placed on the candidate's demonstrated ability to work in a team environment.

☐ Tell us about yourself
☐ Describe your most rewarding college experience.
☐ Describe your most challenging college experience
☐ What three words would a past supervisor or professor use to describe you?
☐ How do you currently use the library?
☐ What do you hope to learn from your library employment?
☐ Tell us about a time you worked on a team. What went well and what challenges did you face? How did you manage the challenges?
☐ Why do you think you would be successful at this job?
☐ What student organizations or activities have you been involved in on campus?
☐ Of the six identified characteristics that describe a strong user services employee. Choose one that is your greatest strength and one that you would need to improve.

Figure 1.3. Sample interview questions.

Orientation, Training, and Development

Once new employees are hired, they participate in a multi-phase training process. During the first phase, new employees participate in an orientation where they are given an overview of library operations and discuss the role of the academic library. Student employees also have the opportunity to meet and interact with the dean of the library, library staff, and librarians. Additionally, students review the student manual, discuss expectations and responsibilities, and are tested on policies and procedures.

Next, new employees shadow returning student employees on various job tasks. New employees are given a copy of the manual and a checklist of tasks to learn. Schedules are intentionally designed for new employees to shadow multiple employees with various tasks and shifts.

The weekend before the semester begins, all student employees (returning and new) are required to attend a mandatory half-day retreat.

Student managers are primarily responsible for planning the retreat agenda. The main goals of the retreat are to build relationships and enhance teamwork skills. The day begins with a series of interactive team builders designed to test team communication and their ability to work together. These activities are completed as a group and students are asked to draw connections to their work environment. All students are required to set personal goals for the semester and undergo training to refresh knowledge of tasks or learn new tasks.

The final phase occurs about a month after new employees start employment. Supervisors and student managers shadow employees, conduct checks on various tasks, and ask students to explain the process to evaluate mastery. Additionally, secret shoppers are sent in at various times to assess customer services skills. If an employee performed less than satisfactorily, additional training was provided.

In addition to the training process, learning and development is ongoing. We implemented mandatory monthly staff meetings that give students an opportunity to provide feedback, network with peers, and take on various projects. Student managers run the meetings and often include team-building or other skills-based activities, such as customer service activities. Regular staff meetings also provide an opportunity to discuss changes and make corrections with the entire staff while promoting peer feedback and support.

Reference Training

At the time the employment program was being revised, the library was struggling to staff the library's reference desk, which had seen declining use. Librarians were increasing instruction and outreach efforts, and staffing a seldom-used desk, located five feet from the circulation desk, became increasingly hard to justify.

After researching alternative models, we decided to expand student support at the reference desk and move to a peer-to-peer reference model to capitalize on peer learning. We removed the reference desk and went to a one-desk service model with librarians on-call should patrons need advanced reference assistance. The positive effects of using undergraduate students in a peer-to-peer reference model have been well-documented. Student benefits include impressive résumés, increased pride in work, and improved researcher skills.[2] Libraries also experience benefits beyond relieving staffing issues, including access to the student point of view and improved morale.[3] Additionally, peer reference services better match student patron needs, as students feel more comfortable approaching a peer.[4]

This move required student employees to have basic reference training. Sagmoen created a three-tiered training program that serves as continuing education for student employees. During the second half of a new student employee's first semester, they complete the first tier of training. The second tier is completed during their second semester, and the third tier during their third semester.

Reference Training Tiers:

- Tier 1: Known item searching (two ninety-minute sessions)
- Tier 2: Basic searching skills and understanding library search tools (five sixty-minute sessions)
- Tier 3: Advanced searching and reference interviews (five sixty-minute sessions)

The curriculum, which utilizes active learning techniques, is taught by a combination of student managers, circulation supervisors, and librarians. Student learning is assessed at the end of each tier before a student employee moves on to the next tier. The impact of this training is not limited to the library. While students become better equipped to answer basic reference inquiries at the desk, they also increase the research skills needed for their course work. In her exit survey, student employee Emma stated, "I owe a lot of my academic success to the reference training I received. Research assignments are less intimidating because I'm familiar with the library's resources and I can navigate the library's collection with confidence."

Student Managers

Our initial changes and efforts in training and increased responsibility provided us with a solid base from which the new employment model could grow. As student employees were given more responsibility, those who excelled took on an active role in training new student employees and were given special projects. This quickly opened up leadership opportunities. Not surprisingly, leaders emerged quickly and leadership positions were formalized through the creation of two student manager positions in the fall of 2013.

In addition to serving as team leaders for the student employee team, student managers are fully trained circulation supervisors. They open and close the library, perform supervisor-level tasks at the desk and throughout the library, train student employees, work on special projects, and help plan and facilitate staff meetings and retreats. They participate in department meetings and serve on library committees, providing a student voice to departmental and library decisions.

House Cup

To enhance our team-based model and simultaneously update our ineffective "three strikes and you're out" disciplinary model, we created our version of the House Cup. Taking inspiration from the House Cup in the Harry Potter book series, the program allows us to reward those modeling good behavior by awarding them positive points, as well as issue negative points for infractions. Using a point system allows us to address small infractions early before they become habits and place students at risk of being terminated.

At the beginning of each semester, students are divided into four teams, or houses: Gryffinbook, Ravenbook, Booklepuff, and Shhhlytherin. Throughout the semester they are awarded points for going above and beyond, or docked points for infractions. As students accrue points, they are added to those of their housemates to tabulate a house's points. Totaling individual student points as house points provides a common goal and encourages housemates to work as a team to help individuals who may be struggling. When ten negative points have been accrued by an individual, the student meets with a supervisor and is placed on probation. During the probation meeting, supervisor and student work together to create a plan of action that will help the student meet expectations and job responsibilities more successfully. When the plan has been met, the probation status is removed. Each student's progress is tracked using a spreadsheet and incorporated into annual evaluations.

Additionally, houses serve as small groups in which the students often complete activities during the monthly staff meetings. Individual point leaders and the house leader are recognized at staff meetings each month and congratulated for their hard work. The program has helped students succeed by reinforcing expectations consistently and fairly and acknowledging those who are modeling good behavior.

Student Evaluation

In addition to the House Cup, students are assessed using an annual formal review process. Students first complete a self-assessment of their performance. Meanwhile, the student managers and supervisor complete a similar assessment, which includes knowledge of duties, reliability, quality of work, customer service, and judgment. The student employee and supervision team have a formal meeting to compare results, discuss personal goals, and offer feedback. Although this is an annual process, new employees have an initial evaluation at the end of their first semester to provide formal feedback early in their time at the library.

Recommendations for Implementing a Student-Centered Employment Program

Many of the elements created for the student employment program at Brookens Library can easily translate to other libraries and be scaled based on institution size. Through researching, building, and continuously evolving the program at Brookens Library, we have established seven recommendations for libraries wanting to implement a robust, student-centered program:

1. Put students first.
2. Find the right people.
3. Identify competencies and outcomes.
4. Develop clear policies and procedures.
5. Provide opportunity for continued learning and advancement.
6. Build a team atmosphere.
7. Create a cycle of assessment and evaluation.

The remainder of this chapter will provide suggestions for successful implementation of each recommendation.

Put Students First

The first step when creating meaningful student employment opportunities is to commit to a *student first* mindset that puts student learning and success at the forefront of employment. Consider employment through the lens of holistic learning and development[5] and identify a philosophy that places student outcomes above organizational outcomes. Find ways to integrate student involvement into all phases of the employment process, from hiring to evaluation. Provide avenues for student input and involve experienced student employees in the hiring process for new team members. Identify students that excel at certain tasks and assign them to train new hires. Think about designing programs that gradually add more responsibilities for students such as employee scheduling, staff training, reference support, facility management, and peer supervision.

Central tenets of our philosophy include believing student employees could perform advanced tasks, act autonomously, supervise peers, and create connections between employment and coursework. We actively promoted these tenets to library staff and current student employees to increase buy-in for the changing program.

During our process, some colleagues expressed concerns that students would be unable to take on additional responsibilities because in the past they witnessed students producing mediocre work with fewer responsibilities. We argued that students were underperforming in the old model because of a lack of trust and low expectations. Students were falling prey to a self-fulfilling prophecy and only achieving the low expectations the position required.

As student employees learned more about the library and were trusted with more responsibilities, their sense of belonging and commitment to the library grew. We quickly discovered that by putting students first, many began to excel as employees and as students. Matt, a former student manager stated, "Working at Brookens was an integral part in my academic success. My supervisors and co-workers motivated me to work at a higher level, and were there to support me in every way. Without Brookens Library I would not have graduated."

Find the Right People

The program's success and ability to continue to grow and evolve is due in large part to the strong foundation provided by Hoag and the continued support of the library dean. Brookens Library was lucky in that it was able to bring in a professional to help in this endeavor. Bringing in a professional is certainly an easy recommendation to make, but it may not be feasible for all libraries. There are, however, alternatives that could benefit you greatly.

Within your institution there are professionals who could serve as excellent allies. Start by reaching out to colleagues in student affairs with whom you have a working relationship. While they may not be the right people, they should be able to point you in the right direction. If you do not have a colleague to contact, here are some common student affairs departments who may be willing to help:

- Student Life/Student Activities
- New Student Programs and Orientation
- Career Services
- Student Union
- Recreation Services

If your institution has a College Student Personnel/Higher Education degree program, consider providing an internship or graduate employeeship for a student who is working toward a degree in college student personnel or other relevant areas of the higher education field.

Identify Competencies & Outcomes

When designing an employment program, it is important to start with the end in mind. Identify competencies and learning outcomes you want students to achieve and design a program to fulfill these outcomes. Consider using existing frameworks or institutional learning outcomes to guide your program. The National Association of Colleges Employers (NACE) identified seven competencies that are essential for new college graduates: (a) critical thinking/problem solving, (b) oral/written communication, (c) teamwork/collaboration, (d) information technology application, (e) leadership, (f) professionalism/work ethic, and (f) career management.[6] These competencies could be used as a guide to integrate student employment, academic learning, and career readiness.

Additionally, the Association of American College and Universities (AACU) identified essential learning outcomes as part of their Liberal Education and America's Promise (LEAP) initiative (AACU, 2005). These sixteen outcomes serve as guideposts for liberal education and include skills such as inquiry/analysis, teamwork/problem solving, information literacy, and intercultural knowledge and competence. AACU also provides assessment rubrics for each outcome.

As we designed our program, we identified several core competencies that we wanted students to achieve through their work at Brookens Library, including teamwork, oral communication/customer service, professionalism, leadership, and information literacy. These competencies served as a roadmap for our decision making. When designing the reference training component, we utilized ACRL's *Information Literacy Competency Standards* and *Framework for Information Literacy in Higher Education* as a starting point and incorporated institutional information literacy outcomes.

Develop Clear Policies and Procedures

In order to set students up for success, it is important to create a single written guide/manual/wiki that contains employment expectations and policies. Think about your employment manual as a class syllabus that outlines individual and group expectations and provides all relevant employment policies. Ensure the manual is reviewed with students during orientation and revisited by staff and updated regularly.

When creating an employment manual, start by conducting an analysis of any existing employment policies and expectations. Consider the following questions when reviewing policies:

- Is it necessary?
- Is it up-to-date?
- Is it practical?
- Do students know the policy exists? If so, is it easily accessible?
- Is it streamlined?
- Why does it exist? Does the policy articulate a rationale?
- Does this policy encourage students to take ownership of the task/action?

Our first policy change was to implement a *shift coverage policy* that placed responsibility on the student employee and not on the supervisor. Students were welcome to switch shifts or cover for each other at will, provided they do not exceed maximum hours allowed per week. Shift coverage did not need to be pre-approved by a supervisor, but students were asked to send a confirmation of their shift coverage to the supervisor. This change in the coverage procedures forced students to be more responsible when planning days off and encouraged students to work together to find coverage solutions. Prior to this change, we found many shifts were left vacant because the supervisor did not have adequate time to assign a replacement. Following the implementation of the policy, unstaffed shifts drastically decreased and students who wanted more hours were accommodated.

Once policies are created, routinely discuss them with students and address infractions immediately. When reviewing policies, provide rationale and background to contextualize the policy for students. Although, some policies and expectations may be inflexible (e.g., tardiness, break time, FERPA), others may be able to be discussed and decided as a group (e.g., dress code, switching shifts). Consider having the student employees create group expectations they will collectively uphold.

Finally, compile a list of common procedures (charging/discharging books, inter-library loan processing, building rounds checklist) and provide detailed instructions in the manual. Although initially time consuming, this is invaluable for on-boarding new employees, and students are empowered to teach themselves if they need to brush up on how to read a call number or process an inter-library loan book.

Provide Opportunities for Continued Learning and Advancement

As you create/update your employment program, you will find a variety of opportunities for continued learning. Continued learning can occur during training retreats, staff meetings, or as a part of a larger training program such as the reference training program utilized at Brookens. Customer service, communication, critical thinking, or advanced job knowledge are excellent topics as they are always areas of growth.

Numerous studies have shown that students learn best from peers;[7] due to this, we emphasized a peer-led approach to training. When new students are hired, they shadow returning employees and are trained on processes by student managers. Students have found this process to be less intimidating than learning from staff members and have effectively mastered procedures. This method has also provided seasoned student employees the opportunity to strengthen their knowledge of the position and improve oral communication skills.

Similarly, there are a myriad of formal and informal opportunities for advancement. Creating positions such as team leaders or student managers allows for students to be promoted within the program. The benefits of creating formal leadership positions for student employees impact both the student and the library. While serving in this role, student managers are able to develop valuable skills such as peer supervision, conflict management, leadership, and critical thinking, all while freeing up time for professional library staff to undergo new initiatives.

As students demonstrate strengths and express interests, consider providing them the opportunity to take on a special project or serve as a library ambassador at campus events.

Projects and events student employees have assisted with at Brookens include:

- Planning library events (e.g. Annual Haunted Library)
- Creating and facilitating activities for new student orientations (e.g. mini-golf tour of the library)
- Staffing the library's table at information fairs for prospective or new students and families
- Providing library tours
- Serving as assistants during library instruction
- Creating book or DVD displays

Providing opportunities for students to take on special projects and serve as library ambassadors provides them with skill sets desired by employers. Skills such as the "ability to verbally communicate with persons inside and outside of the organization" and "ability to plan, organize, and prioritize work."[8]

Build a Team Atmosphere

As students graduate and enter the workplace, they are increasingly expected to excel in a team environment. In a 2015 survey of employers, 79 percent indicated they were looking for candidates that clearly demonstrated the ability to work in a team environment.[9] Collaborative work teams have been known to increase service delivery[10] and employee satisfaction.[11] Equally, it is important to develop a culture in which students feel connected and supported by the organization and colleagues.

An essential step to creating a team environment is to devote training time to team-building activities. Reach out to student affairs professionals in areas such as student activities, leadership programs, new student program, or recreational sports, who actively engage in team-building activities, to suggest examples, or assist with facilitation. Additionally, there are numerous online resources and books that provide activities aimed at developing stronger teams.

Prior to changing our employment model, students primarily worked in isolation, only seeing colleagues during shift changes. As we implemented regular team meetings and emphasized a team approach to projects, students began to help one another and better serve patrons. Laura, one former student employee, commented on the change, "I remember coming back to the library after the summer for fall 2013 staff training and one student said that the main change is, 'We actually talk to each other now!' I enjoyed working at the library before the changes, but after that summer I think a new sense of teamwork, leadership, and communication really entered the student workers and library staff."

Create a Cycle of Assessment and Evaluation

Effective evaluation programs include individual performance assessment, reflection, and goal setting. Evaluation forms and processes should be presented to students upon hiring. This provides students with a clear understanding of performance expectations and helps students identify growth areas. Students should also be provided the opportunity to set personal learning goals throughout the academic year.

Create an evaluation program that allows you to provide feedback in the moment as well as formal review meetings. Using a points system, like the House Cup used at Brookens, allows you to issue points, both positive and negative, that match the action. Small infractions result in one negative point, while large infractions result in upward of ten negative points. When creating a points system, start with a list of expectations and assign points values for common actions to ensure consistency. Additionally, create a scale for negative points to be issued for minutes late to work. For example:

Minutes Late Scale: 1–10 = –1, 11–20 = –2, 21–30 = –3, 30+ = –5

Issuing points in the moment and then tracking them throughout the semester will allow you to continuously provide feedback and build data to be used for formal evaluations.

Formal reviews should be conducted annually and focus on student development. Involve appropriate supervisors, staff, or student leaders who can speak to each student's performance when preparing the review. Reflection can be incorporated into the evaluation process by requiring students to self-assess their performance in preparation for the review. Comparing the scores from all parties provides an opportunity for reflection and discussion.

In addition to assessing student success, it is important to assess the overall effectiveness of the employee program. Provide opportunities for students to provide regular feedback on the program through informal and formal channels. Engage student managers and supervisors in reflection and seek to actively improve your model. Examine data from library surveys and assessments to provide insight on student employment. Finally, have student employees conduct exit surveys upon graduation to encourage personal reflection and to gather data on desired outcomes.

Conclusion

The impact of a student-first employee program on libraries can been profound. By putting students first, both student employees and staff become more engaged and dedicated to improving library services. Giving students more responsibility frees staff time for new initiatives and increased services, especially at times when staffing and budgets are flat. Most important, taking an active role in student success outside of the traditional academic role shows students that the library is invested in their whole college experience.

Notes

1.   Tracy Klum and Sheren Cramer, "The Relationship of Student Employment to Student Role, Family Relationships, Social Interactions, and Persistence," *College Student Journal*, 40 no. 4 (2006): 927–938; George Kuh, Jillian Kinzie, Ty Cruce, Rick Shoup, and Robert Gonyea, *Connecting the Dots: Multi-faceted Analyses of the Relationships Between Student Engagement Results from the NSSE, and the Institutional Practices and Condition that Foster Student Success.* (Bloomington, IN: Indiana University Center for Postsecondary Research, 2007); Ernest T. Pascarella and Patrick T. Terenzini, *How College Affects Students vol. 2.* (San Francisco: Jossey-Bass, 2005); Gary Pike, George Kuh, and Ryan Mass-McKinley, "First-Year Students' Employment, Engagement, and Academic Achievement: Untangling the Relationship Between Work and Grades," *NASPA Journal* 45 no. 4 (2008): 560–582.
2.   Allison Faix, Margaret Bates, Lisa Hartman, Jennifer Hughes, Casey Schacher, Brooke Elliot, and Alexander Woods, "Peer Reference Redefined: New Uses for Undergraduate Students," *Reference Services Review* 38, no. 1 (2010): 90–107, 99–100.
3.   Ibid., 101.
4.   Susan Gardner and Susanna Eng, "What Students Want: Generation Y and the Changing Function of the Academic Library," *portal: Libraries and the Academy* 5 no. 3 (2005): 405–420, doi: 10.1353/pla.2005.0034, 413.
5.   Richard Keeling, *Learning Reconsidered: A Campus-Wide Focus on the Student Experience.* (Washington, DC: National Association of Student Personnel Administrators, & College Personnel Association, 2005) https://www.naspa.org/images/uploads/main/Learning_Reconsidered_Report.pdf.

6. "Career Readiness for the New College Graduate: A Definition and Competencies," *National Association of Colleges and Employers*, http://www.naceweb.org/knowledge/career-readiness-competencies.aspx.
7. Ernest T. Pascarella and Patrick T. Terenzini, *How College Affects Students vol. 2.*
8. National Association of Colleges and Employers, *2015 Job Outlook.* (Bethlehem, PA: National Association of Colleges and Employers, 2014).
9. National Association of Colleges and Employers, *2016 Job Outlook.* (Bethlehem, PA: National Association of Colleges and Employers, 2015).
10. Priscilla Wohlstetter, Courtney Malloy, Guilbert Hentschke, and Joanna Smith, "Improving Service Delivery in Education through Collaboration: An Exploratory Study of the Role of Cross-sectoral Alliances in the Development and Support of Charter Schools," *Social Science Quarterly* 85, no. 5 (2004): 1078–1096.
11. Jeanne Steffes and Richard P. Keeling, "Creating Strategies for Collaboration," *Learning Reconsidered 2* ed. Richard P. Keeling (Washington, DC: American College Personnel Association, Association of College and University Professionals-International, Association of College Unions-International, National Academic Advising Association, National Association for Campus Activities, National Association of Student Personnel Administrators, & National Intramural-Recreation Sports Association, 2006).

Bibliography

"Career Readiness for the New College Graduate: A Definition and Competencies." *National Association of Colleges and Employers.* http://www.naceweb.org/knowledge/career-readiness-competencies.aspx.

"Essential Learning Outcomes." *Association of American College and University.* https://www.aacu.org/leap/essential-learning-outcomes.

Faix, Allison, Margaret Bates, Lisa Hartman, Jennifer Hughes, Casey Schacher, Brooke Elliot, and Alexander Woods. "Peer Reference Redefined: New Uses for Undergraduate Students." *Reference Services Review* 38, no. 1 (2010): 90–107.

Gardner, Susan, and Susanna Eng. "What Students Want: Generation Y and the Changing Function of the Academic Library." *portal: Libraries and the Academy* 5, no. 3 (2005): 405–420. doi: 10.1353/pla.2005.0034.

Keeling, Richard P. *Learning Reconsidered: A Campus-wide Focus on the Student Experience.* Washington, DC: National Association of Student Personnel Administrators and the American College Personnel Association, 2005. https://www.naspa.org/images/uploads/main/Learning_Reconsidered_Report.pdf.

Klum, Tracy, and Sheren Cramer. "The Relationship of Student Employment to Student Role, Family Relationships, Social Interactions and Persistence." *College Student Journal* 40, no. 4 (2006): 927–938.

Kuh, George, Jillian Kinzie, Ty Cruce, Rick Shoup, and Robert Gonyea. *Connecting the Dots: Multi-faceted Analyses of the Relationships Between Student Engagement Results from the NSSE, and the Institutional Practices and Condition that Foster Student Success.* Bloomington, IN: Indiana University Center for Postsecondary Research, 2007.

National Association of Colleges and Employers. *2015 Job Outlook.* Bethlehem, PA: National Association of Colleges and Employers, 2014.

National Association of Colleges and Employers. *2016 Job Outlook*. Bethlehem, PA: National Association of Colleges and Employers, 2015.

Pascarella, Ernest T., and Patrick T. Terenzini. *How College Affects Students vol. 2* San Francisco: Jossey-Bass, 2005.

Pike, Gary, George Kuh, and Ryan Mass-McKinley. "First-Year Students' Employment, Engagement, and Academic Achievement: Untangling the Relationship between Work and Grades." *NASPA Journal* 45, no. 4 (2008): 560–582.

Steffes, Jeanne, and Richard P. Keeling. "Creating Strategies for Collaboration." In *Learning Reconsidered 2* edited by Richard P. Keeling, 69–74. Washington, DC: American College Personnel Association, Association of College and University Professionals-International, Association of College Unions—International, National Academic Advising Association, National Association for Campus Activities, National Association of Student Personnel Administrators, & National Intramural-Recreation Sports Association, 2006.

Wohlstetter, Priscilla, Courtney Malloy, Guilbert Hentschke, and Joanna Smith. "Improving Service Delivery in Education through Collaboration: An Exploratory Study of the Role of Cross-sectoral Alliances in the Development and Support of Charter Schools." *Social Science Quarterly* 85, no. 5 (2004): 1078–1096.

CHAPTER 2

THE LIBRARY AS LEADERSHIP INCUBATOR:

A Case Study of Towson University's A-LIST Program

Carissa Tomlinson and Sara Arnold-Garza

Introduction

Towson University, Maryland's largest comprehensive university, sets itself apart in higher education by placing a priority on leadership development and connecting the classroom to real-world experiences through experiential learning, student research opportunities, internships, and co-curricular opportunities.[†] In this context, librarians at Albert S. Cook Library looked to develop an opportunity that would contribute to this institutional priority while also helping the library enhance visibility and promote academic success. The result was the Albert S. Cook Library Leadership Institute (A-LIST), a program that offers student participants experiential

---

† Read more about Towson University's educational experience at http://www.usmd.edu/institutions/profile/?Inst=TU.

learning opportunities in leadership, research, writing, teaching, outreach, and project management.

While an increasing number of libraries are offering unique opportunities for students in the library, positions typically fall into only one of three categories: peer research assistants (at the reference desk or in the classroom), library ambassadors or advisory board members (focusing on library outreach or user experience), or library as client (where the library hires students from a class to accomplish a related task). The A-LIST program incorporates all three of these responsibilities and puts an emphasis on student leadership responsibilities in all areas. A-LIST students do not simply execute programs or initiatives, they develop, plan, implement, and are accountable for the outcomes of programs. Rather than employees, we see the A-LIST students as paid participants in a year-long leadership institute, where both the library and the students equally benefit from the program. Annually since 2014, the Cook Library has hired three A-LIST students per cohort. These students are expected to commit to ten hours a week for two semesters (spring and fall). After receiving in-depth training, students represent the library through peer research help and library outreach events and initiatives—many that they develop themselves. A-LIST students also have the opportunity to choose projects and work with various library departments to improve library services both internally and externally.

Hiring

Due to budget constraints, the majority of student employees at Cook Library are work-study students. This has always meant that our pool was small and our employment process not necessarily selective. The A-LIST program is different. Fortunately, the library dean set aside endowment funds to pay for the program. Because A-LIST is not funded by work-study funds, the pay is more competitive. The pay, along with the emphasis on leadership training and real-world experience, has helped us annually recruit twenty to thirty highly qualified candidates. The application process requires students to have already completed at least one semester at Towson, hold a minimum 3.0 GPA, and to be able to commit to a year-long program. Additionally, applicants are required to answer short essay questions about their ideas for the library, how they use the library, and why they are interested in the position, giving us insight into their motivations, experience, and creativity. Students also must include two references, including at least one Towson University staff or faculty member. Through a search committee, the top five to ten candidates are brought in for a short interview.

With student outreach in mind, the search committee has always been interested in hiring students who are active on campus and represent diverse backgrounds. While this continues to be a priority, we have learned that students who are active in many things on campus may have a hard time juggling their priorities. Therefore, we have turned down candidates with many obligations in favor of outgoing and enthusiastic students who are involved in one or two unique student activities. In order to grow outreach in certain areas, we also have purposefully sought out students with particular interests or backgrounds. For example, Towson has a very large transfer student population, and we felt that hiring a transfer student might help with this initiative.

While Towson does not have a library science program, we have had students with an interest in becoming librarians apply for the position. While of course an asset, it is more important to us that A-LIST participants are outgoing and connected on campus. As of now, we have never had a student graduate A-LIST with an interest in working in libraries, but we do not see this as a failure. We do not see A-LIST as a librarian training program, but instead, an opportunity for students with a variety of majors and interests to gain real-life experience working collaboratively, leading projects and initiatives, and helping others.

Training

The leadership responsibilities required in the A-LIST position come with extensive guidance and support through a purposeful training program that continues through the whole year-long institute. By framing the program as a leadership institute, we are able to take the time to focus on the process of becoming a leader, not simply the required tasks of a job. The institute model helps student participants think of their role equally as employee and student leader. Our training philosophy is that we focus less on training our students how to do a specific task and more on helping them build capacity to be able to make good decisions, be innovative, and understand how the library can support the needs of students and the university. This is accomplished through an intensive program that requires students to think critically about academic libraries, higher education, and the needs of students, and how we can support them.

A-LIST students start the program by learning about the library, our values, our roles in higher education, and how they can contribute. Students receive a training book with a checklist of modules that are to be completed during the first semester of the program. The modules fall into one of five categories: Library Background, Information Literacy, Research Assistance, Leadership, and Library Outreach and Marketing. Module activities range from reading articles and professional best practice documents, to meeting with representatives from each library department to understand the library's functions. Trainees spend time observing in the classroom and at the Research Help Desk, and they read through documentation of past A-LIST projects while exploring other academic library websites and publications for interesting new ideas. The majority of modules require a reflective blog entry intended to get students to internalize what they are learning and better understand how they, as A-LIST students, can contribute to the library's mission. For example, students are introduced to the big picture of academic libraries and their role by reviewing the university's strategic plan, the library's strategic plan, and a document outlining A-LIST responsibilities and goals, then responding to prompts in a blog post:

- How do you see the A-LIST program supporting the university and the library's goals?
- Brainstorm specific projects and/or programs that you think the A-LIST group could accomplish in order to meet these goals.
- Outline at least one project and/or program in depth.

The full list of modules and their associated reflective components can be found in Appendix 2A. These blogs are read by their supervisor and an assigned librarian mentor and are used for discussion points in individual and group meetings.

Mentorship is another aspect of the A-LIST program which provides a supportive introduction to the library. Each A-LIST student is paired with a librarian mentor. The pair meet regularly, one-on-one, to build a personal connection and support outside of the supervisor relationship.

Early Projects, Initiatives, and Growth Opportunities

The A-LIST students are often excited to get working long before they have completed the modules, so the training is supplemented by projects or goals with increasing responsibility throughout the first semester. During the first few weeks of the institute, the trainees spend their time primarily on their modules, but they also begin developing material to promote their research assistance activities, which usually starts about a month into training. For example, the first cohort worked together—along with guidance and technical assistance from library staff—to produce a commercial* that played on the library's website and in the library lobby. They also designed their own t-shirts and several fliers to hang around campus. A-LIST students also begin small library projects, such as themed book displays or assisting at library open house events. Early in the program, most students expect considerable structure and guidance. Thus, our goal over the course of the first semester is to build confidence and ability through the training book and structured, assisted, hands-on activities, so that in semester two they are able to develop and manage projects, programs, and other initiatives more independently.

Another early training goal is to get the students familiar with the research help desk quickly. In complement to the module readings about providing quality research assistance, trainees spend substantial time shadowing and building confidence at the research help desk. They also spend time reviewing past A-LIST research questions and answers to help them understand the kinds of questions they will need to answer. When they feel ready, the students must complete a short, hands-on quiz with their supervisor. The students answer questions that are similar to ones they might get at the desk. Once they pass the quiz, they begin working four hours a week each, either at the Research Help Desk or at the Writing Center. Because our Research Help Desk is also staffed by another library employee, the A-LIST students rove around the building each hour to see if anyone needs help on other floors.

---

* Watch the commercial at https://youtu.be/KjM_QeCcHoo.

Leadership Conferences and Workshops

The A-LIST program not only works to provide leadership opportunities for participating students, it also has a leadership training requirement. Students are required to attend a minimum of six leadership programs throughout the year and then reflect on their experiences by answering the following questions in their blog:

- What was the purpose of the program?
- What surprised you?
- How will you implement what you learned in this program?

The programs that students attend most often are those coordinated out of the University's existing Initiatives for Leadership Education and Development (iLEAD) program,* offered by the University's Division of Student Affairs. Examples of iLEAD program topics include: cultural competency, achieving group synergy, effective communication styles, active listening, and leadership styles. Additionally, the University holds student-focused leadership conferences that also can be used toward the six required activities. An added bonus of the A-LIST leadership requirement is that it gets our students halfway to an iLEAD Certificate, which requires a total of twelve iLead activities. Finally, by connecting the A-LIST students with other university leadership initiatives, it helps spread the word around campus that the library is actively supporting university priorities through creative means.

Taking the Lead

While training continues throughout the year, at the start of the second semester, students are mostly done with their modules, are offering research assistance, and working on guided projects. The second semester is when students generally have built their confidence and knowledge and are ready to take a leadership role on a variety of things. Students are still working ten hours a week, with four hours scheduled for research assistance. An additional hour is scheduled for a weekly group meeting. That leaves five hours a week for students to work on their own initiatives during times that they schedule themselves. Giving students the opportunity to self-schedule

---

* iLEAD program information here: http://www.towson.edu/studentlife/activities/engagement/leadership/certificates/ilead.html.

allows flexibility for meetings with library and university staff and empowers students to manage their time and balance their priorities.

All of this freedom is carefully nurtured through formal and informal mentoring and extensive, purposeful communication. Each week, the group meets with their supervisor to brainstorm ideas, discuss their plan of action, get direction from their peers and supervisor, and discuss collaboration opportunities. A-LIST students are also asked to report on all of their work from the past week and their plans for the upcoming week. While some students have a never-ending supply of ideas, many need a basic concept to get started. This meeting is a time for the group to brainstorm new ideas, but is also an opportunity for the supervisor to bring possible projects to their attention. In addition to the group meeting, students meet with their mentor and supervisor about once a month. The mentor role is an informal way for students to get feedback. Mentors also look for opportunities to include the A-LISTers in their own projects, when appropriate. By doing so, the pair can spend more time getting to know each other, the A-LISTer may be exposed to a wider variety of project opportunities, and more library activities get the benefit of input from a student.

In addition to the personal support, students are also given tools to manage their work. One tool that students have particularly appreciated is Microsoft Outlook. At Towson University, students use Gmail and faculty use Microsoft Office, but students who work for the university get access to Outlook. The feedback from our students is that the calendar functions in Outlook, such as the ability to see availability for all university staff and library classrooms, makes scheduling appointments much easier. Requiring students to use a calendar for all of their work has helped them understand the value of this time management tool. The tool makes it easy to share calendars, so A-LIST students, their supervisor, and mentors can all easily see what others are up to. Additionally, since Outlook calendars are already part of the regular work habits in our library, use of this tool seamlessly incorporates A-LIST students into the culture and work of the library.

Student Initiatives

Over the last two cohorts, A-LIST students developed a number of successful events, programs, and initiatives. They have helped the library develop new partnerships and reach new students in a variety of ways. Below are some examples of new campus partnerships, library initiatives, and events all brainstormed, developed, and implemented by A-LIST students.

New Campus Partnerships

- Greek Life: Several A-LIST students have been involved in Greek Life, an area of student life with which the library was not well connected. By working with the Greek Life director, an A-LIST student was able to secure funding to support a Finals Study Lounge with snacks and research help (staffed by A-LIST students) in the library for the fraternity and sorority with the most improved GPA each semester.
- The Writing Center: While writing assistants were already holding hours in the library, the library was not offering assistance in the Writing Center. A-LIST students developed a program to staff the Writing Center four hours weekly, offering research assistance to students and training to writing assistants on library resources. Recently, the Writing Center held a "mixer" for A-LIST students and writing assistants to casually get to know one another and discuss how they can work together to help students.
- Athletics: One of our A-LIST students was a former athlete and wanted to help the library connect with new athletes. While athletes at Towson have extensive academic support and orientation, the library was not officially involved. Our A-LIST student coordinated a meeting between the library and Athletics, and a library orientation for all new students was born. Our student helped design an iPad-based scavenger hunt game that athletes completed in teams.

New Library Initiatives

- Student Group Spotlight Program: All of our A-LISTers are involved on campus in a variety of student groups. The library is always looking to connect with these groups in new ways. One of our A-LIST students came up with a formalized, mutually beneficial program called the Student Group Spotlight Program. On a monthly basis, the library features one student group using a combination of programming, library displays, and social media.

The goal is to help promote the selected student groups, while also drawing new students into the library.

- Social Media: A-LIST students assist with social media and have helped the library change its voice to be more student friendly. They introduced the popular "throwback Thursday" post, which showcases photos from the library's Special Collections.

Events and Displays

- Events: As a part of their training, A-LIST students are asked to explore other libraries' outreach initiatives. This gives students a lot of great ideas for events such as "Mugshots with Banned Books" and a "National Library Week Button Contest."
- Displays: In addition to the many themed booked displays that A-LISTers have curated, they also develop a monthly student and student group-focused display using historical photos from the library's Special Collection.

Feedback from A-LIST Graduates

At the time of publication, Cook Library has graduated two A-LIST cohorts for a total of six students, two of which have graduated from Towson as well. Their feedback about the program has been overwhelmingly positive. They mention three main areas of growth as a result of the program: communication and collaboration skills, research and information literacy skills, and increased confidence in leadership abilities. Conor Reynolds, from the first cohort, told us about the benefits of research skills:

> The research skills I learned during my time in the A-LIST have been extremely helpful to me as I've entered my career. Whether I had an interview for an internship—or ultimately the interview I had that landed me in my current position—the fact that I have experience with applied research always opens the door to a strong conversation with the interviewer. In my opinion, being able to effectively find information is valuable in any field and employers realize that.

Kelly Langford, also from the first cohort, explained how she gained leadership and communication skills:

> Being a member of the A-LIST taught me the difference between being an employee in the workplace and being a leader in the workplace. The program gave me experience in creating my own schedule, planning my own initiatives, and budgeting my time and resources to see a project through to completion. Now as a graduate in my first job, I find myself adding this kind of leadership structure to my work days, dedicating certain hours to specific projects to make sure they all get done. A-LIST also allowed me to gain experience in coordinating meetings and planning across departments. This skill has been particularly applicable in the post-graduate workplace, and each time I send an introductory email to someone I want to meet with or set an agenda for a meeting, I am thankful for the advantage A-LIST gave me by allowing me to learn these skills while still in college.

Melanie Lutz participated in the second cohort and found the practical learning components of A-LIST most helpful:

> A-LIST gave me the unique opportunity to implement my ideas and creativity into actual events and projects. This leadership experience was more realistic and useful than any part of my undergraduate career. As a result of A-LIST, I am prepared to enter my graduate studies with the confidence to make a significant difference in my program and in my profession as a whole.

The A-LIST program strives to give students meaningful experiences that fulfill the university's priorities of offering experiential learning and leadership opportunities, and our students have illustrated the potential for success in these initiatives. Our A-LIST graduates have attested to their own growth through participation, and the impact can be seen in the amazing results they produce to improve the library and their own résumés.

Challenges and Best Practices

Challenges

Overall we have been very pleased with the A-LIST program, but we have learned some things over the last two and a half years of running the program, especially about the undergraduate student participant. While no two students are alike, below are some of the challenges we have come across, which may be generalized across most students.

- Scheduling and time management: Even the best, most organized student still struggled with scheduling and time management. This, in part, is because we are asking them to do things they have never done before, and sometimes they have unrealistic ideas about how long it takes to plan and execute an event, collaborate with other departments, or complete a library project. We have found that weekly meetings in which students report their plans for the week are useful. At these meetings, a supervisor can adjust time expectations. Additionally, we have found calendar sharing to be very helpful. Requiring students to put all of their activities on their calendar and share it with their supervisor can be an unobtrusive way to monitor time management.

- Maturity and confidence: Just because our students tend to be overachievers does not mean that they are at a maturity level of a library staff member. We learned early that it is their overachieving nature that actually makes them uncomfortable appearing to not know something. As much as we tell students that the role of an A-LISTer is to learn and grow, they often do not ask questions when they have them. While an ongoing challenge, we try to overcome this by reassuring students that questions are an important part of learning as an A-LISTer, and we give them a variety of opportunities to ask questions, such as group meetings, meetings with their mentor, meetings with their supervisor, and time among themselves.

- Supervisory requirements and supportive guidance: Our goal with the A-LIST program is to help the students build capacity as leaders in the library, but this takes time and effort. Not only do we need to help students learn about our mission and goals, but we also need to build their confidence in working without constant supervision. In our experience, students often want extensive guidance and reassurance in the first semester of the program. If they have had jobs in the past, they likely have been very task oriented and straightforward. The A-LIST program requires students to be innovative and try new things. It is our job to help them feel that they are in a safe, supported environment. This will mean more "hand holding" by their supervisor and more support from their mentors their first semester. While the time required to manage the A-LISTers in the first semester is not small, we have found it to be a worthwhile investment. The confidence and creativity they exhibit in carrying out unique projects for the library could not be replicated by other library staff members. The value A-LIST delivers is irreplaceable, despite the costs.

Best Practices

Over the course of three A-LIST cohorts, we have adapted some of the best practices for working with students in this unique role and developed our own best bets for running a smooth leadership development employment program in the library.

- Communication: Frequent and structured communication among students and their supervisors, mentors, and each other is crucial to a success for programs like A-LIST. Not only should communication be encouraged, it should be scheduled through regular meetings and required progress reports. Students may not feel comfortable asking questions or getting clarification on their own and therefore need explicit opportunities to do so.

- Ease students into independence and leadership: Rarely do typical undergraduate jobs require students to take significant leadership or ownership on projects or programs. Students need help transitioning from highly structured responsibilities to independent leadership. This is accomplished through strong communication and support alongside opportunities for students to better understand the culture and mission of academic libraries. Only after they feel comfortable asking questions and trying new things can they be creative and innovative in their project leadership.

- Give them mentorship opportunities outside of the supervisor: Allowing students to develop relationships with different individuals across the library and learn about different perspectives of the library's mission are great ways to encourage the student to develop independent thinking about their leadership role and how they can contribute to library goals. Supervisors, mentors, and other library staff working on projects that include A-LIST students can each contribute to their growth in skills and confidence, since the student must integrate their different perspectives and negotiate their own time and participation with these individuals.

- Get started with projects as soon as possible: While significant training is a part of the program, students often want to dive into "real" work as soon as possible. If there is a team of students, having them work together on simple, task-oriented projects early on can be a great way to help them build their relationships with each other while helping them feel productive.
- Keep your department and library in the loop: Regular reminders will result in more library staff contributing ideas for A-LIST roles in the library. Staff are also more comfortable interacting with A-LIST students when they understand their own role or relationship to the program, which means they will feel comfortable giving direction or suggestions to students and the A-LIST supervisor or mentor.

Conclusion

The A-LIST program was created to support Towson University's institutional priorities for student learning experiences, and to emphasize the library's role in helping make these priorities successful. We started by planning for a competitively paid, uniquely structured program with a selective hiring process. By training academically oriented, outgoing, and connected students to think creatively about library services and programming, developing their capacity for leadership and independent decision making, and systematically engaging them in various projects, we end up with outstanding results. Our A-LIST students have created new partnerships on campus, enhanced our social media presence, and brought relevance for their peers to many of our programs. By doing so, they have also developed their own skills and capacity to be successful after leaving college. This experience has been challenging at times, but mostly rewarding for all involved. Students lead the library at Towson University, and we are better for it!

APPENDIX 2A	
Module	Reflective Question/Activity
Library Background	

Understanding the Big Picture and Your Role in it.	Review the following documents:
	
	    A-LIST Responsibilities and Goals
	    Towson University Strategic Plan
	    Library Strategic Plan
	
	Answer the following questions in your blog:
	
	☐ How do you see the A-LIST program supporting the university and the library's goals?
	☐ Brainstorm specific projects and/or programs that you think the A-LIST group could accomplish in order to meet these goals.
	☐ Outline at least one project and/or program in depth.

What is the Value of Academic Libraries?	Read *The Value of Academic Libraries* sections on Student Retention and Graduation Rates, Student Engagement, and Student Learning (pp. 32–45). Answer the following questions: ☐ What surprised you? ☐ What things do you think are especially important regarding these topics and the library? ☐ Are there things that Cook Library should be doing (don't worry if you aren't exactly sure what we are doing already)?
How has the Academic Library Changed?	Read *The Changing Academic Library*, Chapter 1: Introduction and a Little History. Answer the following questions: ☐ What surprised you? ☐ How has the academic library changed over time? ☐ What challenges do you see the academic library of today facing? ☐ How can A-LIST help the library and university meet those challenges?
Getting to Know Cook Library	Review the library's organization chart then meet with a library staff member from Technical Services, Research and Instruction, Interlibrary Loan, Administration, Circulation, and Special Collections. Answer the following questions: ☐ What does each department do? ☐ Do you have ideas for how A-LIST could work with any of these departments?

APPENDIX 2A	
Module	Reflective Question/Activity
Information Literacy	
Information Literacy Instruction at Cook	Observe a library session. Pay attention to what is taught and how it's taught. Think about why the library teaches what it teaches. Then read the ACRL Information Literacy Competency Standards for Higher Education. Answer the following questions: ☐ Define information literacy in your own words. ☐ Why is it important th at people are information literate (both as students and throughout life)? ☐ Based on what you know so far about the library, how does Cook Library help students with information literacy? ☐ Are there ways that A-LIST could help with this mission?
Project Information Literacy- Freshman	Watch the short clip, "Major Findings: PIL's Freshmen Study" and read the corresponding study: *Learning the Ropes: How Freshmen Conduct Course Research Once they enter College.* Answer the following questions: ☐ Do you identify with the student quotes? ☐ Do you think the transition to college is difficult for students when it comes to the academic expectations for research and research papers? ☐ Based on what you know about the library so far, how is the library helping with this transition? ☐ What do you see as your role as an A-LISTer in helping with the freshman transition?
Project Information Literacy- Graduates	Watch the short clip, "Major Findings: PIL's Day after Graduation Study (2012)" here: https://youtu.be/5gOtjexhyvE and read the corresponding report, Learning Curve: How College Graduates Solve Information Problems Once They Join the Workplace. Answer the following questions: ☐ What surprised you? ☐ Based on the ACRL Information Literacy Competency Standards for Higher Education, the freshman study and the day after graduation study, why is information literacy important?
Research Assistance	
Getting Familiar with Information Needs	Spend an hour walking around the library. Make a list of people that you see that look like they might need help. Answer the following questions about them: ☐ Where did you see them? ☐ What kind of help do you think they might need? ☐ Did you see students asking their friends/ other students for help?

APPENDIX 2A	
Module	Reflective Question/Activity
Research Assistance (continued)	
RUSA Guidelines	Read the *Guidelines for Behavioral Performance of Reference and Information Service Providers*. Answer the following question: ☐ What are the five basic guidelines in your own words?
Shadow Desk 1 (just observing)	Shadow the Research Help desk during a busy time. ☐ Keep track of the kinds of questions the librarian received. Make a list of those types of questions. ☐ Which questions/types of questions do you feel comfortable answering now (if any)? ☐ Which questions/types of questions do you think you should be able to answer? ☐ Which questions/types of questions would you refer to a librarian?
Roving Reference in the Library	Read "Rolling Out Roving Reference in an Academic Library" from the book *Leading the Reference Renaissance*. Answer the following questions: ☐ What do you see as the biggest challenges to "roving" while giving research assistance? ☐ What are ways we can make roving more successful?
Read last year's A-LIST questions, take notes	Read over last year's A-LIST questions/answers. Take note of the questions you think you could answer now and the questions you still need to learn how to answer.
Shadow desk 2 (complete A-LIST Students Research Assistance Training document)	Shadow the Research Help desk during a slow time. Work with the librarian on duty to learn these tasks. You will be asked to demonstrate/explain these skills.
Library of Congress call number activity	The Library of Congress classification system is how our books are organized in the library. In order to assist patrons in finding books, you will need to know how it works. Read and complete the enclosed Library of Congress worksheet.
Research Assistance Quiz	Sit with your supervisor to complete the research assistance quiz.
IM Reference Best Practices	Read the *IM Reference Best Practices & Etiquette*, then sit with a librarian to get an overview of how the system works. ☐ How might an IM question be different than an in-person question? ☐ When should you answer a question and when should you let a librarian pick up the question?

APPENDIX 2A	
Module	Reflective Question/Activity
Research Assistance (continued)	
Connecting with the Writing Center	Read the Writing Center FAQ and then read *A-LIST Students Working at the Writing Center: What to Expect*. In your blog, write your thoughts about working at the Writing Center. ☐ What are the advantages of this collaboration? ☐ Do you see any possible issues? ☐ Do you have questions?
Leadership	
iLead Programs or Leadership Conferences	For each program, answer the following questions: ☐ What was purpose of the program? ☐ What surprised you? ☐ How will you implement what you learned in this program?
Library Outreach & Marketing	
Library Outreach	Review the list of outreach activities that the library has done over the last few years. Also, look at other libraries' web pages and social media as well as the books we have on library outreach to see what others are doing. Answer the following questions: ☐ What are your ideas for library outreach? ☐ Are there departments we could work with? ☐ Events we could support/host? ☐ Ways for us to help students with their research?
Social Media and the Library	Read the following articles: *20 Ways to Make People Fall in Love With Your Instagram: A Guide for Libraries and Other Cultural Institutions* *Social Media and Libraries: 5 Quick Tips for Using Instagram* *10 Twitter Best Practices for Nonprofits* *Social Media Best Practices: Facebook* Then, spend time looking at Cook Library's Instagram, Facebook, and Twitter Accounts. Answer the following questions: ☐ What are your ideas for helping Cook Library connect with students through social media? ☐ Outside of Twitter, Instagram, and Facebook, is there another social media platform that you think could be successful for connecting with students? How would you use it?

Bibliography

Albert S. Cook Library. "A-LIST: Student Research Assistants." *YouTube* video, 1:25. July 31, 2014. https://youtu.be/KjM_QeCcHoo.

Towson University. "iLead Certificate." Accessed June 8, 2016. http://www.towson.edu/studentlife/activities/engagement/leadership/certificates/ilead.html.

University System of Maryland. "Towson University." Accessed June 8, 2016. http://www.usmd.edu/institutions/profile/?Inst=TU.

CHAPTER 3*

THE FRONT FACE OF LIBRARY SERVICES:

How Student Employees Lead the Library at Grand Valley State University

Kristin Meyer and Jennifer Torreano

Introduction

Academic libraries have always been involved in student learning, but our profession has perhaps failed to recognize that the students who work for us every day are likely the ones we can impact the most. Librarians and library staff have a tremendous opportunity to contribute to the professional growth of the students they employ. Historically, academic libraries have defined student learning in terms of librarian instruction, collections, and providing study space. While these remain important aspects of what libraries do, student employees benefit from intentional, empowered roles and, in turn, libraries are enriched when student employees take on leadership roles.

When walking into the Mary Idema Pew Library at Grand Valley State University, students surround you. As you walk through the library's main corridor, students are staffing the service desk on your right, and the Knowledge Market on your left is bustling with students engaged in peer consultations. Professional staff are not visible. To students entering the building for the first time, the immediate impression is that students are front and center within the facility. Placing students in these leadership roles visually cues student patrons that the space is theirs and encourages them to manage their own learning. Additionally, this model provides high-impact learning experiences for the student employees themselves and positions them to make significant contributions to the library.

Research consultants and user experience (UX) student assistants are the two groups of student employees that serve as the front face of library services in the Mary Idema Pew Library. UX students staff the single service desk, and research consultants provide one-on-one peer consultations in the Knowledge Market. Both groups perform high-level work not traditionally entrusted to student employees.

Background

Various components of Grand Valley State University's institutional mission, makeup, and culture, as well as the culture of the University Libraries, have contributed to the formation and the success of these student employee programs. Grand Valley State University is a Carnegie classification "Master's Large" university located near Grand Rapids, MI. Eighty-five percent of the university's 25,000 students are undergraduate students, and the university is a liberal education teaching institution. Grand Valley is student-centered, and the institution values informed risk-taking. The Dean of University Libraries, Lee Van Orsdel, describes the culture of the university as "confident and innovative" and has surmised that this gives library faculty and staff the confidence to try new initiatives, including those involving student employment.[1]

As a result of the university's makeup and culture, the library strives to be user-centered with a focus on undergraduate students. Students are the front face of library services in an effort to capture the benefits of peer learning[2] and to visually illustrate to student patrons that library space is their space. "For students, by students" is the way that we often think about library services and spaces. This thinking did not happen in a vacuum, however, and was the result of a long discovery process that was tied intrinsically to the design process of the new library facility.

Grand Valley opened the Mary Idema Pew Library Learning and Information Commons in 2013. The new library has been called a model of twenty-first century learning and is a radically student-centered space.[3] Students are encouraged to manage their own learning—furniture is mobile and there are few rules or directives for the space. Prior to the design process that started in 2010, Dean VanOrsdel started to share her vision for creating a new kind of library using the analogy of a shopping mall. In shopping malls, students and young adults are highly self-directed and self-motivated, and this is all visually evident. Part of the library design process included adding elements that would encourage that kind of self-direction and self-motivation. The vision for the building included the notion of student empowerment. Over time, staff started applying that thinking about student empowerment to student employment. Throughout the new building design process, staff started to rethink not only library spaces, but also library services. Dean VanOrsdel suggests that the design process "allowed us to move beyond the patterns that we already knew."[4]

Prior to utilizing students as the front face of library services, University Libraries had already made several bold changes to library services and, in particular, to service desk staffing. By 2010, liaison librarians were no longer working regularly scheduled shifts at the service desk. This decision was based on statistical data that indicated that most service desk transactions did not require the assistance of a professional librarian.[5] This change allowed librarians to concentrate on instructional sessions and faculty outreach. From 2010 to 2013, full-time support staff took the lead at the service desk. When the Mary Idema Pew Library opened, UX students started to staff the service desk, supported primarily behind the scenes by support staff. While these changes were not always easy, the "why" behind them seemed to resonate with library faculty and staff and, over time, most library employees have come to see the value of a student-led service desk. By witnessing firsthand the benefits of peer learning and the high quality of service provided by student employees, staff received a powerful confirmation of the advantages of this service model.

During the design process, the library also identified that employers often seek skills that students may not be able to master in the traditional classroom setting, such as identifying and synthesizing relevant information, writing clearly and concisely, and speaking persuasively. Grand Valley had a well-established Writing Center in a building housing the university's writing program, and the library envisioned bringing a second Writing Center location into the library, where it would be in the heart of campus, alongside consultants ready to assist students with presentations and library research. Providing one location in the library for students seeking assistance with their assignments would ensure that the services would be visible to students in all disciplines. This space would eventually be coined the "Knowledge Market."

Research Consultants

A central feature of the Mary Idema Pew Library is the Knowledge Market, a space for students to seek assistance in researching, writing, and delivering presentations, skills that employers desire and evaluate but are not always explicitly taught by classroom faculty.[6] The consultants are intentionally visible from the building's main entrance, and the space is open with a receptionist staffing a small counter instead of an imposing desk. The idea of the Knowledge Market was inspired by kiosks at shopping malls. Designed to surprise you with products and services you did not know you needed, kiosks provide an opportunity for serendipity, and the Knowledge Market is designed to do the same for students who might desire assistance with their assignments.

Peer consultants exist in a space that faculty cannot. Students and teachers operate in different discourse communities, and students often struggle to understand the language faculty use to describe assignments and provide feedback.[7] Additionally, regardless of the tone or approach taken by faculty, students are aware of the inherent authority imbalance between them. Peer consultants are able to exist between teachers and students, translating assignment instructions in a non-evaluative context.[8] If, as Bruffee posits in "Peer Tutoring and the Conversation of Mankind," becoming a member of a community is dependent on learning its discourse, and the ability of students to practice normal discourse is paramount to their success,[9] such a process can be made easier when fear of "looking stupid" is minimized.[10] Peer consultants can provide this safe space for students to learn the language and values of their academic communities through trial and error using the medium of conversation.

Writing and presentation support are offered by peer consultants at the Writing Center and Speech Lab, and the University Libraries employs twenty research consultants to offer a parallel service for research assistance.[11] Originally, the library had intended to utilize reference librarians in the Knowledge Market to work with students. However, the library had recently transitioned librarians away from the reference desk so they could focus more deeply in a liaison capacity, emphasizing outreach and targeted instruction.[12] That transition, combined with research on the benefits of peer learning, led the library to join the Speech Lab and Writing Center in offering an academic support service for students, by students in the Knowledge Market.[13]

Research consultants are highly trained,[14] primarily undergraduate students who meet one-on-one with other undergraduates to talk them through the research process. Students can make thirty- or fifty-minute appointments in advance or drop in for a thirty-minute consultation. The consultants work independently; librarians and professional staff are not present in the Knowledge Market. Professional support staff are available behind the service desk, but because the Knowledge Market is intended to be a safe space where students can feel vulnerable improving their discourse, there is no intrusive presence from librarians or professional staff by design.

Though consultants offer reference assistance, they do not replace librarians, both in the theoretical context mentioned previously and a practical one. Research consultants and librarians do not compete, for they are entirely different kinds of student support, and students manage their own learning experience by deciding what kind of support to request each time they seek it. Librarians offer targeted instruction and expert assistance in consultations, a fundamentally different kind of interaction than a peer conversation. The two kinds of assistance are complimentary and fluid; library services are designed so students can never make the wrong choice. A student can ask anyone—UX students, research consultants, librarians, and any other library staff—for help, and that person will find the resources the student needs. Sometimes those resources are other people.

Librarians work closely with the research consultants, mentoring them and providing a variety of training opportunities which, in turn, leads to referrals from research consultants. In fact, the number of librarian consultations has gone up since the research consultant program began in the fall of 2012. We do not currently have a way to track whether students who meet with consultants and librarians overlap, but we suspect the consultants are acting as a gateway to library services for students who would be unlikely to request a meeting with a librarian. It is possible that consultants are easing such interactions by offering low-pressure consultations and referring to librarians regularly.

As part of the Instructional Services department of the library, research consultants are supervised by the Library Research Consultant Manager, who oversees the program and collaborates with directors of the Writing Center, Speech Lab, and newly-created Data Inquiry Lab. Successful administration of the programs requires harmony and consistency among the services. Knowledge Market consultants regularly pull in consultants from other services to assist when questions veer outside the scope of their work, so a unified vision and collaboration, including some shared trainings, are paramount to the Knowledge Market's successful operation. The consultants enjoy working together closely, and the collaboration reflects to students the recursive nature of the work happening in the Knowledge Market.

UX Students

The term *user experience* has become increasingly popular in libraries as well as the corporate sector and can be interpreted in a variety of ways. One definition is that user experience characterizes how a person feels about using a product, system, or service.[15] Aaron Schmidt and Amanda Etches state that "Ideally, all of your library's touch points—the places where your users come into contact with your library—will be aligned and well-designed. This means that creating a holistic and positive user experience includes designing great print materials, signs, customer service, facilities, reference workflows, programs, collections, and services."[16] We recognize that user experience should be holistic, and many faculty and staff within University Libraries are involved in some type of user experience-related work. Our User Experience Team, however, specifically focuses on front-line customer service and experiences within the physical library space.

Our Operations and User Services Department is the area traditionally known as Access Services. The department is split into two teams—the User Experience (UX) Team and the Access and Delivery (A&D) Team.

UX focuses on "front-of-the-house" services while A&D focuses on the "back-of-the-house" processes. The UX Team is led by the User Experience Librarian and is composed of four full-time support staff and twenty-five UX students. UX students report directly to one of the UX staff, and this staff member and the UX Librarian work collaboratively on student employee program elements. All UX staff and most of the A&D staff work regularly scheduled shifts at the "Perch," an area behind the service desk. When staff work at the Perch, they oversee the services provided by UX students and are available to help with difficult questions and situations, assist with training initiatives, answer telephone calls, and respond to text and chat questions. The service desk is open and staffed with UX students during all open library hours; currently, the library is open until 2:00 a.m. Sunday through Thursday and until 9:00 p.m. on Fridays and Saturdays. At least two staff members from the Operations and User Services Department are also typically in the building during all open library hours.

The primary function of the UX students is to staff the single service desk. They welcome patrons and answer a variety of directional, circulation, basic reference, and technology questions. At the service desk, they often serve as an entry point to library research services, answering basic reference questions and showing students how to get started searching, but also by promoting and referring students to research consultants or liaison librarians whenever it benefits the end-user.

The UX students also roam the library each hour, assisting patrons who may need help at the point of need, checking that everything in the building is running smoothly from an operational standpoint, and collecting data on how students are using library space. Additionally, UX students conduct building tours, often for high-profile visitors from educational institutions and corporations from around the world. UX students also occasionally assist with user experience research techniques. For example, two UX students assisted with conducting wayfinding usability tests that were implemented in order to better understand how our digital displays were being used by students. Another UX student worked with the User Experience Librarian to conduct ethnographic touchpoint tours aimed at understanding student perception of library space.

By helping fellow students with their various needs at the service desk, UX students engage in peer learning. Whether it involves demonstrating how to print, how to search for a particular article, or how to find a book in the stacks, UX students often share knowledge with their peers. UX students who have worked for multiple semesters are also involved with various components of the training plan, giving them opportunities to help orient, train, and informally mentor new UX students.[17]

Recruitment and Hiring

Setting high expectations for our student employees begins with the recruitment process. Job advertisements and interviews are as much a time for prospective student employees to learn about the work and library culture as they are a time for employers to evaluate candidates. We think carefully about what we want to convey to candidates in our job advertisements and interview questions and devise them accordingly. Unlike many libraries, GVSU is not limited to hiring only work-study students, and typically only a small percentage of UX students and research consultants have awards. Regardless of any library's applicant pool, a deliberate hiring and recruitment process can benefit both the library and prospective hires.

To begin setting high expectations, the research consultant's job application is rigorous. Modeled after the GVSU Writing Center's application, it requires responses to scenario questions, two writing samples with research, and a faculty recommendation. The time and energy investment needed to complete the application filters those who are not motivated, and the rigor makes it clear that we are looking for academically focused students who are serious about research. Similarly, the UX students also go through an elevated application process, including an application with scenario questions and a required letter of recommendation.[18]

We also involve the UX students and research consultants in the hiring process which, in addition to being a learning opportunity for the student employees themselves, demonstrates to candidates that we regard the student employees as professionals with valuable perspectives. Hiring managers and student employees use rubrics to evaluate applications, and the research consultants also complete training on inclusive hiring practices before participating. Because student employees have a different perspective than program managers, their input has been quite helpful.

Student employees also participate in candidate interviews. The research consultants review and assist with revising the interview questions each year, and they also ask half of the questions during the interviews.

They complete an evaluation sheet during every interview, and their comments and recommendations for hire are weighted heavily by the Library Research Consultant Manager when making hiring decisions. The UX Team uses a similar process, and former UX students have indicated that participating in the interviews was a valuable experience. For candidates, learning about the jobs from student employees during the interviews introduces the concept of peer learning and the value we place on peer mentoring relationships. This method also conveys that student employees have some ownership of the work: student employees help to shape the programs and are invested in their success and future as a result.

Being thoughtful about what messages our application materials convey and how we utilize student employees during the hiring process ensures that we are selecting highly motivated, serious students with the potential to become leaders on campus. The rigor and behavior modeled by student employees during the process also sets expectations of professionalism for candidates selected for hire, changing our work during orientation from setting expectations to reinforcing them, a more manageable objective.

Contributions to the Library

The library has benefited greatly from having students play a leadership role as the front face of library services. Empowering student employees has given them a feeling of ownership toward the library, making them natural ambassadors among their peers. Their work has also helped the library demonstrate its value to the campus in new ways and has created extra time for faculty and staff, resulting in new library endeavors and, ultimately, positive publicity for the university.

Student patrons view the library as their space, and the visibility of student employees appears to have contributed to this perspective. The library has become an extremely popular place on campus; more than one million people visit the library per academic year, and 600–900 students are often in the building at once. Students are empowered here: they regularly move furniture and modify the environment to fit their own needs. While this is undoubtedly due to a number of factors, it seems that putting students in highly visible leadership roles has made an impact. "From the beginning, we intended that the building would be theirs," Dean VanOrsdel said. "We wanted both the building and its programs to be radically student-centered, and we have been true to our word. I don't know how we can get much more radical than to put students in charge of our main services on the floor of the library. I think that speaks volumes about our confidence in their ability, their need to manage their own learning environments, their ability to help one another, and the social nature of learning."[19]

One unexpected result of implementing this service model is that these students serve as a built-in marketing tool. Our student employees are wonderful ambassadors of the library to their fellow students, and they frequently promote the library and library services as they go about their own campus experiences. We have often witnessed the power of peer-to-peer endorsements. For example, student patrons have commented during focus groups that they learned about the library through their friends and often through connections with library student employees. Employing a greater number of students, empowering student workers so that they have a sense of pride in their work and in the library, and ensuring that their training includes a deep understanding of library services and resources helps promote positive messages about the library to the rest of the campus community.

In addition to serving the library by promoting the library among their peer groups, UX students are in a position to provide valuable feedback on library policies, services, and spaces. They are constantly observing what is happening in the building, and they routinely share what they think works well and what could be improved. Their perspectives and experiences as students are different from those of library employees, and they often provide unique and valuable insights on a wide range of issues.

We can also demonstrate to the campus community that the library directly impacts student learning in an unexpected way: these student employment opportunities themselves are learning experiences that help our students gain professional skills that they are unlikely to learn in the classroom. Sharing these insights with campus faculty and administrators can be useful for library advocacy efforts.

The data we gather from research consultations is also used to demonstrate the impact that the library has on students. In addition to the obvious benefits of students talking through their research process, data recorded during consultations suggests that students are reassured by their interactions with research consultants. Each consultation ends with a short survey asking whether students felt comfortable, found the consultation helpful, and feel more confident going forward. The data indicates that 98 percent of students feel more confident about completing their assignment after working with a research consultant. This measure is a specific way that the library can demonstrate its relevance and value to the campus community.

The campus has also noticed that the library is engaged in new kinds of interesting work, which is only possible because the work of student employees has allowed library faculty and staff to focus their time on other initiatives. Since moving away from the reference desk, liaison librarians now have more time for instructional sessions and to support faculty in their areas of responsibility. The Operations and User Services staff members also have time to devote to new projects and initiatives as a result of the work of the UX students at the service desk. For example, the Mary Idema Pew Library includes event space, and UX staff started coordinating and assisting with event support when the new library opened. The team assists with approximately 200 educational events each academic year. These events support campus-wide values and would not be possible without UX staff being able to devote some of their time to this type of work.

Our UX students have also helped us understand how students use the library by collecting space usage data on their hourly roams. This information has been valuable for a variety of purposes, including policy decisions, decisions on when and where events and special activities should be hosted within the library, and in helping to determine how to best utilize space. UX students staffing the service desk has also given staff the time necessary to implement various research techniques aimed at better understanding how students perceive library space. For example, we recently conducted cognitive mapping with student patrons, during which we asked students to draw maps of the library and then explain their maps. We gained valuable insights pertaining to how students describe library space, their familiarity with individual spaces and services, and why they tend to gravitate to particular areas. This also helped us to identify possible marketing opportunities. If our UX staff spent all of their time at the service desk, projects like this would not be possible.

One risk of experimenting with such a radical service model is that we could not guarantee that this model would positively impact satisfaction among library users. However, anecdotal as well as quantitative data indicate that the campus community is more satisfied than ever before with library services. Students, faculty, staff, and community members alike have made many positive comments about the service they have received from student employees, and their service has even been highlighted in the student newspaper. Additionally, the library conducted the national LibQUAL+ Lite survey* in 2015 and received higher scores in the Affect of Service dimension than in previous surveys when professional staff were at the service desk. In particular, we scored higher in the "Employees with knowledge to answer questions" category, indicating that our UX students are answering questions satisfactorily. While there could be a number of factors involved in these scores, we view this as a preliminary positive affirmation that the model is working.

Finally, our approach to student employment has also helped the library earn awards which have ultimately resulted in positive publicity for the university. For example, University Libraries received the Michigan State Librarian's Excellence Award in 2014, which is an award for a library of any type that exemplifies excellence in customer service. In the award application, we highlighted our approach to student employment and, specifically, our research consultants and UX students. Our student workers were undoubtedly part of the reason that University Libraries won this award, and the university received positive publicity as a result.

Benefits to Student Employees

Empowered student employees become better students and are more prepared for life after graduation. The information they learn and skills they develop while working front and center in the library go beyond what student employees gain from traditional roles in academic libraries. In addition to the skills they could learn at any job—punctuality, honesty, time management—empowered library student employees develop transferable skill sets in addition to professional poise.

Research consultants and UX student assistants have an advantage as students on campus. Because their work involves helping others with research and answering questions about campus resources, they have a solid grasp of information that we struggle to share with every individual student on campus. Library student employees know about opportunities for undergraduate research, who to ask for assistance with fellowship appli-

---

* "LibQUAL+," *Association of Research Libraries*, accessed January 8, 2016, https://www.libqual.org/home.

cations, resources provided by the Office of Multicultural Affairs and the LGBT Resource Center, and numerous campus events that could expand their worldview outside of their own discipline. They are also trained and practiced in reference interviews and search strategies, and they have an awareness of library collections that many students lack. A significant portion of their work is informing others, and the foundation of knowledge required to do that benefits student employees academically.

Complex work provides an opportunity for student employees to develop skills that will transfer to any career. For research consultants, learning how to ask strategic questions to solve miscommunications is a skill useful in any future position. Consultants also hone the skill to apply familiar methodology to unfamiliar disciplines and bridge communication gaps. Consultants learn how to read others and gain strategies to help those feeling disappointment, embarrassment, and apprehension. They also practice turning emotional conversations into productive ones, a skill that has the potential to be useful in a variety of future endeavors.

UX students develop a slightly different skill set, gaining customer service skills and valuable experience in a fast-paced service environment. The user-centered philosophy that the department advocates is applicable in a variety of settings. UX students cultivate observational skills and get practice offering solutions for the pain points that they discover. They are also involved in UX research, such as usability testing, and practicing methodical research and analysis teaches them useful problem solving skills. UX students also have regular opportunities to interact with highly accomplished professionals, giving tours to senators, CEOs, and government officials from other countries. Dean VanOrsdel recalled an anecdote about a student employee who answered questions in a meeting with officials from the Russian Ministry of Education. She noted, "The student didn't hesitate to make a comment. He didn't blink. We've seen students do that over and over again. We're either just hiring really poised students, or we're hiring good students whom we have given a chance to become poised in the face of interest in the building."[20]

The student employees also recognize the benefits of these experiences. At the end of their employment, UX students are given an anonymous exit survey that asks them to reflect upon their employment and how they see their experiences being relevant to their future careers. Students often indicate that their face-to-face communication skills have improved as a result of their employment. One student wrote, "Working with executives when giving tours has benefited me in so many ways. Being able to communicate and carry myself in a professional manner is truly a remarkable experience and characteristic to possess." The level of professionalism that UX students are expected to maintain will likely benefit them in any future profession.

Research consultants offer similar comments when asked about what they have gained while working for the University Libraries. One consultant encourages other students to apply for the job by saying, "Not only do you get to help fellow students feel better about their research abilities, you also continuously hone your own skills and become much more effective with research, communication, and collaboration." The consultants understand the impact they have on students and they see how their contributions affect the library, but they sometimes struggle to fully connect their activities to graduate work or future employment in different fields. To guide them through this thought process, consultants participate in a résumé workshop each year so they can break down what they have learned on the job and how those skills can translate to their future endeavors.

Conclusion

Although we felt confident about some aspects of this new student employment model during the design phase, in many ways it was an experiment that we are still adjusting and evaluating. Broad support for these student employment groups did not happen overnight, but developed over time as library faculty and staff observed the tangible benefits of this approach. Throughout our journey, we have made a few large changes, such as the administrative structure of the research consultant program, and we have made slight modifications to the daily work of our students, our recruiting and hiring methods, training plans, and our communication strategies. We anticipate that this work will never be finished. We will continue to identify ways to improve this service model, and we must be vigilant and responsive to changing needs on campus.

What we believe to be most successful is the abandonment of our preconceived ideas about what student employees are capable of accomplishing. Being imaginative about new ways to approach student learning and keeping an open mind about the possibilities of what roles could be given to students allowed us to push beyond the limits of tradition. We put our faith in the students, trusting that they would meet our raised expectations. They have.

We are not advocating for all libraries to replicate our model. These particular student employment groups will not work everywhere; in fact, we use a different service desk model at two other library locations because they serve different student populations with unique needs and, frankly, this model is a costly way of doing business. However, we do believe that thinking intentionally about student employees as leaders has value in every academic library. The possibilities for student contributions extend far beyond the boundaries of what are traditionally seen as the role of student employees.

Reflective Activity

While adopting GVSU's particular model of student employment may not make sense for many institutions, reconsidering the role of student employees and moving to a model that emphasizes student learning and leadership can benefit all academic libraries. To begin thinking about potential roles for your student employees, consider the following questions:

- Why does your library exist?
- Why do you employ students?
- What do your student employees learn throughout their employment experience?
- What are the current campus needs that your library could meet?
- How could student employees help the library to meet those needs?

Whether you have identified opportunities for a new student employment group or want to enhance existing student roles and practices, consider the following questions:

- What do you want prospective student employees to know about your library and the position?
- What skills do you need to identify throughout the hiring process?
- What will new student employees need to learn to accomplish their work?
- What elements could be included in a comprehensive training plan?
- What other learning opportunities could students be given along the way?
- How could you assess your training plan?
- How could you measure success for this student employment group?

Notes

1. Lee VanOrsdel in interview with authors, October 27, 2015.
2. Nancy Falchikov and Margo Blythman, *Learning Together: Peer Tutoring in Higher Education* (New York: Routledge/Falmer, 2001); Muriel Harris, "Talking in the Middle: Why Writers Need Writing Tutors," *College English* 57, no. 1 (1995): 27–42, doi: 10.2307/378348; Kenneth Bruffee, "Collaborative Learning and the 'Conversation of Mankind,'" in *The Allyn and Bacon Guide to Writing Center Theory and Practice*, ed. Robert W. Barnett and Jacob S. Blumner (Boston: Allyn and Bacon, 2001): 206–218.
3. Pete Daly, "Newsmaker of the Year: GVSU Adds to its Facilities in Allendale and Downtown," *Grand Rapids Business Journal* (Grand Rapids, MI), Jan 17, 2012.
4. Lee VanOrsdel in interview with authors.
5. Lynn Sheehan, "Re-Inventing Reference," in *Declaration of Interdependence: The Proceedings of the ACRL 2011 Conference*, ed. Dawn M. Mueller (Chicago: Association of College and Research Libraries [ACRL], 2011): 384–89.
6. Ellen Schendel, et al., "Making Noise in the Library: Designing a Student Learning Environment to Support a Liberal Education," in *Cases on Higher Education Spaces: Innovation, Collaboration, and Technology*, ed. Russell Carpenter (Hershey, PA: Information Science Reference, 2013), 290–312.
7. Harris, *College English*, 36–40.
8. Ibid., 38.
9. Bruffee, "Collaborative Learning and the 'Conversation of Mankind,'" 211–213.
10. Harris, *College English*, 28.
11. Mary O'Kelly, et al., "Building a Peer-Learning Service for Students in an Academic Library," portal: Libraries and the Academy 15, no. 1 (2015), https://muse.jhu.edu/journals/portal_libraries_and_the_academy/v015/15.1.o-kelly.html.
12. Sheehan, "Re-Inventing Reference," 385.
13. Mary O'Kelly, *portal: Libraries and the Academy*, 165.
14. Mary O'Kelly, "Research Consultants at Grand Valley State University: Developing Intentional Peer Support," in *Training Research Consultants: A Guide for Academic Libraries*, ed. Mary O'Kelly (Chicago, IL: Association of College and Research Libraries, forthcoming).
15. Aaron Schmidt and Amanda Etches. *User Experience (UX) Design for Libraries* (New York: Neal-Schuman Publishers, Incorporated, 2012): 1.
16. Ibid., 2.
17. Kristin Meyer, "User Experience at Grand Valley State University: Training Students Who Take the Lead in Staffing the Library's Single Service Point," in *Training Research Consultants: A Guide for Academic Libraries*, ed. Mary O'Kelly (Chicago, IL: Association of College and Research Libraries, forthcoming).
18. Ibid.
19. Lee VanOrsdel in interview with authors.
20. Lee VanOrsdel in interview with authors.

Bibliography

Bruffee, Kenneth. "Collaborative Learning and the 'Conversation of Mankind.'" In *The Allyn and Bacon Guide to Writing Center Theory and Practice*, edited by Robert W. Barnett and Jacob S. Blumner, 206–218. Boston: Allyn and Bacon, 2001.

Daly, Pete. "Newsmaker of the Year: GVSU Adds to its Facilities in Allendale and Downtown." *Grand Rapids Business Journal* (Grand Rapids, MI), Jan 17, 2012.

Falchikov, Nancy and Margo Blythman, *Learning Together: Peer Tutoring in Higher Education*. New York: Routledge/Falmer, 2001.

Harris, Muriel. "Talking in the Middle: Why Writers Need Writing Tutors." *College English* 57, no. 1 (1995): 27–42. doi: 10.2307/378348.

"LibQUAL+." *Association of Research Libraries*. Accessed January 8, 2016. https://www.libqual.org/home.

Meyer, Kristin. "User Experience at Grand Valley State University: Training Students Who Take the Lead in Staffing the Library's Single Service Point." In *Training Research Consultants: A Guide for Academic Libraries*, edited by Mary O'Kelly. Chicago, IL: Association of College and Research Libraries, forthcoming.

O'Kelly, Mary. "Research Consultants at Grand Valley State University: Developing Intentional Peer Support." In *Training Research Consultants: A Guide for Academic Libraries*, edited by Mary O'Kelly. Chicago, IL: Association of College and Research Libraries, forthcoming.

O'Kelly, Mary, Julie Garrison, Brian Merry, and Jennifer Torreano. "Building a Peer-Learning Service for Students in an Academic Library." *portal: Libraries and the Academy* 15, no. 1 (2015): 163–82. https://muse.jhu.edu/journals/portal_libraries_and_the_academy/v015/15.1.o-kelly.html

Schendel, Ellen, Julie Garrison, Patrick Johnson, and Lee VanOrsdel. "Making Noise in the Library: Designing a Student Learning Environment to Support a Liberal Education." In *Cases on Higher Education Spaces: Innovation, Collaboration, and Technology*, edited by Russell Carpenter, 290–312. Hershey, PA: Information Science Reference, 2013.

Schmidt, Aaron, and Amanda Etches. *User Experience (UX) Design for Libraries*. New York: Neal-Schuman Publishers, Inc., 2012.

Sheehan, Lynn. "Re-Inventing Reference." In *Declaration of Interdependence: The Proceedings of the ACRL 2011 Conference*, edited by Dawn M. Mueller, 290–312. Chicago: Association of College and Research Libraries, 2011.

CHAPTER 4*

ALIGNING VALUES, DEMONSTRATING VALUE:
Peer Educator Programs in the Library

Krista Bianco and Joannah O'Hatnick

HOW DO PEER educator programs—long established in higher education in North America, yet relatively new to library settings—find their "fit" in academic libraries? What values do peer educator programs contribute to libraries, and how do they demonstrate their value in this setting? Through an examination of our peer educator programs, which have been fully integrated into our university's library for close to ten years, we propose to address these questions about the overlap and juxtaposition of values and value between academic libraries and peer educator programs. Note that we, the authors, are not librarians, but rather higher education professionals with graduate-level education and experience supporting the academic success of students on our campus. Consequently, we provide an external perspective on the operations of our library; our colleagues in the field of academic support at other institutions tend to work in student affairs. In this chapter, we provide context for our services and institution, before describing the values that underpin our peer educator programs and how they align and intersect with those of our library. We discuss how the concept of value is assessed and demonstrated differently by libraries and peer educator programs. Throughout, we offer insights and recommendations for those who may be considering the development and implementation of peer educator programs within an academic library environment.

Peer Educators in the Library at the University of Guelph

Context and Overview

The University of Guelph, a public institution of 22,000 undergraduate and graduate students in southwestern Ontario, Canada, is known for its many student-focused services and programs. It recently received the highest student satisfaction rating from among similar Canadian institutions in a national survey[1] and has a rich history of student volunteerism.* Our Learning Commons, established in 1999 and one of the oldest in North America, is among the many services which students perceive as contributing to a supportive and student-focused atmosphere on campus.

Our Learning Commons began as a part of Student Affairs in the 1980s as Learning and Writing Services (LWS), and was dedicated to supporting students' academic skill development. In 1999, LWS moved physically from a building which housed most Student Affairs units to the library, and became the core of the new Learning Commons, whose mandate was "to offer students a coherent and integrated approach to learning, writing, research and technology support."[2] In 2007, the Learning Commons was incorporated administratively into the University of Guelph's McLaughlin Library. Despite these transitions, peer educator programs continue to be fundamental to our services.

Peer Educators in the University of Guelph's Library

Although six peer educator programs have been housed in our Learning Commons over the past thirty years (see Table 4.1), we focus here

---

*An informal campus survey in 2014 revealed that 64% of responding students reported currently volunteering either on or off campus.

on the three peer educator groups with the longest history: the learning peer helpers, the writing peer helpers, and the supported learning group (SLG) peer helpers. The learning peer helpers and writing peer helpers provide assistance to undergraduate students through individual consultations, workshops, and resource development, such as the creation of handouts or other tools. The learning peer helpers focus on skill development in study strategies and time management, while the writing peer helpers assist students at all stages of the writing process. The SLG peer helpers implement the Supplemental Instruction (SI) model by facilitating weekly group study sessions for historically challenging undergraduate courses.[*]

Peer Educator Group	Established in	Part of the Peer Helper Program	Current Number of Peer Educators
Learning Peer Helpers	mid-1980's	yes	13
Writing Peer Helpers	1994	yes	11
Supported Learning Group Leaders	1998	yes	45
Student Technology Consultants	2001	yes	0 (program ended in 2004)
Student Athlete Mentors[1]	2009	no	13
Engineering Peer Helpers[2]	2008	yes	9

[1] The Student Athlete Mentor (SAM) Program training and supervisory model is largely based on the Peer Helper programs housed within the Library, but, unlike the Peer Helpers, the mentors are paid on an hourly basis and do not receive a notation on their transcript.
[2] Co-supervised between Learning Commons staff and the University of Guelph's School of Engineering (SOE), these Peer Helpers are primarily located within the Engineering building.

Table 4.1. Overview of Peer Educator Groups in the Library at the University of Guelph

These three peer educator groups are all part of the University of Guelph's Peer Helper Program (PHP), one of the oldest and largest of its kind in Canada. Established in 1984, the Peer Helper Program provides a

---

[*]The SI model, established in 1973 and now practiced around the world, aims to support student retention and engagement in high risk courses, which are considered to be those courses with a combined "drop," fail, and letter "D" grade rate in excess of 30% over time. Peer educators facilitate study sessions using collaborative learning strategies to help students master the course content while also developing effective learning strategies and metacognitive awareness.

multi-semester experiential learning opportunity for students to volunteer five or ten hours a week in a paraprofessional, peer-to-peer helping role on campus. The PHP includes a competitive application process for students, and Peer Helper supervisors, who are typically professional staff on campus, must commit to providing ongoing training and professional development opportunities for their peer helpers. Although peer helpers do not receive payment for their service, they do receive a non-credit notation on their transcript and a small honorarium per semester. Our long-term collaborative partnership with this larger, volunteer-based program has had a significant impact on many of the values inherent in our library-based peer educators.

The Core Values of Peer Educators and Programs

The success and effectiveness of peer-to-peer academic support services in a post-secondary context have been well established for many years;[3] these programs enable many peer educators to develop leadership, metacognitive, and professional skills, while students receiving services often experience gains in increased motivation and metacognitive skills.[4] Peer-to-peer support acknowledges that students may feel more comfortable approaching another student for assistance compared to an "expert" staff person who may differ from them in age, education, and experience. Having peer educators assist in the delivery of services thus makes the services more approachable and relevant, provides students with visible role models for personal and academic success, and expands the institution's capacity to support students.[5]

In the University of Guelph's Learning Commons, we have always taken a great deal of care in selecting those students who act in peer educator roles within our units. Our experience has shown us that students with specific values not only tend to excel in these roles, but also to benefit the most from the experience. The values that we look for in prospective peer educators include openness to self-growth and development, inclusivity, a belief in the importance of community, a commitment to service, and a non-hierarchical approach to service delivery. Not surprisingly, these values mirror those that guide our own work and also the work of many student affairs professionals.[6]

Self-Growth and Development

As part of the broader Peer Helper Program, our peer educators must understand their role within the framework of experiential learning, in which they are expected to reflect on their experiences and view challenges as opportunities for personal, academic, and professional growth. In our experience, peer educators who are committed to this perspective not only serve as strong role models to the students they serve, but also fully engage in the training and development opportunities we provide them. Practically, there are a number of strategies we use to find students who embody this value and to help foster it through our training and operational practices.

We use an intensive hiring process, in which prospective students submit cover letters, resumes, references, and an application. We look for evidence of an interest in self-growth and development in cover letters and resumes, including participation in activities that demonstrate their broader interests. We seek applicants who can transfer their prior experiences to the role of a peer educator, and can clearly describe what they learned from those experiences. Successful candidates must participate in an hour-long interview which usually includes at least one supervisor and one current peer educator. Interview questions probe applicants' love of learning and their ability to reflect critically on their experiences. In addition, every two semesters, peer educators complete a reflection on their own learning and skill development in key areas; this reflection has been found to be essential to lifelong learning.[7] We encourage ongoing growth and reflection in our peer educators by regularly soliciting their feedback regarding training content and processes. This critical reflection also inspires us to grow and develop as professionals alongside them.

An Inclusive Approach to Working with Students

Given the high level of contact that our peer educators have with students, we believe it is paramount that they are aware of how issues of diversity, power, and privilege intersect in our everyday lives. In the interview process, we assess this value through questions and scenarios which help us understand each candidate's assumptions about how and why students learn. We want to know if candidates are aware of different learning preferences and if they have considered the many factors which can influence academic achievement. Above all, we seek to find out if applicants assume others learn and live like they do, or if they are aware of a plurality of equally valid experiences. Through the careful construction of interview questions and behaviorally based scenarios, the presence of this value can be elicited.

In our daily operations, we incorporate training practices focusing on inclusivity. We aim to create an inclusive environment for peer educators to grow, and to enable them to help their peers grow as they provide services for the broader student population. When they are designing and delivering programs, peer educators are asked to wrestle with ideas about inclusivity, such as, *"How do a student's social locations influence them in the broader context of university learning?"* and *"What are this student's experiences of marginalization and/or privilege?"* More formally, all of our peer educators are required to participate in a training session on diversity and an online module about providing services to people with disabilities. Within the Learning Commons, we also bring in guest speakers and use scenario-based training simulations to build awareness, expand their skill set, and highlight inclusive approaches to serving students.

The Importance of Community

An orientation towards community is also an essential value for successful peer educators. Students who understand the broader context of their impact on other students, and their own ability to create a supportive work and academic environment, inevitably become committed peer educators who shape and grow our programs. Being part of a larger community of students helping students gives value and meaning to their work, even when demand for services is slower or when their own class schedule becomes more hectic. As supervisors of peer educators, we make the establishment of community a priority because we know how much it contributes to our services' effectiveness.

In the application and interview process, we look for students who participate in community-based experiences, such as being part of a sports team or working as a camp counselor. We also seek evidence of having learned within a community, such as forming a study group for a challenging course, or mentoring co-workers. We hold regular meetings with our peer educators which incorporate intentional community-building activities, and we include information about the history of our services so that they understand how our community has developed over the years. One way we promote community-building is by providing two large workrooms for the peer educators in our library. These workrooms, accessible to our peer educators whenever the library is open, provide them with space for work and study and also a physical location for community-building. Many peers socialize and study in the workrooms between classes, and many comment on the friendships that they have formed through the shared space. Food, noise, and visual stimuli (quote boards, photographs, and message boards) contribute to an energized, informal atmosphere which is atypical of many library settings, but is a crucial component for our programs' success.

Commitment to Service

Peer educators who value service to others demonstrate a dedication to the role that exceeds the standard expectations for a part-time volunteer position. In fact, because most of our peer educator positions are unpaid, we find that many applicants come with a service-oriented approach. (In library settings where peer educators are paid, supervisors should still seek out evidence of a service orientation.) In applications, we look for demonstrations of increasing responsibility over time in a service-oriented position, or for multiple service-oriented experiences, such as participation in high school clubs, tutoring experience, or jobs with an emphasis on serving clients. We also look for a service-oriented perspective in their interview responses. Although many candidates can articulate how they will benefit from being a peer educator, we only hire those candidates whose primary reason for applying is to help their fellow students. Day to day, we nurture this value by encouraging our peer educators to assist each other in their roles, by developing semi-formal "buddy" programs within our units, and by sharing student feedback to ensure that peer educators understand their impact on other students.

Non-Hierarchical Approach to Service Delivery

Peer-to-peer support mitigates many of the potential power dynamics between students and helpers,[8] and, as supervisors, we look for potential peer educators who understand that student-to-student dynamics are fundamentally different than professional-to-student dynamics. In the interview process, we look for signs of a non-hierarchical approach to helping. For example, students who understand the nuances between *giving* fellow students the answers and helping students *discover* the answers are often well-suited to the role of peer educator. Scenario-based questions also help us learn more about interviewees' approaches to helping others, as their responses often reveal whether they see themselves as the center of the peer-to-peer interaction or if they recognize when to step back so that others may lead.

We endeavor to adopt a non-hierarchical approach by treating our peer educators as partners in the development and implementation of our services. Although the concept of "students as partners" has been primarily viewed as an opportunity for students to engage in research related to the Scholarship of Teaching and Learning (SOTL) and curriculum development,[9] we follow more closely Wenger's Community of Practice model,[10] in which our peer educators enter into our professional community. We have found over time that working with peer educators allows us to check our assumptions regarding what students might find helpful and enables us to develop more relevant programs. We encourage them to develop and propose new programming ideas, lead meetings, serve on hiring committees, and participate in assessment activities, thus building their knowledge and experience into our supervisory and programming practices. We also invest a great deal of time and effort in supervising these students and ensuring that they have the skills, knowledge, and support to take on such tasks, in order to maintain our reputation for services of high quality. We are fortunate at the University of Guelph to have a strong history of administrative support for this intensive supervisory process, and to work within a wider institutional culture which values student volunteerism and engagement outside the classroom. In libraries that are developing new student-led programs, we encourage staff to speak with supervisors of peer educators in other departments at their institution, and to connect with other libraries with well-established student-led programs. These conversations are essential to having realistic and concrete information about the amount of supervisory and training time needed to have a well-run program.

The Values of Peer Educator Programs and Academic Libraries: Alignments and Intersections

At first glance, our peer educators' values, and the values inherent in the programs that they deliver, align with many of the values traditionally held by academic libraries. Our own library underwent an organizational re-structuring process in 2008, which identified a new set of guiding values: learning, service, intellectual freedom, stewardship, access, innovation, communication, and integrity.[11] Values such as learning, service, access, and innovation certainly correspond with the values that we have previous-ly discussed. Despite these similarities, tensions have become apparent over time, in which seemingly complementary values have been interpreted in different ways. These tensions highlight both the challenges and opportuni-ties that accompany the development of peer educator programs in a library environment. Ultimately, we have learned that a holistic approach that com-bines these different interpretations is not only possible, but preferable.

Inclusivity: Individual Access vs. A Systems Approach

The positioning of inclusivity is one area in which the values of our library and our peer-to-peer support programs do not completely align. With-in our library's statement of values, the notion of inclusivity is addressed through an examination of access—to resources, to services, and to the collection—as well as through the notion of intellectual freedom. These values address equal access and freedom of thought amongst a popula-tion of *individuals*; consideration of the impact of broader social forces is less apparent. In contrast, our peer educator programs address inclusivity through the lens of systems-based thinking about the complex and inter-connected environment in which we live.[12] As professionals trained in the fields of counseling and education, we assume that the systems in which students experience their lives have a significant impact on their engage-ment with academic support. This is not to say that library staff and librar-ians do not ask themselves such questions; indeed, conversations around critical librarianship provide excellent examples of such dialogue in the librarian profession.[13] However, the impact of broader systems on students' engagement with the library needs to be more explicitly acknowledged at both an individual and organizational level. The development of peer ed-ucator programs within a library setting provides an opportunity for the library as a whole to consider how we design programs, deliver services, and interact with students in ways that recognize the value and impact of a plurality of experiences.

Professional Expertise vs. Lived Experience

Another tension arises when we examine the relationship between professional expertise and lived experience. Traditionally, library services to students have been delivered by librarians, who hold advanced degrees and are part of a well-established profession with a long history in higher education. This strong tradition favors the value of the service provider as an expert who reveals knowledge and guides students. Our peer educator-based services, however, stem from the phenomenographic approach, which acknowledges that understanding people's lived experience is an essential element of providing relevant and meaningful services.[14] This approach is important not only when helping students develop academic skills, but also when conceptualizing the programs which peer educators provide. Peer educators' particular type of expertise—that of currently being students—enables them to be more approachable and accessible, and, in some cases, more believable and genuine, to students using the services.

Of course, students also deliberately seek out and value the expertise of professional staff. Peer educators' lived experience and limited training cannot replicate the professional expertise of staff, nor is it meant to. In our supervisory roles, we are familiar with this tension between professional expertise and lived experience; however, we do not view them as competing values, but rather as complementary. When planning new ventures, for example, we deliberately reflect on how we might incorporate peer educators into the process. We consider whether our peer educators will be at the core of service delivery, whether they will act as "behind the scenes" consultants on a staff-led project, or whether they will take on a role somewhere in between. Having peer educators in traditional library settings means there needs to be an acknowledgement that advanced degrees and many years of experience do not always lead to the most appropriate or approachable services. There are many situations in which well-trained and well-supervised students can offer valuable, unique service—not parallel service, but service *different* from that of a professional—within a library setting.

Autonomy vs. Accountability

In keeping with our non-hierarchical approach to service and supervision, the peer educators in our library function with a great deal of autonomy, consulting one-on-one with first-year students regarding learning and writing issues, as well as facilitating study sessions for high-risk courses on a weekly basis. Overall, they provide more than 150 hours of service per week during the semester. Our peer educators are expected to view their work as an opportunity for experiential learning, in which they take risks, develop their skills, and formally reflect upon their progress every semester. Failure is viewed as an opportunity for reflection and growth, rather than as a stigma to avoid at all costs. Having some autonomy in their role is a necessary feature of this experiential learning framework, and we are comfortable placing our trust in our peer educators as service providers because of the strong training and supervision we provide.

While this viewpoint fosters a positive environment for learning, it can conflict with the value of accountability, which favors careful planning, reliability, and professional knowledge. Some staff may not be comfortable with students bearing responsibility for users' experiences within the library; they may believe that students are not as reliable as staff, or that students do not have enough practice and knowledge. However, our experience has shown us that we can give peer educators autonomy without sacrificing accountability. We mitigate this tension by encouraging our peer educators to fully understand their role boundaries, to refer students to professionals when students' needs are beyond their roles, and to communicate with us about challenging situations and potential gaps in their training and support.

Promoting Alignment

Our purpose in highlighting these tensions is to shed light on the juxtaposition of values that can arise when developing peer educator programs in a library setting. Despite having similar goals and accountabilities, traditional library services and peer educator programs do not always "speak the same language." To bridge this gap, we recommend that those developing peer educator programs take deliberate steps to foster the smooth integration of these programs into the library environment. As we noted earlier in this chapter, student-led programs have been long established at most institutions across North America, especially in student affairs units. Use the existing expertise on your campus to find out more about how student-led programs work within your context. What values have your campus colleagues observed in their student leaders, and what values have they nurtured? How have they done so? What conflicts in values have arisen, and how do supervisory staff address those conflicts? Consider as well the values you hold as a professional, and how those might intersect with the values inherent in peer-to-peer support programs.

Also, identify how your peer educator program fits into the broader mandates and priorities of your campus. What are the strategic priorities and missions of your university and library? What are the values of your institution, and how do the values within your program align and intersect with them? Be prepared to articulate how your program supports the institution's and the library's values to all stakeholders—library administration, other senior administration on your campus, library staff, and the peer educators themselves. Well-supported arguments about how peer educator programs enhance organizational values and advance mandates are essential to demonstrating the value of these programs to the larger institution.

Demonstrating Value: The Role of Data and Assessment

Defining Value in Libraries and Higher Education

As post-secondary institutions aim to determine how they can best demonstrate their value to funding agents, so too do academic libraries strive to prove their worth to their institution. Although the term value is often rooted in business literature, the ACRL report "The Value of Academic Libraries" provides a useful perspective for understanding how such definitions of value can be extended to an academic context.[15] At post-secondary institutions, methods of conveying value are influenced by current trends toward evidence-based practices and performance metrics. Publications and citations are used to measure scholarly value and research output; meanwhile, retention and graduation rates, as well as reports of student satisfaction and engagement, are used to measure the educational experience of students. In academic libraries, traditional ways of demonstrating value focus on the use of and access to collections and resources, though there is an acknowledged shift towards including experiences and educational impact as assessment measures.[16] Peer educator programs, as a newer phenomenon in libraries, do not always fit into these established pathways for demonstrating value.

At the University of Guelph, the incorporation of our peer educator programs into the library administrative structure prompted us to reconsider the concept of value. Circulation statistics, building counts, and total number of student contact hours have been historically used in our library to demonstrate value; however, peer educator programs typically convey value through student satisfaction and evaluative questionnaires, as well as impact data related to grade achievement. When our service statistics were first included in the library's report to the Association of Research Libraries in 2010, data related to our peer-educator services did not fit into any existing reporting category. Based on the recent 2014 instructions and definitions from ARL, "instruction," "presentations to groups," and "reference transactions" capture activities related to information literacy efforts,[17] but do not reflect the type of programming and services delivered by our peer educators. The ways in which broader organizations such as ARL recognize and understand the different forms of service occurring within libraries today needs updating, in order to better reflect the evolving nature of the work happening in academic libraries. While we have noted a greater awareness of the value of our peer educator programs within our library over time, the ability to communicate the value of peer educators to the wider library community remains a challenge. This highlights the need to encourage broader, more inclusive conversations about value in the library environment.

Developing a Shared Understanding of Value

Within our context, some tensions arose from different conceptions of value when we initially faced practical concerns related to program implementation. When our peer educator programs first moved administratively to the library, some of our colleagues expressed concern about the sheer number of programs and their resulting need for in-demand resources, such as instructional space. Discussions about the use of space, and the value of the programs requiring space, revealed assumptions that devalued peer educator programs in comparison to librarian-led programs. For us, this conflict highlighted the influence of professional and institutional contexts on perceptions of value. In libraries, it is customary for the work of librarians to be highly valued, given their professional expertise and positions of authority. However, peer educator programs have a collaborative and non-hierarchical foundation. Their inclusion within libraries necessitates both time and open dialogue for staff to develop a shared understanding of the role and purpose of those programs.

As supervisors, we have addressed this need by deliberately considering how to convey our programs' value to others in our library. We look for ways to share data about our programs within the library; recently, we used infographics to share information with both library staff and students, and our library's last annual report prominently featured peer educators. We also strive to integrate our peer educators into the library as a whole by having them serve as social media advisors, library ambassadors to prospective high school students, and student members of hiring committees. Not fitting in the typical library evaluation framework means that we need to be extra diligent in conveying the value of what our peer educators do. Given that some senior library administrators—whose understanding and support is essential to the continuation and development of peer educator programs—have likely had little exposure to student-based programs, we take on the role of "champions" of our programs, and consider regular communication with library administration to be an integral part of our jobs. We have been fortunate to have administrators who have been open to learning more about the unique value that peer educator programs bring to the library, and have been committed to putting us on equal footing with traditional library services.

Demonstrating the Value of Peer Educator Programs in Libraries

Data and assessment are not the only mechanisms through which value can be demonstrated, but they are excellent starting points. For colleagues developing programs at other institutions, we offer several recommendations regarding how to best demonstrate the value of peer educator programs. First, become familiar with your library's existing data reporting structure, and how data from your peer educator programs might fit within that structure. It is also important to collect data that aligns with your program's goals, even if that data is not required by your library. What outcomes do you want your peer educator programs to produce in the students using the programs, in the peer educators themselves, and in your library? How will you assess and evaluate the achievement of those outcomes? With whom will you share this data, and how will your library use it? Consider especially how you will convey data and evaluation feedback to library administration, whose support and endorsement is crucial for setting a tone of acceptance within the library as a whole. These considerations create a solid foundation for transformative change through the inclusion of peer educators in academic libraries.

Conclusion

Although at the University of Guelph peer educator programs originated outside of the library, the values that we have identified within our programs also apply to student-led programs implemented in libraries. We hope that the opportunities and challenges arising in our library from the incorporation of peer educator programs may serve as helpful guideposts for others considering the use of peer-to-peer support in their library. We acknowledge that the values discussed in this chapter are not the only ones that guide student-led programs; these are the values that have had the most profound impact on our work and on the success of our peer educators.

In our experience, the presence of peer educators transforms the library both internally and externally. While we initially were challenged by the integration of our peer educators into the library, we now view that tension as an opportunity to reflect on our collective practices, clarify goals, and discover ways to work together. Recognizing shared values has fostered a greater sense of community, an improved understanding of roles, and better assessment practices. The assessment and subsequent demonstration of the value of our peer educator programs have led many in our library to think more deeply and critically about what we assess in our library, how we assess it, and *why* we assess it.

Perhaps even more importantly, peer educators symbolize stakeholders' changing perceptions of academic libraries. Peer educators, due to the very values inherent in the concept of peer-to-peer academic support, bring with them a different way of supporting and interacting with other students. Far from being academically-minded undergraduate "mini-librarians" who help students with the most basic questions about the library, peer educators use their experiences as students—coupled with extensive ongoing training and active supervision—to assist students in ways that professional library staff cannot. Their presence in the building highlights the shift in libraries' positioning from knowledge repositories with "no talking" and "no eating" signs to bustling, lively centers of academic discourse and learning. At a time in which academic libraries face mounting pressures to demonstrate their relevance and value, we must rise to the challenge and be open to further transformation. We encourage academic libraries to embrace peer educator programs as an effective way of transforming their presence on their respective campuses, and re-thinking how they can be of value in an academic context.

Notes

1. Zane Schwartz, "Students' Choice: Introducing Maclean's Student Satisfaction Rankings," Maclean's Magazine, Rogers Media, accessed January 5, 2016, http://www.macleans.ca/education/students-choice-introducing-macleans-student-satisfaction-rankings/.
2. Nancy Schmidt and Janet Kaufman, "Learning Commons: Bridging the Academic and Student Affairs Divide to Enhance Learning Across Campus," *Research Strategies* 20 (2007): 242.
3. Keith J. Topping, "Trends in Peer Learning," *Educational Psychology* 25, no. 6 (2005): 631-645; Nancy Falchikov, *Learning Together: Peer Tutoring in Higher Education* (New York: RoutledgeFalmer, 2001); Keith J. Topping, "The Effectiveness of Peer Tutoring in Further and Higher Education: A Typology and Review of the Literature," *Higher Education* 32 (1996): 321–345.
4. Falchikov, *Learning Together.*
5. Jaime L. Shook and Jennifer R. Keup, "The Benefits of Peer Leader Programs: An Overview from the Literature," *New Directions for Higher Education* 157, (2012): 5–16, doi:10.1002/he.20002.
6. Council for the Advancement of Standards, "CAS Statement of Shared Ethical Principles," Council for the Advancement of Standards in Higher Education, accessed October 23, 2015, http://www.cas.edu/content.asp?contentid=148.
7. Frederick T. Evers, James C. Rush, and Iris Berdrow, *The Bases of Competence: Skills for Lifelong Learning and Employability* (San Francisco: Jossey-Bass, 1998).
8. Topping, "The Effectiveness of Peer Tutoring."
9. Mick Healey, Abbi Flint, and Kathy Harrington, "Engagement through Partnership: Students as Partners in Learning and Teaching in Higher Education," Higher Education Academy, accessed November 2, 2015, https://www.heacademy.ac.uk/engagement-through-partnership-students-partners-learning-and-teaching-higher-education.
10. Etienne Wenger, *Communities of Practice: Learning, Meaning, and Identity* (New York: Cambridge University Press, 1998).
11. McLaughlin Library, "Vision and Values," University of Guelph, accessed November 24, 2015, http://www.lib.uoguelph.ca/about/about-library/vision-values.
12. H. Gumbrecht, H. Maturana, and B. Poerksen, "Humerbto R. Maturana and Francisco J. Varela on Science and the Humanities: The Poerksen Interviews," *Journal of Aesthetic Education 40*, no. 1 (2006): 22–53.
13. Kenny Garcia, "Keeping Up With… Critical Librarianship," Association of College and Research Libraries, accessed March 22, 2016, http://www.ala.org/acrl/publications/keeping_up_with/critlib.
14. Max Van Manen, *Researching Lived Experience: Human Science for an Action Sensitive Pedagogy* (Albany, NY: State University of New York Press, 1990).
15. Association of College and Research Libraries, "Value of Academic Libraries: A Comprehensive Research Review and Report," researched by Megan Oakleaf (Chicago: Association of College and Research Libraries, 2010).
16. Association of Research Libraries, "ARL Statistics 2013–2014," Association of Research Libraries, accessed January 5, 2015, http://publications.arl.org/ARL-Statistics-2013-2014/.
17. Association of Research Libraries, "ARL Statistics 2013–2014."

Bibliography

Association of College and Research Libraries. "Value of Academic Libraries: A Comprehensive Research Review and Report," researched by Megan Oakleaf. Chicago: Association of College and Research Libraries, 2010.

Association of Research Libraries. "ARL Statistics 2013–2014." Association of Research Libraries. Accessed January 5, 2015. http://publications.arl.org/ARL-Statistics-2013-2014/.

Council for the Advancement of Standards. "CAS Statement of Shared Ethical Principles." Council for the Advancement of Standards in Higher Education. Accessed October 23, 2015. http://www.cas.edu/content.asp?contentid=148.

Evers, Frederick T., James C. Rush, and Iris Berdrow. *The Bases of Competence: Skills for Lifelong Learning and Employability.* San Francisco: Jossey-Bass, 1998.

Falchikov, Nancy. *Learning Together: Peer Tutoring in Higher Education.* New York: RoutledgeFalmer, 2001.

Garcia, Kenny. "Keeping Up With… Critical Librarianship." Association of College and Research Libraries. Accessed March 22, 2016. http://www.ala.org/acrl/publications/keeping_up_with/critlib.

Gumbrecht, Hans Ulrich, Humberto R. Maturana, and Bernhard Poerksen. "Humberto R. Maturana and Francisco J. Varela on Science and the Humanities: The Poerksen Interviews." *Journal of Aesthetic Education* 40, no. 1 (2006): 22–53.

Healey, Mick, Abbi Flint, and Kathy Harrington. "Engagement Through Partnership: Students as Partners in Learning and Teaching in Higher Education." Higher Education Academy. Accessed November 2, 2015. https://www.heacademy.ac.uk/engagement-through-partnership-students-partners-learning-and-teaching-higher-education.

McLaughlin Library. "Vision and Values." University of Guelph. Accessed November 24, 2015. http://www.lib.uoguelph.ca/about-library/vision-values.

Schmidt, Nancy and Janet Kaufman. "Learning Commons: Bridging the Academic and Student Affairs Divide to Enhance Learning Across Campus." *Research Strategies* 20, (2007): 242–256.

Shwartz, Zane. "Students' Choice: Introducing Maclean's Student Satisfaction Rankings." *Maclean's Magazine*, Rogers Media. Accessed January 5, 2016. http://www.macleans.ca/education/students-choice-introducing-macleans-student-satisfaction-rankings/.

Shook, Jaime L. and Jennifer R. Keup. "The Benefits of Peer Leader Programs: An Overview from the Literature." *New Directions for Higher Education* 157 (Spring 2012): 5-16. doi:10.1002/he.20002.

Topping, Keith J. "The Effectiveness of Peer Tutoring in Further and Higher Education: A Typology and Review of the Literature." *Higher Education* 32 (1996): 321–345.

Topping, Keith J. "Trends in Peer Learning." *Educational Psychology* 25, no. 6 (2005): 631–645.

Van Manen, Max. *Researching Lived Experience: Human Science for an Action Sensitive Pedagogy.* Albany, NY: State University of New York Press, 1990.

Wenger, Etienne. *Communities of Practice: Learning, Meaning, and Identity.* New York: Cambridge University Press, 1998.

Part 2

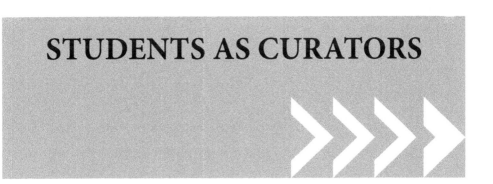

STUDENTS AS CURATORS

CHAPTER 5*

COMMUNITY COLLECTIONS:
Nurturing Student Curators

Julia Glassman, Simon Lee, Danielle Salomon, and Doug Worsham

Introduction

With peer-assisted learning flourishing at many academic libraries, student involvement in reference and even instruction is becoming increasingly common in higher education. But can students play a similar role in collection development? Can undergraduate circulating collections benefit from the involvement of student curators?

In 2012, librarians at the UCLA Powell Library, which supports undergraduate curricula, began to reexamine Powell's popular reading collections. Consisting of recent fiction, graphic novels, and travel guides, the collections were small and had been curated for many years by librarians, with little to no input from undergraduate students. While most undergraduates don't have formal collection development training, multiple factors led Powell librarians to rethink this traditional collection development model.

The first factor was the reimagining of Powell Library's mission, a vision for Teaching and Learning Services (TLS) that included "foster[ing]

undergraduate engagement in UCLA's scholarly community and beyond," "support[ing] the 'whole' 21st-century student," and "building foundations for lifelong learning."[1] The second factor was the need to update Powell's historic Main Reading Room for the needs of undergraduates. The Main Reading Room previously housed bound periodicals and outdated reference materials that were removed due to low use rates, and Miller began to explore the possibility of expanding the popular reading collections to fill the room's now-empty shelves.* This move would turn one of Powell's most popular spaces into a "public library" for over 10,000 students who live on campus.[2] After encountering student groups that were actively curating independent collections, Powell librarians realized the potential of partnering with students to co-create popular collections. Thus, the Community Collections were born.

The value of popular reading collections in academic libraries is well-documented; they make the library relevant and responsive to student interests, and promote lifelong reading habits.[3] However, many recreational reading collections are limited to fiction and popular nonfiction. Powell librarians, on the other hand, have taken advantage of campus-wide initiatives and Los Angeles's creative communities to produce five innovative thematic collections: cookbooks, science fiction and fantasy, sustainability, zines, and travel literature. The Community Collections also include more traditional collections, including the extant recent fiction and graphic novel collections, and a newer collection of career guides. The goal of the Community Collections is to

> support and promote student intellectual growth, health
> and well-being, and creativity. Reflecting the diversity
> of the student population, the collections aim to foster
> curiosity about the world and empathy for others, while
> nurturing lifelong reading habits.[4]

Although the collections developed organically, they fall into roughly three tiers of engagement for students. The highest tier involves identifying existing student-built collections on campus and using the library's

---

* For additional information about Miller's initiatives at Powell Library, see "Imagine! On the future of teaching and learning and the academic research library" in *portal: Libraries and the Academy* 14 (3), 329–351.

resources to make those collections more widely accessible. The second tier involves inviting students to select titles for collections initially built by librarians. Finally, the third tier consists of soliciting student work to add to the collections.

This chapter will describe the inception of each collection, the process of building it, and tips for librarians looking to establish similar collections at their own institutions.

Top Tier: Incorporating Existing Student Collections into the Library

The Enigma Science Fiction, Fantasy, and Gaming Collection

The first collection to incorporate student curation was born in a moment of happenstance. Anyone who has visited the UCLA campus is familiar with the Bruin Walk: a lively path between the student union and the library where student organizations set up sandwich boards, hand out flyers, hold bake sales and singalongs, and promote their activities. One day in 2012, after articulating the new vision for Powell and TLS, Miller noticed one particular organization amid the cacophony: Enigma, the science fiction, fantasy, and gaming club. When she struck up a conversation with the students, they told her that the organization had a library of more than 1,000 titles, along with an elected club librarian to keep track of the collection. The problem, though, was that they had no space to permanently house the collection, so it was stored in approximately forty-five banker's boxes that migrated from apartment to apartment as students joined the club and then graduated. Although the club librarian kept careful inventory of the collection and each box was accompanied by an item list, the arrangement made the collection virtually inaccessible to most students.

It was decided that in order to promote the club and increase access to the collection, Powell Library should house it. Librarian Simon Lee, who took on a liaison role with Enigma and became Powell's science fiction and fantasy selector, and Lise Snyder, Powell's collections manager at the time, took on the logistics. The UCLA Library's acquisitions policies, coupled with the large size of the collection, complicated the process of transferring the collection to the library. There were no procedures in place for moving and cataloging an independent campus collection, so the collection had to be treated as a gift to the library, with the rationale that it would increase curricular ties with the teaching and learning community while giving students leadership experience by engaging them directly with collection development. The Enigma officers signed the deed of gift and the boxes were "donated."

One of the most rewarding aspects of ingesting the collection was the inclusion of Enigma's club librarian in the process. The student, who was interested in pursuing librarianship as a career, worked with library staff to design an independent study in which she helped process the collection, learning about librarianship and receiving course credit for her work. Through the combined efforts of the UCLA Library, the student librarian, and the Enigma membership, which was kept abreast of the process through updates to its Facebook page, the collection was completed in May of 2014.

Meanwhile, collections funds were allocated, and the Enigma membership began selecting new releases to add to the collection. The student librarian, whose club duties had evolved into a liaison role with Powell Library, used multiple methods to engage the Enigma community. She photocopied reviews from *Booklist* and distributed them at their weekly meetings, and posted calls for title suggestions on the group's Facebook page.

Four years later, the collection has grown to more than 2,000 items. Under the leadership of a new student librarian, Enigma formed a book club to promote and have discussion sessions around the collection, and worked with Powell to put on events tied to the collection, such as a reading by science fiction author, Greg Van Eekhout. During every step of the process, the librarians were delighted and gratified at the skill the students demonstrated in selecting titles and facilitating the workflow. Although processing could be a challenge at times, especially when dealing with brittle or damaged items, the students laid the conceptual groundwork for the collection years before librarians ever knew of its existence. Rather than "letting" the students build the collection, the library supported them in work in which they were already engaged. Not only did this project help the library offer a popular reading collection that was demonstrably of interest to undergraduates, it also served as a teachable moment, allowing students to look behind the scenes at their campus library and take the lead in shaping its offerings. The message it sent to the undergraduate population was a powerful one: *This is your library, and we see you as equals.*

The Sustainability Collection

In 2014, UCLA launched the Grand Challenges, a series of large-scale research projects aiming to solve societal problems. The first Grand Challenge, Sustainable LA, focuses on achieving water and energy sustainability in Los Angeles and improving the city's ecosystem by 2050. The university describes the Grand Challenges as "the biggest, most collaborative, and potentially most transformative efforts UCLA has undertaken to date,"[5] and campus departments are encouraged to weave them into their instructional activities.

Powell librarians decided to add a new collection to the Community Collections, with a focus on sustainability. Following the success of the Enigma Collection and the Zine Collection (discussed below), Julia Glassman, the selector, approached student organizations to gauge their interest in helping to build the collection. She first contacted E3, a student sustainability organization. That organization was unable to help build a collection, but their president introduced Glassman to another group: the Sustainability Resource Center (SRC), run by two graduate students and an undergraduate assistant. Upon meeting with the SRC, Glassman discovered another hidden collection: a multidisciplinary student-built library consisting of titles on ecology, climate change, economics, human rights, social justice, urban planning, and other topics. The thought and experimentation that had gone into the collection were impressive. Rather than reducing sustainability to questions of recycling and limiting carbon emissions, the collection presented the concept as a broad mosaic of interconnected issues, from sweatshops to income inequality to the military industrial complex. The collection was more than a compilation of resources for students studying sustainability, it was a political statement, put forth by students, which expands the conception of sustainability so often espoused in popular media.

Like Enigma, the SRC suffered from a lack of accessible space. The collection was kept in the SRC's office, which had to be locked whenever the student leadership wasn't working there. Furthermore, the office itself was hard to find, as it was tucked away in a seldom-used hallway of an administrative building. The original SRC leadership had envisioned the collection as an open resource for the entire student body, but few people even knew it existed, and would be largely unable to browse it even if they did.

Because Powell Library had already started building its Sustainability Collection, the process of ingesting the SRC's collection differed from that of Enigma's. Glassman took inventory of the SRC's titles, and any titles that were already in Powell's stacks were moved to the Community Collections. The remaining 200 titles, as of this writing, are being processed; however, in the spring of 2015, Powell and the SRC were able to collaborate on a soft launch of the collection in the form of a social media contest in which students described what sustainability meant to them. The winners, chosen by the SRC leadership, won gift cards to the UCLA student store.

One challenge that the SRC's collection posed was the rotating student leadership. In Enigma, an officer might be elected as an underclassman and serve for three or even four years, which gives librarians time to form solid relationships. Officers in the SRC, however, are limited to a one-year term, and the undergraduate leadership volunteers on an informal basis. This system delayed the process of ingesting the collection, as the project had to be re-introduced to the new leadership multiple times. It also poses a challenge to having students continue to curate the collection by selecting new titles, as the students need to be re-trained every year, and the collection may not be a priority for every new set of officers. A nine-month school year is simply not enough time for students and librarians to get to know one another.

However, the Library has still greatly benefited from incorporating the SRC's collection into the Community Collections. Not only does the collection make the same statement as Enigma's, it has also enabled librarians to view sustainability in new and interesting ways. Would a librarian have selected Barbara Ehrenreich's *Blood Rites* or Noam Chomsky's *Necessary Illusions* for a sustainability collection? Probably not. The students' selections transformed the collection into something more ambitious and thought-provoking than it would have been had librarians acted as gatekeepers. Now, as those titles sit alongside books on urban gardening and permaculture, the collection invites students and other patrons to consider the myriad issues that contribute to problems like climate change. The SRC students have benefited from the increased visibility of their hard work, and the Library has benefited by pushing the boundaries of what a collection can do.

Second Tier: Student Selectors
The Cookbook Collection

The idea to start a community cookbook collection was sparked by a convergence of two related initiatives: the Library's annual Edible Book Festival, in which students and staff prepare dishes and desserts based on books and the UCLA Healthy Campus Initiative, a set of programs designed to improve the health and wellness of UCLA students and staff. At the 2012 Edible Book Festival, the president of the student Bruin Culinary Community (BCC) served as a judge. He and Associate University Librarian Kevin Mulroy struck up a conversation, and the BCC president said that interest in food was "definitely taking off" among students at UCLA. Mulroy put the student in touch with Powell librarian Danielle Salomon to discuss possibilities for collaboration. Together, they developed a cookbook collection co-curated by the Library and the Culinary Community, tying it into the Eat Well part of the Healthy Campus Initiative by providing students with materials to learn how to cook for themselves, try new cuisines, and explore healthier food choices.

In contrast to the existing cookbooks held at UCLA, which are housed in the Research Library and used for research and instruction, the Powell Community Cookbook Collection was envisioned as a working collection—one that would go home with students, get splattered with cooking grease, and be used for practical purposes. Academically, it would provide an entry point for undergraduate students to become interested in the study of food and culture, a cross-disciplinary field that is examined in courses in different departments. When it came time to begin ordering titles, the Library provided seed money ($2,500) and the Culinary Community students compiled a list on Amazon of cookbooks they wanted. Salomon ordered the books and the club president organized the initial display on the shelf.

The following year, Snyder attended UCLA's Enormous Activities Fair, at which student organizations seek to promote their activities and attract new members, and she discovered a second organization: the Cooking and Baking Club. In contrast to the Culinary Community, which was interested in modern, sophisticated cuisine, the Cooking and Baking Club focused more on everyday cooking. Salomon formed a relationship with the organization and, like the Culinary Community, the Cooking and Baking Club students compiled a list of titles on Amazon. The title list from each organization reflected that organization's interests: the Culinary Community, for example, selected *The Professional Chef* by the Culinary Institute of America, while the Cooking and Baking Club selected titles like *All About Braising: The Art of Uncomplicated Cooking*. Interestingly, the two organizations had little interaction with each other, so each worked independently with the Library.

In addition to selecting titles, the presidents of the two organizations have continued to serve as judges at the Edible Book Festival, and since the launch of the Cookbook Collection, the festival has served as a showcase for new titles, which are displayed near the contestants. Salomon still solicits title recommendations from students, although the number of recommendations has shrunk since the initial title lists from each organization. Because the students and the librarian all had busy schedules, and the students' interests lay primarily with cooking instead of library collections, it proved difficult to coordinate collection development among all three parties—especially since the students were essentially asked to perform unpaid labor for the library. Challenges such as this one are discussed in more detail below.

Nevertheless, the Cookbook Collection may never have come to be if it weren't for the involvement of the BCC president and other student cooking enthusiasts. It's one thing for librarians to be aware of and involved in campus initiatives like Eat Well, it's quite another to be able to see these initiatives from a student's perspective. Communicating and working with students ensures that libraries build collections that are truly responsive to undergraduate interests.

The Zine Collection

In 2012, the first annual Los Angeles Zine Fest launched at The Last Bookstore in downtown Los Angeles. Although zines (often thought to be killed off by blogs and other new media) had been increasing in popularity over several years, LA Zine Fest arguably marked the beginning of a zine renaissance in Southern California. Enthusiasm for zines blossomed at UCLA as well, and multiple student groups began to create and distribute them.

Among these groups were the Bad Art Zine Collective (BAZC) and the Student Committee for the Arts (SCA). Although the SCA was primarily an arts organization with some interest in zine culture, BAZC was a collective of student *zinesters* who were committed to bringing a greater awareness of zine culture to campus. In a stroke of good fortune, after the Library decided to create a zine collection, Glassman, the zine selector, discovered that a student circulation desk worker was a member of the collective.

Selecting and purchasing titles for a zine collection can be more challenging than for a collection of more traditional items like monographs. These challenges have been described in chapter 6 of Julie Bartel's *From A to Zine: Building a Winning Zine Collection in Your Library* (2004). Simply put, librarians cannot rely on infrastructures like approval plans or purchase orders to acquire small-scale, self-published materials like zines. Thus, when the UCLA Library began the Zine Collection, it was decided that items for the collection would be purchased by hand at the various zine fests, and online from vendors like Etsy or Quimby's Books. Although the process of selecting zines one by one—not to mention meeting and forming relationships with zinesters—is immensely enjoyable, it can be time-consuming. Furthermore, Glassman faced the added challenge of tabling at LA Zine Fest herself, limiting her ability to browse other booths. So, in preparation for the 2014 Zine Fest, she approached the student worker for help with purchasing.

Because the vast majority of vendors at zine fests only accept cash, asking a student to purchase items on a librarian's behalf requires a good deal of trust. At the 2014 Zine Fest, Glassman brought personal funds, which would later be reimbursed by the Library, and gave the student cash and a receipt book for use in purchasing. The student then walked the floor and searched for zines to purchase while the librarian worked her own table. Although this arrangement isn't necessary at every zine fest, it is useful because, as with other student-curated collections, the library is able to make selecting decisions from a student's perspective.

However, even though enlisting student assistance for purchasing is helpful, student involvement in the Zine Collection truly becomes a symbiotic relationship in programming. The Library has hosted several events connected to the Zine Collection, all of them either proposed by or coordinated with students. For example, in the fall of 2013, the People of Color Zine Project, a collective of writers and performance poets, performed at the library. Glassman invited the performers to campus and coordinated logistics for the event. Then, after the performance, BAZC led a zine-making workshop, guiding their peers through the creation of original zines.

Third Tier: Soliciting Student Work for Collections

In the previous two tiers, students have taken a decisive leadership role, actively building and shaping collections. On the surface, including student work in existing collections may not seem to be a leadership opportunity, but when it's part of a larger practice of putting students in leadership positions within the library, it supports the philosophy that the library values students' knowledge and contributions. The practice allows the library to include student voices in scholarly and creative conversations, which in turn allows students to share knowledge and creative work with their peers, bolstered by the institutional weight of the library.

The Zine Collection Revisited

As discussed above, involving students in purchasing and programming is an integral part of the Powell Zine Collection. However, what makes a zine collection stand apart from more traditional collections is the ease with which students can contribute their own work. Zines are cheap, easy, and enjoyable to produce, which means that librarians have access to a wealth of creative work by students. The Powell Zine Collection benefited from three groups in particular: a student collective authoring a zine series called *Nothing New*, and two classes, one on writing and another on race and the sex industry.

Nothing New's inclusion in the Zine Collection was relatively straightforward: the students approached Glassman and donated a copy of the first issue to the library. From then on, Glassman acquired new issues through a combination of donations and purchases at zine fests, where the students frequently tabled. (The students offered to donate every issue, but considering the extremely low cost to the library versus the relatively high cost of production for the students, it was decided that the library would purchase issues whenever possible.)

The process of collecting zines originating from classes was more complex. It is difficult to say how many instructors at UCLA use zines as assignments. A challenge for librarians—as in so many other aspects of academic librarians' work—is making faculty aware of opportunities to collaborate with the library. For example, faculty may know the Zine Collection exists, but have no idea that student work is welcome in it. Thus, the Powell librarians found that in order to collect zines resulting from coursework and add them to the collection, it was necessary to form a relationship with the instructor and students, and provide library resources to help students create the zines.

The first instructor Glassman worked with taught upper-division thematic writing courses: one focusing on water and the Los Angeles Aqueduct, and another on cities in literature. For each of these classes, the instructor had students create art and poetry to compile into a group zine. The second instructor was a teaching assistant for a year-long freshman lecture course that broke into seminars in spring quarter. Instead of assigning a traditional research paper in her seminar on race and the sex industry, the teaching assistant had students compile research, interviews, and creative work into individual zines. For each class, Glassman took an active role from the beginning. Early in the quarter, she visited each class to talk about zine culture and show the students samples from the collection. In the writing courses, the librarian returned for the final class session to help the students compile their poems and drawings into a master copy, then made copies for each student—plus one for the collection. In the race and the sex industry seminar, Glassman encouraged students to make an extra copy of their zines for the library. Thirteen out of twenty students donated copies to the library. In each instance, she was proactive in offering help and resources to the instructors and students. It is important to note, though, that each instructor had a preexisting relationship with the library. It is crucial to perform outreach and establish relationships ahead of time, rather than wait until an instructor happens to assign work that the library would like to collect.

The Travel Collection

As one of Powell's extant popular reading collections, the Travel Collection was originally launched and developed with little to no student involvement and without direct ties to campus community groups. In the fall of 2015, librarian Doug Worsham, who took over selection duties for the collection, began to address this by revising and updating the collection's mission statement and seeking out opportunities for community engagement. The new vision for the collection shifts the focus from "travel guides" to "the traveler's experience" and aspires to continue to "help travelers prepare for their journeys," while also exploring the experience of travel from diverse perspectives and sparking community conversations about travel, world languages and cultures, and study abroad. The collection includes guidebooks, travel writing and narratives, photography collections, and language learning resources for destinations worldwide as well as local travel in the greater Los Angeles area.[6]

Early partnerships have included a collaboration with UCLA's International Education Office (IEO), which coordinates study abroad initiatives on campus. Shortly after the launch of the re-envisioned collection, the IEO and Powell Library co-curated a library exhibit of exemplary travel photography by students, with each photograph accompanied by a brief narrative and a related set of travel books from the collection. This exhibit was a promising first step in collecting student work. In addition to the physical exhibit, the event featured social media marketing focused on students and student groups (primarily through Facebook and Twitter), as well as a website allowing UCLA students and the broader community to view and vote on their favorite student photographs.[*]

The juxtaposition of student-generated digital travel photography and social media engagement alongside the print collection led to a number of brainstorming sessions in which Worsham worked with the IEO to explore possibilities for incorporating digital and multimedia student work into the collection. Moving forward, Powell librarians plan to work with the IEO as well as directly with study-abroad students to collect, preserve, and share the photography, video, audio-recordings, and multimedia travel narratives already being created by students. Often posted to course blogs for study-abroad students, these UCLA student-generated digital ephemera have potential long-term relevance for University Archives, as well as immediate applicability for students interested in embarking on a study-abroad experience. Powell librarians are exploring the possibility of publishing collections of these born-digital creations in both print and e-book formats.

In addition to generating many new ideas and directions for collection development, the student photography exhibit and associated online engagement led directly to increased circulation for the collection, and paved the way for other campus partnerships, including the International Student

---

[*] See https://www.wishpond.com/lp/1163006/.

Ambassadors program in UCLA's Dashew Center for International Students & Scholars. Given the many community groups on campus, librarians see opportunities to foster face-to-face and online ties with student groups focused on world cultures, multiculturalism, internationalism, as well as travel writing and narratives by authors from traditionally underrepresented communities.

Challenges and Tips for Co-Curating with Students

As with any new initiative, developing the Community Collections has been a process of trial and error, with successes and setbacks. Below are some of the lessons Powell librarians learned from working with students to build collections.

Identifying Campus Partners

Both existing student libraries, the Enigma Collection and the Sustainability Collection were happened upon through word of mouth: in the first case, stopping to chat with students on campus, and in the second, reaching out to student groups and being referred to the group that happened to maintain a collection. Librarians would never have found out about these collections had they not been proactive in forming relationships with student groups. Indeed, there may still be student libraries on campus that the Powell librarians don't yet know about.

Thus, it is crucial for librarians to form a robust outreach strategy. Mutual trust and goodwill should be established before attempting to enlist students in curation. Furthermore, it's much more effective to work with student groups rather than individual students; individuals may be busy with coursework and other obligations, but groups have both a clear mission (promoting science fiction, achieving sustainability, etc.) that may align with the library's interests, and an infrastructure that mitigates the challenges of individual schedules.

Furthermore, tying thematic popular collections into campus-wide initiatives can vastly increase interest in those collections. Is your campus launching a major social justice initiative? If so, start a social justice collection and ask student social justice organizations for their input. The benefit of this strategy is twofold: the library both demonstrates that it is an integral and engaged part of the campus community, and establishes the mutually beneficial relationships described above.

Training Students

After spending years as an MLIS student and then a library professional, it's surprisingly easy to forget what one didn't know about libraries as an undergraduate. Undergraduate students can't be expected to know the basics of collection development, and so must be assessed and trained.

Interestingly, the main challenge that arose when working with students at Powell was that they proved to be more timid than expected. For example, when Glassman asked the student to purchase zines at LA Zine Fest, the student came back an hour later with five or six zines, which she had painstakingly selected from the hundreds of zines offered. However, because of the ample budget and the massive size of the fest, Glassman was looking to purchase at least twenty to thirty zines in that amount of time—and many more before the end of the day. Similarly, when asked to recommend titles, students tend to suggest only a small handful at first. The scale at which libraries acquire materials is not apparent to library users, and librarians must give students a firm grounding in collection scopes and sizes, purchasing policies, and other aspects of collection development. Don't assume that the inner workings of the library will be intuitive for students simply because those inner workings are familiar to you. Of course, adequate training may require a larger commitment than volunteer curators are prepared to give, which makes the following issue central to working with students.

Compensating Students for Their Time

There are several reasons why you should avoid, if at all possible, asking students to work for free. First, as mentioned above, effective student curators should receive some level of training, and volunteers may not have the time to devote to that training. Furthermore, that training may go to waste if volunteers quit unexpectedly. Students' priorities change, and student organizations can be ephemeral. For example, as of this writing, the Bad Art Zine Collective is defunct. Secondly, although student organizations can benefit in the ways described above, the individual students performing the work may experience burnout if they don't feel they're deriving any personal benefit from it. Finally, although it may sound obvious, collection development is work—enjoyable work, yes, but still work. If a task is worth someone's time and effort, then it's worth compensation. Librarians would balk at performing collection development for free, so we shouldn't expect it from students.

One common mistake librarians and other professionals make is telling students that volunteer work will look good on their résumé. This is not a compelling rationale for students. There's no shortage of unpaid work that looks good on a résumé. Happily, there are several ways that libraries can compensate students. As mentioned above, Enigma's student librarian received course credit in the form of an independent study. The library may be able to offer internships for credit. If maintaining a collection is integral to a student organization's mission, the library can work with that organization to formalize the task in their bylaws and assign it to an officer. And, of course, there's always the holy grail of student work: money. This chapter has mainly discussed student organizations, but student staff positions can be reserved for curators—and a job like that genuinely *does* look good on a résumé.

Conclusion

The effort, time, and care librarians put into campus collections cannot be overstated. However, inviting students to take the lead in collecting and curation efforts doesn't detract from the valuable work that librarians do. Instead, student curators augment librarians' efforts by bringing fresh and interesting ideas into the library and giving librarians a "student's eye view" of campus trends and initiatives. Furthermore, students can benefit greatly from the expertise and leadership opportunities that collection-building provides. When students and librarians work side by side to build vibrant collections, everyone on campus wins.

Notes

1. Kelly Miller, "Vision Statement: UCLA Library's Teaching and Learning Services" (UCLA Library unpublished internal document, Los Angeles, 2011).
2. Kelly Miller, e-mail message to authors, January 14, 2016.
3. Pauline Dewan, "Why Your Undergraduate Library Needs a Popular Reading Collection Now More Than Ever," *College & Research Libraries* 17 no. 1 (2010): 44–66.
4. "Community Collections," UCLA Powell Library, accessed January 15, 2016. http://library.ucla.edu/powell/collections/community-collections.

5.   "UCLA Grand Challenges," UCLA, accessed January 15, 2016. http://grandchallenges
      .ucla.edu.
6.   UCLA Powell Library (2015). "About the Travel Collection," UCLA Powell Library,
      accessed January 15, 2016. http://guides.library.ucla.edu/communitycollections/
      travel.

Bibliography

Bartel, Julie. *From A to Zine: Building a Winning Zine Collection in Your Library.* Chicago:
    American Library Association, 2011.
Dewan, Pauline. "Why Your Undergraduate Library Needs a Popular Reading Collection
    Now More Than Ever." *College & Research Libraries* 17, no. 1 (2010): 44–66.
Miller, Kelly. "Vision Statement: UCLA Library's Teaching and Learning Services." Unpub-
    lished internal document, UCLA Library, 2011.
UCLA Library. "Community Collections." *UCLA Library.* Accessed January 15, 2016,
    http://library.ucla.edu/powell/collections/community-collections.
UCLA Library. "About the Travel Collection." *UCLA Library.* Accessed January 15, 2016,
    http://guides.library.ucla.edu/communitycollections/travel.
UC Regents. "UCLA Grand Challenges." UCLA.edu. Accessed January 15, 2016, http://
    grandchallenges.ucla.edu.

CHAPTER 6

"LEAVE YOUR LEGACY":
Student-led Contributions of University Experience to the Special Collections and Archives

Ashley Todd-Diaz, Shari Scribner, and Kylie Lewis

Introduction

Academic special collections and archives act as institutional memories, safeguarding and sharing the vibrant history woven together from the diverse voices within a college or university community. This memory often contains the meticulously collected official records generated by departments and offices. However, an important and often challenging group of voices to capture is those of the students. Swain describes student culture as dynamic—something that "must be examined, engaged, and explored regularly."[1] However, Wagner and Smith note that pursuing this task is like "hitting a moving target,"[2] suggesting that special collections and archives need to pay careful attention to collecting student materials.

Much of the existing literature regarding students' interaction with archives has been centered on their use of materials and not what students can lead the library and archives toward. Woodward writes, "While the library may have been instrumental in their successful academic career, alumni, more often than not, feel no loyalty to it, as they might to their department, school, college, or even sports team."[3] This can be said for current students as well as alumni. Research has provided some clues as to how special collections and archives can encourage students within their own institutions, but there still is a level of individuality with each university that requires specialized strategies for encouraging students to donate their materials. In a collaborative effort to raise awareness of the value and benefits of contributing to the institutional memory, and to get students involved in both documenting unique perspectives and enhancing research resources for their peers, the Emporia State University (ESU) Special Collections and Archives and the Associated Student Government developed an initiative called "Leave Your Legacy."

Lacking Legacies

Emporia State University (ESU) is a Midwestern regional university with approximately 6,000 students. Traditionally, ESU has been known for its strong education program stretching back to its roots as a normal school, though today it offers more than 75 degree programs across the bachelors, masters, and doctoral levels. In 2013, ESU celebrated its sesquicentennial year. This celebration led to numerous retrospective initiatives across campus, as well as in the library. In an effort to coordinate campus-wide activities such as homecoming and alumni reunions, the Special Collections and Archives decided to focus its fall exhibit on the topic of the first 150 years of athletics at the University. Beginning in the spring of 2013, the full-time and student staff of ESU Special Collections and Archives began researching potential topics, stories, primary sources, and artifacts to include in the exhibit. As with most research projects, we used an iterative strategy and started with a broad lens: athletics in general. We amassed a list of student names and events to investigate further, and then dove back into the available resources for a deeper round of research. We quickly realized that beyond a potential mention in yearbooks and newspapers, there was not much information about specific students to be found, especially during the last fifty years.

During the course of this process, a student assistant approached the curator of special collections and archives with a question about why very few of the collections included items from the recent past. The curator explained that most donations are from people cleaning out attics, garages, and estates. People who have recently graduated are usually either not ready to part with materials that relate to fond memories, or they simply do not view themselves as a part of the University's history. The student reflected on this and acknowledged that they did not consider themselves to be a part of the University's history either. This statement surprised the curator and compelled her to start considering how this sentiment could be modified.

Engaging with Students

At colleges or universities, students are the focus of the institution. Although the records of the faculty, offices, and departments are important, it is the student experiences and initiatives that tell the story of the school. A university archives can be considered a research resource, and it can also be viewed as a collective effort to maintain an institutional memory. According to archivist Michele Christian, "Despite the fact that students constitute the largest group of any college or university community, very few records and papers of students generally exist outside the registrar's office."[4] This statement is true of Emporia State University; even the Special Collections and Archives maintains very few records that relate to students outside of personal collections. One problem that Christian discusses is the "continuous turnover of students,"[5] which can have a lasting and powerful impact within small university communities such as ESU. She asks how we might impress upon students that their materials are worthwhile and have historical value even when they see none. Christian writes, "Active documentation in a university and college setting is essential to ensure that we record what it means to be a student. Otherwise, the history of the university will remain the story of the administration without regard to the student population the university was created to serve."[6]

Within the Special Collections and Archives at ESU, many of the patron research requests we receive come from family members wanting personal information of their relatives' time at the University. Unfortunately, we face the issue that these students did not leave large legacies of personal materials and information for us to reference in depth. Without these materials, we have only the bare information found in official records to draw on, which makes it difficult for us to provide extensive details about their individual experiences at the university. Encouraging current students to leave materials would aid in creating a more dynamic history of the university.

Considering the value of students to the collective effort of documenting campus life, the curator started to consider how students could be encouraged to realize their role in the history of the university. Ellen Swain suggests the creation of a student advisory committee, composed of representatives from groups like Greek life, student organizations, and student leadership, to act as a "sounding board for new programs" so that archives can better reach their students.[7] To get a better grasp on students' perspectives, the curator reached out to the president of the ESU Associated Student Government (ASG). The president was receptive to discussing the idea of how students could contribute to the Special Collections and Archives, but admitted she did not know much about the resource and had never used it in her four years at the University. This lack of awareness is consistent with Wagner and Smith's survey that revealed the majority of students (63 percent) did not know university archives existed or that they accessioned new materials on a regular basis.[8] Another deterrent to student use of the archives is public perception of and stereotypes surrounding these resources. Swain writes, "The archives is generally depicted as a dark, dusty, isolated room, usually in a remote area, that contains forgotten and unimportant mementos of times past. It is a place of noncurrent, cast-off materials managed by quiet individuals who revel in the past."[9]

At ESU, the Special Collections and Archives was closed for four years during 2008–2012 due to a mold infestation within the collection. The department was effectively forgotten by the University and its students. After being closed for years on end, the shroud of mystery has to be drawn away from these resources. With a basic level of understanding of special collections and archives, students not only gain access to a new research resource, but they recognize the significant role and unique perspective they alone can offer to the history of the university. Through this recognition, students are not only empowered to contribute to the University's memory by leaving their individual legacies, but also to embrace the opportunity of leading their peers by example.

Seeing the ASG president's unfamiliarity with the resource as an opportunity to highlight the benefits and details of what a special collections and archives is, the curator invited her for a personal tour. The tour featured a timeline of notable student manuscript materials that reflected the rich history of student life from the 1870s through the 1970s, including photos, clothing, artifacts from sports events and Greek life, and personal memories captured in diaries and correspondence. Unfortunately, due to a lack of donations of student materials in recent decades, the timeline of student life dwindled by the 1980s. The ASG president immediately related to the materials and enjoyed recognizing buildings and names, comparing past activities to what is being planned now, and realizing that ESU students since the nineteenth century have remained very similar. However, when the curator reached the end of the tour and discussed the last of the materials she had pulled, the president asked if there were any materials from the 1980s, when some of her relatives had attended the University. The curator stressed this gap in donated materials, and emphasized the need for current students to be aware of the important role they play in contributing to the institutional memory and to feel empowered to donate materials to enrich the documented memory.

Following the tour, the ASG president invited the curator to an ASG meeting to raise awareness among the other student senators. The curator and the assistant archivist developed a short presentation that featured historic student manuscript materials, reinforced the value of current students contributing to the history of the University, and encouraged the students to leave their legacy. While the tour and presentation planted the seed of awareness and interest, the next step was taking action to continue the momentum.

Establishing "Leave Your Legacy"

Following the presentation with ASG, Special Collections and Archives designated May 5–9, 2014, as "Leave Your Legacy Week." Our goal was three-fold:

- Intentionally and actively interact with students in an environment where they were likely to be found.
- Promote the donation of materials by students currently enrolled at ESU.
- Increase awareness of Special Collections and Archives across campus.

As this was "Dead Week" on campus—the last full week of classes, when students begin cleaning off their desks, packing up their dorm rooms, etc.—it seemed an ideal time to talk to students, faculty, staff, and leaders of campus organizations about donating materials to the university archives.

Wagner and Smith assert that as archivists we must "insert ourselves into the student environment to make them aware of our existence, our mission, and our symbiotic relationship with them."[10] One of the most common methods of interacting with students and advertising activities on campus is to "table" in the student union's Main Street, an area commonly used by students traveling to and from class or just relaxing. With this in mind, we reserved a table each day. Student-to-student interaction is a very different dynamic than faculty-to-student or staff-to-student contact, so we scheduled a student assistant to help staff the table each hour. A student assistant created a brightly colored paper banner that drew attention and stated our theme: "NOW is the time to Leave Your Legacy at Emporia State University!" Flyers and business cards were handed to everyone with whom we spoke, and file folders, boxes, and labels were available to collect donated materials right at the table. Each day a campus-wide email announcement was published advertising the campaign and encouraging students and recognized student organizations (RSOs) to bring materials for donation or transfer to the archives. These announcements were emailed to every student, faculty, and staff member. Photographs of items students had donated in the past were printed and used to decorate the table. These items were eye-catching, showcased our current collections and student life from the past, and naturally led into conversations as students passed the table.

The benefits of having students (rather than only full-time staff) at the table were immediately apparent: they had the greatest number of connections across campus, easily attracted and engaged their peers in conversation, and had experience tabling. One student assistant was especially outstanding in this area. While all the other staff had been sitting behind the table, trying to catch the eyes of passers-by and offering flyers and business cards to anyone who stopped, she grabbed the flyers, stationed herself in front of the table in the flow of students, and distributed flyers to just about every person walking in the area. She had several years of experience tabling for different student organizations and demonstrated that waiting for someone to come to the table was a less effective way of spreading our flyers than proactively engaging students as they moved naturally through the area.

Collecting Legacies

During this initial effort, we distributed more than 150 flyers, resulting in the donation of three collections of student personal papers. While this number included two collections from Special Collections and Archives' student assistants, the third collection was donated by a student introduced to our department through the Leave Your Legacy initiative. Additionally, eleven campus organizations transferred records, which included some that had not previously contributed materials to Special Collections and Archives. These results provided evidence that our initiative was working and students were interested in being a part of history, which motivated us to start planning for the next academic year.

The second "Leave Your Legacy Week" was held May 4–8, 2015, and closely followed the previous years' design, but this year we took advantage of two additional promotional activities. At the beginning of each fall semester, complimentary student planners are published that provide students with a calendar of important dates and campus-wide events. In the 2014–15 academic year, Leave Your Legacy Week was included as a scheduled activity, which potentially put free advertising in the hands of approximately 3,800 students. We also had the opportunity to participate in the "E-Experience," an orientation event that welcomed more than 500 incoming freshmen to campus during the summer for special activities, including a tour of University Libraries and Archives. The focus for the 2014 E-Experience was student success, so as each group spent twenty minutes in our department, we talked to them about how they would be creating a legacy on campus over the next few years, encouraging them to be mindful of that legacy, and encouraging them to leave evidence of it at the Special Collections and Archives prior to graduation. This discussion included examples from the alumni manuscript collection of Brigadier General Art Bloomer. This former outstanding student athlete also had a stellar military career, served Emporia State University as its Foundation president, and donated ESU and military memorabilia to Special Collections and Archives in 2001. Utilizing this collection allowed us to illustrate evidence of student success leading to a prosperous career, service to one's alma mater, and how the donated materials have been used by recent students completing research assignments.

One of the benefits of spending a full week in the student union is that we talked with and collected materials from many student organizations that were also tabling. It is amazing what can happen when you get out of the building and become a presence across campus, making connections and promoting a campaign that potentially affects every student, faculty, and staff member at the university. One visitor to our table was a professor who happened to be on her way to teach a leadership class and was excited to share our initiative with her students as a leadership opportunity. Another visitor was a local high school teacher who brought a group of students for a campus tour. She also asked for flyers to share with her class. During this second campaign, we distributed approximately 150 flyers, one student donated personal papers, and four campus organizations transferred records to Special Collections and Archives. Although we were pleased with continued success, these lower numbers challenged us to consider new strategies for bolstering the initiative as we moved forward.

Positive observations we noted during the year included an awareness that the student assistants in the Special Collections and Archives became enthusiastic in the promotion and development of Leave Your Legacy and were often caught talking to patrons about donating their student papers and artifacts. They also expressed interest to full-time staff regarding additional ways to promote Leave Your Legacy and Special Collections and Archives throughout the year, rather than just during certain weeks. Some of their creative ideas included: purchasing swag that could be handed out at the table, such as decks of cards, flash drives, or water bottles marked with the Leave Your Legacy logo; exhibits and games in the library's 24/7 Learning Commons; and increased use of social media and our department's blog to highlight student donations.

Expanding Legacies

As we assessed the challenges and successes of the second Leave Your Legacy campaign as well as the input of our student assistants, the consensus of the department was that we needed to expand its impact across campus. In the fall of 2015, Special Collections and Archives had the good fortune to hire two students with experience, education, and interest in marketing, one of whom agreed to assume responsibility for moving Leave Your Legacy forward. She began by learning all she could about the history of the initiative, then sharing her perspective of what would be most successful with students. Some of her ideas included: creating an artifact timeline of ESU history with a big question mark for current items to represent the need for current students to fill in the blank; creating drop-off locations across campus; offering incentives, such as buttons, pens, or stickers; advertising with chalk on campus sidewalks; promoting via digital bulletin boards; combining with special events such as homecoming or organization anniversaries; and targeting specific groups to work with, including leadership, student government, ambassadors, RSOs, resident life, Greek life, athletics, the Honors College, and alumni.

After meeting with Special Collections and Archives' full-time staff, we all agreed that she should pursue her ideas with the assistance of one of the department's graduate assistants. Immediately, the student assistant set up a new schedule for the initiative. Rather than spending a full week at the end of each semester tabling in the student union, one to two days each month would be designated "Leave Your Legacy days" and specific advertising would be developed for each event. Student-designed posters were created for each Leave Your Legacy day, and the student leader also worked with the marketing department to develop a logo and professionally produced flyer for the campaign. This flyer highlighted how easy it was to donate materials to Special Collections and Archives and featured a student-donated item from the 1970s to provide an example of what current students could consider contributing (see Figure 6.1).

Donate in 4 easy steps:

1

Consider what items you have in your dorm room, apartment, or house such as photos, t-shirts, flyers, artwork, notebooks, etc.

2

Bring your item(s) to Special Collections and Archives, located in room 119 of the William Allen White Library.

3

Tell us a little about your item(s): what it is, how you used it, dates, memories about the item, etc.

4

Complete some quick paperwork to transfer the item(s) to our care.

LEAVE SPECIAL COLLECTIONS & ARCHIVES *Your* LEGACY

WHERE: Memorial Union
WHEN: Thursday, November 12   10:00-2:00

ESU Special Collections and Archives
620.341.6431 · archives@emporia.edu · WAWL room 119

EMPORIA STATE
U N I V E R S I T Y

Image 6.1. The Leave Your Legacy campaign flyer.

She identified target programs, offices, and organizations across campus and met with them to talk about embedding Leave Your Legacy into their curricula, initiatives, and events. The student leader met one-on-one with the director of the Alumni Association and the PanHellenic Association president. Many alumni approach the Alumni Association to donate their materials, so furthering this relationship presents an opportunity to ensure these materials will ultimately be placed within the Special Collections and Archives for use by students and researchers. The PanHellenic Association provides a closer collaborative opportunity with Greek organizations that do not meet on campus but have a wonderful wealth of materials relating to student life and the University. Additionally, the public services supervisor joined the student leader to meet with a class of leadership students and the Student-Athlete Advisory Committee (SAAC). Most notably, the meeting with the leadership class was an opportunity for the students to see the donation process in action when their professor donated materials during the presentation. This was especially beneficial since it showed the students that the process of leaving their legacies is not difficult. It also opened up the floor to many more questions that arose from the students' curiosity. For the SAAC, the presentation was adapted to illustrate materials that are unique to student athletes such as apparel, equipment, or rosters. These students are often the face of the university and are underrepresented within student-donated materials for ESU. Over the course of the semester, the student leader's interactions resulted in personally inviting seven departments and more than forty students to leave their legacies with Special Collections and Archives.

A special Leave Your Legacy Week was included in our celebration of Archives Month in October, with blog posts highlighting Leave Your Legacy and videos of Special Collections and Archives' student assistants sharing their favorite student-donated collections. Leave Your Legacy days were held three times during the fall 2015 semester. Knowing the effectiveness of student-to-student communication, a focus was placed on encouraging meaningful conversations about their unique legacies and their opportunity to donate materials, rather than relying on flyers to impart the message. With this new strategy in place, we distributed flyers to the sixty-five students with whom we conversed, and received personal papers from two students and records from seven campus organizations.

Lessons Learned

Every year, approximately 1,000 new students arrive on campus who have never heard of Special Collections and Archives. We need to be an active part of their university experience, or every four years an entire generation of students will pass through ESU without utilizing our services. Some students have heard of Special Collections and Archives but have no idea what we do—including that we collect materials from current students and RSOs—or where we are located on campus.

By talking to students, we have learned that many of them are focused on the present and future, not thinking about the past. The idea that they are living history and building the legacy of ESU with the classes they take, organizations they join, and the activities in which they engage, is foreign to them. Introducing (and then repeating) the message that each student is creating their own legacy at ESU is how Special Collections and Archives helps them develop a different perspective of their ESU experience. This new perspective changes the conversations we are able to have with students, and they more easily recognize the value of donating mementoes of their student experience to Special Collections and Archives.

The student assistant leading the fall 2015 initiative suggested that in today's climate of convenience and instant gratification, students do not usually go out of their way to do things. She pointed out that donating materials needs to be easy and should not take much time. Promoting the initiative in the student union is one step we have taken to become more accessible and visible to students, but we have also discussed visiting other locations including residence halls, other academic buildings, or locations where student organizations are meeting.

Students will want to keep their most treasured memorabilia, and that's okay. We want to encourage, not extort, donations; however, items they might be discarding could easily be transferred to Special Collections and Archives instead of being trashed or recycled. Although students might not think to keep flyers for events they have attended, projects they have completed, photos they have taken, or university t-shirts they have received, all of these items reflect the unique student experience and are important to university archives.

We have observed that once students become invested, they will share their positive experiences and encourage others to join them in the enterprise. We have witnessed this phenomenon with our student assistants; the ones who are most enthusiastic about Leave Your Legacy are the ones who have either already donated materials or who plan do to so before they graduate. We have also seen this when a student we have talked to about Leave Your Legacy pulls a friend over to our table in the student union to meet us and learn more about the initiative. This is very rewarding!

Special Collections and Archives staff and student assistants need opportunities to personally interact with students beyond the walls of the library. Positive things happened when we got out from behind our table and approached students at the Memorial Union. We have found different ways to successfully connect with students across campus: Leave Your Legacy days, presentations at meetings of different student groups, informal discussions with researchers visiting the Special Collections and Archives, and scheduling one-on-one information sessions with faculty members and students. With the changes to the initiative implemented this semester, our student assistants met with seven professionals and faculty members across campus, as well as one student group and one leadership class. This effectively laid a foundation for future interactions with the University's leadership program, student athletes, Greek life, alumni association, and the office of Marketing and Media Relations.

Utilizing a variety of staff members—faculty, full-time staff, and students—allowed us to connect with the greatest number of people passing through the student union. Students had the largest number of connections, and other students were more likely to approach the table when there was at least one student working at it. This reinforced the value of what is possible when students step up to a leadership position within an initiative like Leave Your Legacy.

The Future of "Leave Your Legacy"

One of our major visions for the future of the Leave Your Legacy campaign is further embedding the campaign into the University culture through programs and classes. In the future, we would like to speak to all freshmen, transfer, and nontraditional students, and begin to impress upon them early in their educational experience that their materials have value and can be left for the future. By speaking to them earlier, we can encourage student investment and empowerment over those materials. In an ideal setting, students would donate materials throughout their university experience and not just in fifty years when they feel the pressure to get rid of the old memories. Student empowerment and investment on all levels could also aid the university in retention and alumni activities. This approach would embed the Special Collections and Archives more deeply within the university's culture.

While tabling and speaking with students, we observed that many hold the stereotype that the Special Collections and Archives are old, dusty places, shrouded in mystery. A major step for the future of the initiative is to overcome those stereotypes held by students. Similar misconceptions are held by staff and faculty, many of whom must be reeducated on what a special collections and archives holds, collects, and displays. Overcoming the stereotypes will lead to increased awareness of the available primary sources, and students will turn to us as a useful information resource. With more student-related primary sources held by the ESU Special Collections and Archives, there is a higher probability that students will see the materials as relevant to their papers and projects, aiding in the awareness that we wish to encourage in students. We often receive research requests from the children of alumni who are searching for a record of their parents' time at the university. Considering that collecting policies did not prioritize student life materials in the past, we can only provide a basic level of information to those researchers. Acquiring more student-related primary sources allows us to better serve current and future students, alumni, community members, and outside researchers through richer collections, broad ranging exhibits, outreach initiatives, and instructional programs.

Conclusion

Our initial data and observations indicate that an outcome of Leave Your Legacy is the empowerment students achieve by donating their personal papers to the Special Collections and Archives. Through this act they have the opportunity to contribute to the collective memory of the university and a shared resource that will benefit future students and researchers. Although current students might not see immediate return on the importance of their materials, they will know that someone in the future will see the importance. While tabling during the Leave Your Legacy campaign, we have found, as Wagner and Smith suggest, that most students "were surprised at the notion that materials belonging to them might be 'worthy' of inclusion in an archival collection."[11] Students see their materials as things they work on and experience, but not something that others would find useful in the future as a research resource. What we would like to see in the future is a student understanding that, even if they do not see their papers or organizational materials as being important, by leaving those materials for others, they proactively contribute and preserve their unique, individual legacies.

Notes

1. Ellen D. Swain, "College Student as Archives' Consultant? A New Approach to Outreach Programming on Campus," *Archival Issues: Journal Of The Midwest Archives Conference* 29, no. 2 (2005): 124.
2. Jessica Wagner and Debbi Smith, "Students as Donors to University Archives: A Study of Student Perceptions with Recommendations," *The American Archivist* 75 (October 2012): 539.
3. Eddie Woodward, 2013. "Building a Donor Base for College and University Libraries," *College & Research Libraries News* 74, no. 6 (June 2013): 308.
4. Michele Christian, "Documenting Student Life: The Use of Oral Histories in University Archives," *Archival Issues: Journal Of The Midwest Archives Conference* 27, no. 2 (2002): 111.
5. Ibid., 111.
6. Ibid., 117.
7. Swain, "College Student as Archives' Consultant," 117.
8. Wagner and Smith, "Students as Donors to University Archives," 545.
9. Swain, "College Student as Archives' Consultant," 115.
10. Wagner and Smith, "Students as Donors to University Archives," 557.
11. Ibid., 549.

Bibliography

Christian, Michele. "Documenting Student Life: The Use of Oral Histories in University Archives." *Archival Issues: Journal of The Midwest Archives Conference* 27, no. 2 (2002): 111–124.

Swain, Ellen D. "College Student as Archives' Consultant? A New Approach to Outreach Programming on Campus." *Archival Issues: Journal of The Midwest Archives Conference* 29, no. 2 (2005): 113–131.

Wagner, Jessica, and Debbi Smith. "Students as Donors to University Archives: A Study of Student Perceptions with Recommendations." *The American Archivist* 75 (October 2012): 538–66.

Woodward, Eddie. "Building a Donor Base for College and University Libraries." *College & Research Libraries News* 74, no. 6 (June 2013): 308–311.

CHAPTER 7*

WE DIDN'T BREAK TWITTER:
Student Control of the Library's Social Media Channels

Jamie P. Kohler

Introduction

Facebook, an undergraduate student reported to me, is for old people. When pressed, this student acknowledged that by "old people" she meant people in their 30s. At Westminster College, a small, undergraduate, liberal arts institution in Pennsylvania, students seem to live and breathe social media, where change is the rule, rather than the exception. Just because librarians understand and use social media does not mean that they are a part of the thriving and evolving student social media culture that lives on a college campus. Do we understand the (sometimes elaborate) etiquette and social codes that students follow in their social media interactions? Are we adequately reaching students without seeming nosy or creepy? The answer is oftentimes either "no" or, more likely, "we are not sure."

One of the first question libraries ask when embarking on a social media program is: Which social media platforms should we use? The popularity of

---

each site seems to change so quickly, and our target audience, undergraduate students, use social media sites in very different ways than we do as librarians. There has been much discussion in the literature about why and how academic libraries use various social media outlets. In addition, academic libraries are making more effective use of the unique functionalities of each social media outlet, and also keeping up with the changes in platform popularity to reach their target audiences most effectively. Keeping up with rapid change is challenging, and knowing where our students are going and what they are doing online continues to be a daunting prospect.

To address these uncertainties, our library instituted a program in which the library's social media channels are largely populated with content and monitored by student employees. The program, though not without its terrors, flaws, and setbacks, provides benefits to both our library and our student employees. The library gains an opportunity to work and develop relationships with motivated students, and, most important, the ability to more effectively and appropriately connect with our students. Students gain valuable leadership opportunities, a way to more fully participate in the life of the library, and valuable experience in managing a social media campaign.

Literature Review

There is strong evidence that the undergraduate student population is using social media platforms. According to the PEW Research Center in 2015, Facebook remains the most popular, with eighty-two percent of the traditional undergraduate population (eighteen to twenty-nine-year-olds) participating. Thirty-two percent of eighteen to twenty-nine-year-olds are using Twitter, and fifty-five percent of twenty-nine-year-olds are using Instagram. A higher than average percentage of this age group are using each of the platforms as compared to the adult population as a whole (ages eighteen to fifty-six-plus).[1] All of these platforms fulfill a need for undergraduate students. According to Swanson and Walker in their 2015 article, many undergraduate students' "relational connections are conducted via technological tools."[2] Social media is a part of the fabric of life, especially for our target population.

Academic library use of social media platforms for these various purposes is well documented in the literature, especially in recent years.

Hofschire and Wanucha found that "the majority of libraries…had at least one social media account."[3] And Rossmann and Young state that "the question of social media in libraries is no longer 'should?' but 'how?'"[4] Undergraduate students are using these platforms in their daily lives.

Library student employees do not typically play a significant role in coordinating and posting to academic library social media sites, such as Facebook, Twitter, and Instagram. At Ohio University's library, as well as perhaps a handful of other institutions, student interns do play a large role in the library's social media program, but this seems to be the exception, and even in these programs, librarians hesitate to give students significant control and responsibility.[5] Usually, there is either a single librarian or a team of librarians and library staff who coordinate, populate, and assess social media activity.[6] At many libraries, this seems to be a successful way to run a social media program, as librarians have been publishing research and case studies presenting the intricacies and successes of their social media programs for the past ten years.

Although there is enthusiastic support for social media programs at academic libraries, there isn't often space or time in staff schedules to squeeze in this time-consuming responsibility. Zohoorian-Fooladi and Abrizah conducted a study that examines reasons that libraries do and do not participate in social media. Time is a key component of many of the deterrents discussed in this study.[7] There is almost unanimous support for this conclusion throughout the literature written about social media use in libraries.[8] Managing social media is a huge responsibility and time commitment for any group or individual.

Why is the responsibility for a social media program so time-consuming? Because it takes effort and thought, not only in the choices of which social media platforms to use, but also in thinking about, creating, and posting appropriate content to these platforms. The success of a particular post on a social media site depends, in part, on the platform to which you are posting content.[9] For each social media platform, however, posting frequently and maintaining an active presence is one of the key features of a successful social media program.[10]

The literature suggests two other important aspects of a successful library social media page: interactivity and authenticity. Several studies have addressed the need for interactivity on any library's social media site.[11] Using Twitter as a bulletin board is not worth a library's time. Useful content should go beyond the announcement of events and promotion of library resources and services. Library social media pages are successful if they are able to achieve a high degree of interactivity[12] and make connections with their target audience. In addition to being interactive, libraries should be posting content that "is fashioned in such a way as to invite interaction by providing a strong sense of relevancy and personality,"[13] write Young and Rossman. How to accomplish this with a Twitter post or an Instagram photo is less clear. Some emerging library literature attempts to decode why some posts are successful and others are not. Most seem to agree that libraries should work towards "personality-rich, two-way interactions"[14] in social media posts. Social media should be a tool that encourages community building between the library, its users, and the campus community at large.[15] To develop a "personality" for a social media page is no easy task, however, and creating an authentic voice can be a challenge.

Summarizing the literature reviewed above, there are three aspects of a successful social media account: content needs to be timely, interactive, and perhaps most important, creative and full of personality. How to achieve this is less clear, and is likely going to be different depending on the particular institution and audience. Overall, however, the literature on this subject agrees that the maxim "be interesting, be interested"[16] should be the goal of library social media programs.

The way in which our library chose to implement a social media program was to heavily involve our library student employees, who we felt were those best suited at our institution to provide both the level of timeliness, interactivity, and meaningful content that was needed for the program to be successful.

Design and Implementation

In the beginning, there was Facebook—a solid choice, in 2011, for a first foray into the world of social media. In the fall of 2011, we created a Facebook page for the main library. Luckily, our library leadership saw that the page might be left open to possible change and different uses. Without any particular guidelines or restrictions, the philosophy was, "Let's throw something at the wall and see what sticks." From the beginning, it was important that students be at the core of any social media system that we developed.

First Attempts

During the following two and a half academic years (spring 2013 through spring 2015), we attempted several different iterations of social media team structure and workflows. Our first attempt involved working with student interns, who were specifically assigned to manage our social media program. We tried to ensure a steady stream of interns, but after some initial success, quickly discovered that most students were not interested in an intense, unpaid internship. We then tried a team of co-coordinators—paid student employees—which quickly degenerated into chaos without any particular person in charge and with the enormous workload involved. We tried involving all library student employees, no matter what their primary task, with a single student coordinator. This, again, turned out to be too much for a single student to manage, especially with restricted pay and hours. In all of these attempts the following remained true: We always had a librarian or a library staff member as an appointed advisor/coordinator, and we always carefully selected the students who would be involved in any kind of leadership role in our social media efforts. These were all students who had worked for the library in other capacities, and who were known to be responsible, creative individuals with a decent work ethic. Even with these safeguards in place, none of these structures seemed to work well.

Managing undergraduate students has proved to be the most challenging and difficult aspect of this project. Undergraduate students (even good ones) are busy and distracted, and sustaining a vibrant social media program for a library takes more time and effort than most students are willing or able to commit. The students had fantastic ideas and plans, but often these did not come to fruition when coursework, Greek life, or family obligations created conflicts. It wasn't that the social media program wasn't making progress throughout this period—on the contrary. We developed policies, gained followers in leaps and bounds, ran several successful contests designed to gain followers and increase interaction, and were pleased with the amount of activity on our pages. But we were still just "making it work" from semester to semester, without a sustainable plan. Librarians and library staff were often picking up the slack left when students dropped the ball. We needed to make another change to put the students at the center of our social media, while at the same time ensuring that it could be a vibrant, functioning program.

The problems with the library's social media program came to a head in the fall of 2014, when I, as the librarian coordinating and managing the social media program, was gone on maternity leave. When I returned, the program had descended into confusion. The students involved had slowly drifted toward inactivity, and without a designated person to do something about it, the postings all but stopped. Frustratingly, again, our bright, creative, responsible students were too busy to dedicate themselves to the library's social media program. How could we create a program that reached our goal of making students central, but also provide structure and oversight? The current iteration of the social media program at our library is a step towards answering this question.

The Plan that Worked

During the waning days of the fall semester of 2014, we established the model that, thus far, seems to fit our library and our followers' needs. It is a hybrid program, with a combination of student coordinators, student participants, and a library staff member, who works with me to oversee student work and to develop requirements and goals. This approach allows for student contribution and for much-needed structure.

First, I work with one other professional library staff member and in coordination with the students, to develop specific policies, targets, and goals for each student involved in the program. For example, each student is expected to generate a certain amount of content for the page each week, and post a certain number of times each week. These weekly goals are set by the full-time staff member in consultation with the student coordinators, but the students actually do the work. Regular meetings are important; students have the opportunity to discuss their ideas and give feedback on library initiatives. (This has proved helpful for not only the social media project. A side benefit is that we have a group of involved students who can give us feedback on all aspects of the library and its role on campus.) We also, in consultation with our student coordinators, set specific policies for our social media accounts. For example, students are expected to post timely updates to Twitter (and not other social media outlets). The students felt that posting such announcements as "The printer is out of paper" was not necessarily appropriate for Facebook or Instagram. These policies help us to better define our purpose in each distinct social media platform, and provide student employees with some boundaries. For additional examples of policies (especially concerning Twitter), see Appendix 7A. For now, these policies are extremely basic and fluid. As a result, there are guiding principles (including a focus on assessment), but not a strict definition of purpose or a hierarchical approval process.

Second, we have a team of three paid student coordinators, who are largely responsible for posting content to the social media pages and monitoring the pages' interactions with followers. This work is both task-oriented and ongoing. Students generate content for the pages as part of their regular hours and regular work duties at the library. They are also expected to monitor the library's pages several times a day. The student social media coordinators are selected from among our general student employee pool, all of which are paid using federal work-study dollars, and as such are not eligible for any special pay or status. This is a bit troubling for us, since we would like to have a way to reward creative and talented students who work hard. So far, however, students have been happy to participate simply for the experience and as a résumé-building opportunity (and of course a little bit of money). Students in the social media coordinator position must be "work-study eligible," and eligibility is based on the students' Free Application for Federal Student Aid (FAFSA) information. This sometimes disqualifies interested and talented students, and this is an issue we would like to address in the future.

Finally, all of the library's student employees are expected to participate in at least some aspect of the social media program. Student workers are the "face" of our library—they staff the main service point for our library, and are therefore exposed first to many of the issues and problems that arise. So, we ask all students to post updates to our library's Twitter account. Everything from "the printer is fixed" to "fresh coffee available now" to "there's a class currently meeting in the computer lab" are appropriate posts. A clear policy sheet and list of suggested posts are provided and updated by the student and staff coordinators (See Appendix 7A). These students have minimal involvement/creative input on the social media content that is posted by the library, but are essential. The posts made by these students on the front lines are the "hooks" that attract followers. Current, timely posts are only possible if those who are physically present and seeing what goes on are able to participate in the library's social media.

Combined, the three aspects of our social media program—guiding principles for social media, a team of student coordinators, and involvement of all front-line student workers—address our target audience's needs and provide appropriate, useful, and attention-grabbing content. And, though we started with Facebook, we now operate three social media platforms, each that has evolved to have its own purposes and goals. We maintain a robust presence on Twitter and Instagram. For each of these three platforms, we have developed a set of policies and objectives that guide student coordinator participation levels. Since each platform is different and used for different purposes, the role of the student in each is slightly different.

For example, we have found that our library's Facebook page is much more effective communicating with members of the local community and alumni. The content of our Facebook page, therefore, is much less geared toward our current undergraduate population. Because of this, it is less important that our students have a direct role in the management of this page. This page is also more slow-moving. Posts, comments, and responses are much less time-sensitive. So it makes sense that this arm of our social media program is largely populated by members of our professional library staff. However, the content included on the page is often collected by student employees. For example, one of our student employees is responsible for assisting in the College Archives, which is housed in the library. One of his duties is to collect and scan interesting archival photos and documents to post to our Facebook page that are either related to campus events or are more generic for "Throwback Thursday."

Our other two main social media platforms, Twitter and Instagram, are driven much more by student-generated content and student input. As mentioned above, all of our student employees are expected to post time-sensitive library happenings to our Twitter page. This moment-by-moment content could only be generated by student employees at our library, since they are the only library staff in the building on evenings and weekends. They operate our main service point during all hours that the library is open, and observe the comings and goings that occur at all hours.

The three student social media coordinators are involved in all three of these platforms, though on different levels and capacities. They are almost solely responsible for content (other than any real-time library updates) posted to both Twitter and Instagram, and they also assist with generating content for Facebook. They do everything from taking photos in the library, to scanning pictures from the archives, to planning and producing short videos, both serious and silly. Our library is fine with silly, which may seem a bit trivial, but it is important to understand in the context of our social media program. Sometimes, the posts that our student coordinators create are not focused on library databases, operating hours, or laptop availability (though all of this is important). The posts are sometimes funny pictures or quotes about libraries, books, or college life in general. Sometimes they are links to ridiculous videos on YouTube. Sometimes they are silly promotions and contests that we come up with ourselves. For example, every Christmas we set up an "ugly sweater" photo booth in the library, and encourage students to take a picture wearing one of our loaner ugly sweaters, against a background of truly ugly decorations, making sure to tag our library's Instagram account. "Silly," un-academic activities like this are essential to our social media campaign's success. Though we are still developing our methods to gather evidence, it seems that our student social media followers like what we are doing. It is difficult to predict, however; some of our less-than-academic posts receive a lot of attention and some do not. The line between "silly" and "weird" is a thin one. This is another place where the input and influence of our student coordinators is essential. They are always the litmus test, to make sure that we do not alienate any of our followers with inappropriate content.

Our student social media coordinators are also important in the specific, targeted campaigns we run once or twice a year to drive more traffic to our pages and posts, and to increase the number of followers of our accounts. Various students have run several very different campaigns, from the initial inception of the idea, to the planning and coordinating, to the assessment of success. Our first campaign was a contest to increase the number of "likes" on our Facebook account. The student running the campaign decided to give away a very small, inexpensive prize to every person who could show that they "liked" our library's account. She found the money in a little-used library restricted account (accessed by a very generous library director) to buy the prizes, then created the promotional material for both online and around campus, and coordinated the prize give-away. As a result of her efforts, we more than doubled the number of "likes" on our Facebook page. More recently, a different student planned and coordinated another contest via Instagram. Students were asked to post a picture of themselves using a new physical technology space in our building. The winner of this contest won a private study room in the library—with a key!—for the entire week of finals. This campaign, again, dramatically increased the number of students following our library's Instagram account. The beauty of these two very different social media membership campaigns was that each was unique. Each was driven by a student's understanding of the motivators and needs of their peers. Each was engaging and fun, and was something that students felt that their peers would participate in and enjoy.

The ultimate goal for our library's social media program is to create a useful and engaging social media presence for our library. We believe this is best accomplished by heavily involving members of our target audience—students at a small undergraduate liberal arts college. By designing the program in this way, library staff and students can cooperate on a project that inspires both parties. It provides students with an invaluable opportunity to demonstrate leadership and flex their creative muscles, and it provides the library with a window into the world of our target audience. We expect to continue the program as it stands into the future, as it seems to be working for librarians, library staff, and students alike.

Assessment and Discussion

There are both benefits and challenges with the social media program described in this chapter. As this is a case study, these lessons learned should be prefaced by two reminders about the situation on our campus. First, this small, liberal arts campus in a rural area is already quite connected without social media. There is a pre-existing sense of community among not only the student body, but between the library student and professional staff. In such a small place, all library groups and departments already must overlap, share news, and work closely together. These important connections that drive the liveliness of social media and the relevance of the content were already in place in our library; we didn't have to build them. This was an enormous help to our program. We had buy-in from the beginning from an enthusiastic library staff and an enthusiastic, if distracted, student employee base.

Second, a major hurdle that did not affect the implementation of this program at our institution was hesitation from library staff. Our director was extremely willing to let go of control in this area and allow the library to experiment. Without this openness and flexibility, this program would have been much more difficult to get off the ground, especially in terms of allowing student employees to have fairly significant control over these very public sites. However, we did have some long-time library staff members who were hesitant, but with the support of our director we were able to move forward.

Our library was fairly late in implementing a social media program, having no social media presence at all before 2011, and not a particularly significant one until late 2014. As such, formal assessment of this program is ongoing, and very few conclusions can be drawn. To this point, the most valuable sources for formal assessment have been the statistics tracked by the social media outlets themselves. Of the three social media sites we currently use, Facebook tracks incredibly detailed data about page usage, but the usage data available via Twitter and Instagram is far less robust. Figure 7.1 shows our Facebook page "likes" as of May 2016.

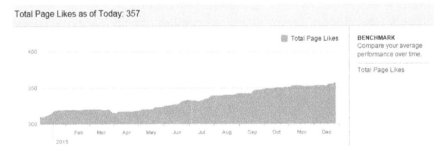

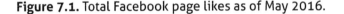

Figure 7.1. Total Facebook page likes as of May 2016.

This chart clearly shows the steady growth of our page over the course of the 2015–16 academic year. The 378 overall "likes" feels very successful to us, as it works out to approximately thirty-three percent of our entire student population. Perhaps more interesting, we can also use this data to see which content and posts were most effective in reaching our audience. During the fall semester 2015, our most popular posts were those that centered on holiday or campus traditions. The following post was the most popular from fall 2015, which reached 526 individuals and was "liked" or commented on by eighteen individuals.

Image 7.1. Librarians ready for #WCMockcon15 cowboy, cowgirls, and corn.

Twitter collects less data and it does not track data over time. Thus, we have started to track some of the basic usage data that is available via both sites in a simple spreadsheet. This data shows very similar patterns to our Facebook page. For our Twitter pages, our overall number of followers has increased gradually over time (See Figure 7.2). This chart also indicates that our Twitter activity is closely linked to our academic calendar, as the rate of increase slows considerably over the winter break and through the summer months.

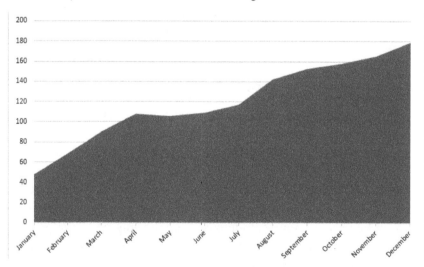

Figure 7.2. New Twitter followers for 2015.

In addition to taking note of this steady growth, data from Twitter usage clearly shows at least an indirect correlation between the number of tweets that the library posts and the overall usage of the Twitter page (See Figure 7.3). There are, however, obvious cases where this does not hold true. Our hypothesis is that these inconsistencies indicate that the tweets being posted are not as interesting or useful to our followers. We hope to use this information to improve the quality of interactions on Twitter.

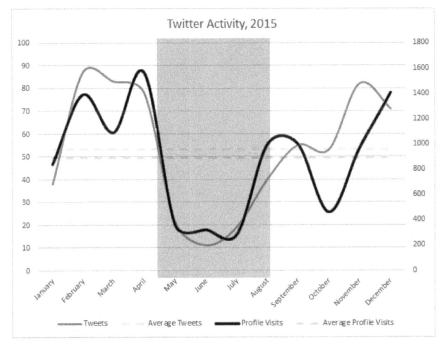

Figure 7.3. Twitter activity in 2015.

The chart in Figure 7.3 also indicates, again, that the busiest times of the year on Twitter coincide with our academic calendar. This makes sense, since our small undergraduate campus offers minimal summer programs. In addition, we are able to see which specific posts are the most popular each month. In November of 2015, our top posts included a photo of one of our student employees, a "thank you" note posted by one of our followers, and the picture celebrating a campus tradition that was also popular on Facebook (See Image 7.2).

Nov 2015 · 30 days

TWEET HIGHLIGHTS

Top Tweet earned 366 impressions

#wcmockcon15 Librarians ready to
represent the Midwest region!
pic.twitter.com/vp7RO7ZZwH

↩ 1   ↻ 1   ♥ 2

View Tweet activity   View all Tweet activity

Top mention earned 60 engagements

 AnDan
@AnDan63   Nov 13

Thanks @Chill_McGill!!!!!
pic.twitter.com/dJRMNhy34b

↩ 1   ♥ 1

View Tweet

Top media Tweet earned 358 impressions

Ben Gaul is the Most Happy Fella that works
in the library basement #seriously and
maybe anywhere on campus
pic.twitter.com/1KA0OfEWMr

Image 7.2. Top tweets on Twitter, November 2015.

Data collected by Instagram is even less detailed than Twitter's data. We have only recently started using and tracking Instagram in earnest, so the data is not particularly useful at this time, though we plan to continue tracking usage and looking for trends. Our most popular post from fall 2015 included a video of one of our student employees riding a hoverboard in the library (see Image 7.3).

Image 7.3. Screenshot of Instagram post, student employee riding hoverboard in the library.

This data shows that the library's social media program is growing and reaching more students. We are also able to use data to see what kinds of posts and what kind of content drive the most activity and growth on the various platforms. We can use this information to create future content. Based on our experience up to this point, it appears that actually posting content that features our student employees and librarians seems to be a useful way of driving usage and adding followers. But all of this information only tells part of the story of the success of this program. As we continue to move forward, we hope to be able to substantiate some of the more intangible benefits of our social media program, such as the benefits to both librarians and library student employees.

Conclusions

The major drawbacks of this program are threefold. First, it is still extremely time-consuming for the library staff to direct and manage this program. One of the initial intentions was that by having students run the social media program, this would save library staff time. The opposite seems to be true. It takes even more time to coordinate the efforts of students. Students must continually be reminded, monitored, and encouraged. As mentioned previously, a student's priority is not often the work of the library, but their own social, extra-curricular, and academic interests (and hopefully not in that order). Second, we continue to struggle with creating and defining the purpose and goals of our social media outlets. As it is, we pretty much do whatever the students are interested in doing—and the students change. There is a fair amount of turnover in the positions, which are responsible for social media; at best, we have students for four years. Students graduate and move on. This creates problems with continuity, and we struggle to adequately define our goals and future plans while leaving enough flexibility to encourage individual student's creativity and enthusiastic new ideas for the project. And finally, it can still seem a little bit scary to some. Giving students control over such a public expression of the library's identity can seem like a big risk. What if they post something inappropriate? Or confidential? In our case, I can report that there have been no surprises. Students have been excellent custodians of the library's social media outlets, and our trust has not been misplaced. We haven't managed to *break* Twitter yet.

Both the library and the student employees benefit from this program. Librarians and library staff gain the opportunity to work closely with some talented and amazing student employees, as well as the ability to more effectively and appropriately connect with our target population: undergraduate students. We gain the ability to reach out to students using an appropriate and familiar "voice." Students know the unwritten social codes of social media, can sound authentic, and therefore can better connect with their peers. Social media platforms change so quickly, and our student employees are always able to explain the latest nuance. Certainly, we are constantly learning from our students. We are also learning more about the campus, and the needs of our student population. As a result of this new source of information about our students, we may be better able to support the goals of our library and our college as a whole. Being better connected to our students, we hope, will lead to improved information literacy, use of library space and technology, and communication with other campus groups and offices.

The student social media coordinators also benefit from this arrangement. They gain valuable leadership experience, a way to more fully participate in the life of the library, and to acquire a set of increasingly useful skills—those of managing a social media program. The students must work with library staff and librarians to coordinate and brainstorm postings for the various platforms. They are required to think creatively and to plan efficiently. The students must also pay much closer attention to the daily life of the library, so that they have ideas about what to post and so that they are able to effectively monitor sites. They must know what the library deems appropriate so that they can edit or take down postings as needed. This is a delicate balance, and requires a close working relationship with the library and the library staff. Working with various groups and managing a project through to its completion are skills that will greatly benefit our students, no matter their majors. Managing a social media page or campaign is a heavy responsibility for undergraduate students, but they can, and do, rise to the challenge.

One of the biggest dilemmas we faced when setting up and implementing this program was hesitation about the extent to which students should be given control of social media outlets that represent the library. Handing over control was a terrifying proposal to some in our institution. Though our director was supportive, a few staff members were less enthusiastic. The endless possibilities of "things that could go wrong" haunted our deliberations when considering how to make this program work. So far, these fears have proved to be unfounded. Students have proved to be excellent custodians of our library's image. Our students did not break Twitter, and our library's social media presence is more robust, timely, and interactive.

Appendix 7A

@Chill_McGill Twitter Account

The @Chill_McGill Twitter account is used to inform followers of things happening in the library in real time!

DURING REGULAR OFFICE HOURS: MONDAY-FRIDAY, 8 AM- 4:30 PM:

- The Help desk Supervisor and the Help desk student workers will provide Kate Ratvasky (ratvaska@westminster) with updates on any issues that are disruptive to library patrons (broken printer, scanner, collaborative tablet etc.) or to the campus at large (Wi-Fi down, my.westminster or D2L down, disruptive maintenance, etc.)

AFTER 4:30 P.M. AND DURING WEEKEND SHIFTS:

Students working at the LIS Help Desk should have the @Chill_McGill Twitter account tab open at all times (just like TrackIt and OCLC tabs).

- Tweet using the Chill_McGill account when the following situations occur. (Not working = you had to put an out-of-order sign on it. Do try and fix stuff first.)
- ALWAYS include #LISHelp at the beginning of each Tweet you send from the Chill_McGill account
  - The printer is not working / printer is back up and running again
  - The Keurig is broken or out of k-cups / Keurig is fixed or when there is a new supply of K-cups available
  - Books scanner is not working / working again
  - If one of the collaborative tables is not working / working again
  - Tweet about anything that Alex specifically tells you to Tweet about, either in person or via e-mail (lishelp@westminster.edu)
    - This may include issues with the Wi-Fi, Internet, website, My.westminster, D2L, cable or phone service, building issues, etc.
- Let your replacement know if the issue is unresolved by the end of your shift so they can continue to provide updates if necessary.
- Follow the @Chill_McGill account, and encourage others to do so. Retweet us too! ☺

DO NOT Tweet anything other than what is stated above and do not let anyone other than LIS Help Desk student employees Tweet using the @Chill_McGill account.

*If you have any questions, comments or ideas, contact Kate Ratvasky (ratvaska@westminster.edu), who monitors all McGill social media accounts

Notes

1. Maeve Duggan, "The Demographics of Social Media Users," *Pew Research Center,* Last modified August 19, 2015, http://www.pewinternet.org/2015/08/19/the-demographics-of-social-media-users/; "Social Networking Fact Sheet," *Pew Research Center,* accessed May 9, 2016, http://www.pewinternet.org/fact-sheets/social-networking -fact-sheet/.
2. Joan Ann Swanson and Erika Walker, "Academic Versus Non-academic Emerging Adult College Student Technology Use," *Tech Know Learn* 20, (2015): 148.
3. Linda Hofschire and Meghan Wanucha, "Public Library Websites and Social Media: What's #trending Now?" *Computers in Libraries* 34, no. 8 (2014): 7.
4. Doralyn Rossmann and Scott W. H. Young, "Using Social Media to Build Community," *Computers in Libraries* 35, no. 4 (2015): 18.
5. Jessica Hagman and Janet Carleton, "Better Together: Collaborating with Students on Library Social Media," *Public Services Quarterly* 10 (2014): 238–244.
6. Rossmann and Young, "Using Social Media," 18–22; Scott Young and Doralyn Rossmann, "Building Library Community Through Social Media," *Information Technology and Libraries* 34, no. 1 (2015): 20–37; Darcy Del Bosque, Sam A. Leif, and Susie Skarl, "Libraries Atwitter: Trends in Academic Library Tweeting," *Reference Services Review* 40, no. 2 (2012): 199–213; David Lee King, "Managing Your Library's Social Media Channels," *Library Technology Reports* 51, no. 1 (January 2015).
7. Niusha Zohoorian-Fooladi and A. Abrizah, "Academic Librarians and their Social Media Presence: A Story of Motivations and Deterrents," *Information Development* 30, no. 2 (2014): 165.
8. Andy Burkhardt, "Social Media: A Guide for College and University Libraries," *College and Research Libraries News* 71, no. 1 (2010): 10–24; Jason Shulman, Jewelry Yep, and Daniel Tome, "Leveraging the Power of a Twitter Network for Library Promotion," *Journal of Academic Librarianship* 41 (2015): 184.
9. Stuart Palmer, "Characterizing University Library Use of Social Media: A Case Study of Twitter and Facebook from Australia," *The Journal of Academic Librarianship* 40 (2014): 612.
10. Del Bosque, Leif, and Skarl, "Libraries Atwitter," 210.
11. Shulman, Yep, and Tome, "Leveraging the Power," 179.
12 Burkhardt, "Social Media," 10–24; Karen Blakeman and Scott Brown, "Social Media: Essential for Research, Marketing and Branding," *Bulletin of the American Society for Information Science and Technology* 37, no. 1 (2010): 47–50; Del Bosque, Leif, and Skarl, "Libraries Atwitter," 199–213; Zohoorian-Fooladi and Abrizah, "Academic Librarians," 159–171; Young and Rossmann, "Building Library Community," 20–37.
13. Young and Rossmann, "Building Library Community," 30.
14. Ibid., 30.
15. Ibid., 22.
16. Harry Glazer, "'Likes' are Lovely, but do they Lead to more Logins?: Developing Metrics for Academic Libraries Facebook Pages," *College and Research Libraries News* 73 (2012): 18–21.

Bibliography

Blakeman, Karen and Scott Brown. "Social Media: Essential for Research, Marketing and Branding." *Bulletin of the American Society for Information Science and Technology* 37, no. 1 (2010): 47–50.

Burkhardt, Andy. "Social Media: A Guide for College and University Libraries." *College and Research Libraries News* 71, no. 1 (2010): 10–24.

Del Bosque, Darcy, Sam A. Leif, and Susie Skarl. "Libraries Atwitter: Trends in Academic Library Tweeting." *Reference Services Review* 40, no. 2 (2012): 199–213. doi: 10.1108/00907321211228246.

Duggan, Maeve. "The Demographics of Social Media Users." Pew Research Center. Last modified August 19, 2015. http://www.pewinternet.org/2015/08/19/the-demographics-of-social-media-users/.

Glazer, Harry. "'Likes' are Lovely, but Do They Lead to More Logins?: Developing Metrics for Academic Libraries Facebook Pages." *College and Research Libraries News* 73 (2012): 18–21.

Hagman, Jessica, and Janet Carleton. "Better Together: Collaborating with Students on Library Social Media." *Public Services Quarterly* 10, (2014): 238–244. doi: 10.1080/15228959.2014.931207.

Hofschire, Linda and Meghan Wanucha. "Public Library Websites and Social Media: What's #trending Now?" *Computers in Libraries* 34, no. 8 (October 2014): 4–9.

King, David Lee. "Managing your Library's Social Media Channels." *Library Technology Reports* 51, no. 1 (January 2015).

Palmer, Stuart. "Characterizing University Library Use of Social Media: A Case Study of Twitter and Facebook from Australia." *The Journal of Academic Librarianship* 40 (2014): 611–619. doi: 10.1016/j.acalib.2014.08.007

Rossmann, Doralyn and Young, Scott W. H. "Using Social Media to Build Community." *Computers in Libraries* 35, no. 4 (2015): 18–22.

Shulman, Jason, Jewelry Yep, and Daniel Tome. "Leveraging the Power of a Twitter Network for Library Promotion." *Journal of Academic Librarianship* 41, (2015): 178–185. doi: 10.1016/jacalib.2014.12.004.

Social Networking Fact Sheet. Pew Research Center. http://www.pewinternet.org/fact-sheets/social-networking-fact-sheet/.

"Status Update." Podcast audio. *This American Life*, November 27, 2015. Streaming audio, 58:41. Accessed January 11, 2016. http://www.thisamericanlife.org/radio-archives/episode/573/status-update.

Swanson, Joan Ann and Erika Walker. "Academic versus Non-academic Emerging Adult College Student Technology Use." *Tech Know Learn* 20, (2015): 147–158. doi: 10.1007/s19758-015-9258-4.

Young, Scott and Doralyn Rossmann. "Building Library Community through Social Media." *Information Technology and Libraries* 34, no. 1 (March 2015): 20–37.

Zohoorian-Fooladi, Niusha and A. Abrizah. "Academic Librarians and their Social Media Presence: A Story of Motivations and Deterrents." *Information Development* 30, no. 2 (2014): 159–171. doi: 1177/0266666913481689.

Part 3

STUDENTS AS AMBASSADORS

CHAPTER 8*

STUDENT TO STUDENT MARKETING & ENGAGEMENT:
A Case Study of the University of Nebraska–Lincoln Libraries Peer Guides

Joan M. Barnes

Introduction

This chapter examines an undergraduate student peer guide employment program that works to promote the University of Nebraska–Lincoln (UNL) Libraries' services and resources. As a part of this program, students engage peers by staffing booths at recruitment events, posting on social media, planning and implementing library events, and gathering feedback from students using surveys or other methods. Each peer guide is assigned to lead an area and to collaborate with the remaining peer guides on projects as needed. There have been challenges and successes within the UNL Libraries peer guide program, including the influence peer guides have on the creation and implementation of the marketing products themselves. The students become de facto advisors to the UNL Libraries' efforts to promote its services to students in their own age group. The UNL Libraries benefit from the advice given by the peer guides and in other ways, such as expanding our outreach to more students, increased publicity of Libraries resources and services, and from the feedback the peer guides get from other students.

Literature Review

Promoting services and resources and engaging constituents have become essential strategic goals for libraries. To achieve these goals, more libraries are employing communications professionals or assigning marketing and communications to current staff members already in the library. Academic libraries offer abundant services, and new students arrive on campus every year, so the need for marketing is constant. Many libraries have turned to student employees or volunteers to make connections with other students on behalf of the library. The expectation is that students will more easily engage and relate to other students, so they may be more successful in promoting the use of the libraries and its resources.

A review of the literature of peer-to-peer models reveals a variety of ways that libraries market library resources and services using instruction, reference assistance, technology assistance, and even as liaisons to student groups on campus. Betz, Brown, Barberi, and Langendorfer reported on the use of student ambassadors to market databases through instruction at the University of Connecticut Libraries in the Scopus Student Ambassador Program.[1] Miller described the library student liaison program instituted at Eastern Washington University and concluded that the program added more "student-friendly tools for communication" (e.g. social media), ways to get feedback from students, and that undergraduates became a focus of a strategic communications plan.[2] Millet and Chamberlain write that their library experienced an increase in the use of particular online databases when they partnered with peer tutors, outside the library, to market those resources.[3] Twait describes the use of a marketing internship and collaborations with student organizations to assist a college library's effort to engage more students.[4]

A literature search did not uncover an exact replica of UNL's peer guides program, but certain elements of the programs reviewed are similar, including use of social media, seeking feedback from students, and making service to undergraduates a focus of the UNL Libraries' strategic plan.

University of Nebraska–Lincoln Libraries

The University of Nebraska–Lincoln (UNL) Libraries is composed of seven libraries on campus that contain almost three million volumes of print books and hundreds of thousands of electronic books, journals, and other resources. We serve more than 6,000 faculty and staff and more than 25,000 undergraduate and graduate students,[5] and we employ 121 faculty and staff and 170 students. Currently, our collections are currently moving into off-site locations, where they can be retrieved when requested. Valuable space within the library is transformed into new study and collaborative areas. In addition, student-centered academic activities were moved into the main library, including the First-Year Experience and Student Success Office, The Explore Center (advisors for undeclared student), and Education Abroad. Thus, two large rooms that once held collections or library offices were turned into study areas, an exhibit space was added, and a new Learning Commons opened within the main library. The Learning Commons, a twenty-four-hour study space, adds a service point offering reference and technology support, a coffee shop, fifteen group study rooms, a testing center, and three large areas of open study space. Within a few days of opening, traffic into the main library increased. After being open two months, it was at 90 percent use capacity several days a week during the late morning to evening hours.

The significant physical changes taking place at the UNL Libraries during the last three years transformed library spaces, services, and products as a result of considering the needs, study preferences, and information-seeking behaviors of undergraduate students. A new team was formed to help the UNL Libraries make these transformations possible and evolve into a student-centered library. The user experience and student success team (UX team), led by the special assistant to the dean for student success and user experience, works with other library departments on projects to improve the delivery of services, make webpages and online resources user-friendly, and transform the physical spaces within the UNL Libraries. Members of the UX team include the community engagement librarian, graphic designer, learning commons manager, staff development program officer, team assistant, web content and design specialist, and web usability and design specialist.

The UX team conceived the idea to establish a Peer Guide Program (PGP), and the program's goal and job description were written by the special assistant to the dean, the chair of the Reference and Instruction Services (RIS) department, and me, the community engagement librarian. Planning for the PGP began during the fall semester of 2013 with the primary goal of promoting UNL Libraries' services in a peer-to-peer format. The program would operate out of the RIS department, which offers research assistance and other front-line services directly to students. Under RIS supervision, the peer guides were to provide roaming reference services and impromptu tours.[6] Secondary goals of the PGP were to solicit feedback from undergraduates and help with library events and outreach. These secondary goals helped the UX team continue to guide the Libraries' student-centered transformation.

Timeline of the Peer Guide Program

In November 2013, advertisements were posted on campus with Career Services and in the student newspaper. A pool of more than fifty students applied for four peer guide positions. Applications were reviewed, eight students were interviewed, and four students were hired to begin work during the spring semester of 2014. The students selected to be the first peer guides were all upper-level students, had high GPAs, and were involved in extracurricular activities. The peer guides were supervised by two RIS department staff members, the instructional support associate, and the research specialist. They trained the peer guides, scheduled their work, and coordinated their assignments. As the community engagement librarian and member of the UX Team, I am responsible for marketing, communications, events, and outreach. As a part of this role, I coordinated the peer guides' work for the UX team.

At the end of the spring 2014 semester, a meeting was held to discuss the implementation of the PGP and determine if any changes to the program needed to be considered. The staff involved in the discussion included both supervisors of the peer guides, the RIS department chair, the reference desk manager, the head of the UX team, and me. Feedback gathered from the peer guides in their duties revealed that roaming reference, their main activity, was not a comfortable practice and they felt that students responding to them were disturbed or "creeped out." Roaming reference was a new service for the UNL Libraries as well as the peer guides. It is possible that support for this new service was not adequate because it was not part of the existing culture or menu of services already offered. An insufficient amount of activities to keep the peer guides busy in RIS was also an issue. Many times, the peer guides filled in at the reference desk and were not fully utilized for their purpose of proactive outreach.[7]

According to an internal document on the summary of activities of the first semester of the PGP, the peer guides spent the majority of their time assisting with events coordinated by me and conducting user surveys requested by other members of the UX Team. The peer guides were doing work that supported marketing and UX team activities, and it was a natural conclusion to move the coordination of the program to me, the community engagement librarian. The peer guides would continue to interact with other students but under the direction of the UX Team. In addition, the Libraries' strategic goal of increasing programming was further reason to move the coordination of the program, a move which was fully supported by the RIS department.

PGP Coordination Transferred to UX Team

When I became coordinator of the program, I had three objectives to accomplish by the end of that summer. The first objective was to break down the broad topics of marketing and communications into four main areas in which peer guides could provide assistance and leadership: outreach, social media, events, and user surveys—one area for each of the four peer guides. This division would make the workload manageable for each peer guide and allow them to develop their leadership skills in that area. While each peer guide leads one of the four areas within marketing, they are encouraged to collaborate on projects that cross multiple areas. Collaboration among peer guides provides them the opportunity to develop the soft skills of leadership, especially delegation, cooperation, and interpersonal communication.

The second objective was to hire new peer guides and promote my current student assistant into the peer guide program. That student had been assisting with publicizing the Libraries' events and social media. She would continue her work in that area, but she needed some additional training to be promoted to a peer guide. Only one current peer guide would continue under my supervision; all other peer guides had left the program. That left two spots open in the program to be filled.

The third objective was to prepare for training and supervision of the peer guides and to line up their projects for the coming year. Gathering ideas for projects from the rest of the UX team, determining a meeting schedule with the group of peer guides, and thinking about the division of labor, set the tone for the program.

Recruitment, Training, and Supervision

In order to have an engaged group, we hire students that are outgoing, take initiative, work independently, and have great problem-solving skills. There is an effort to match the student's area(s) of study or personal interest to the UNL Libraries' needs. Often, their job applications provide clues about their interests, but most often they come out during the interview process. During the job interview, one potential peer guide majoring in environmental science expressed her career goal was to work outside doing something both educational and fun. She was hired and assigned to assist with the SciPop Talks, a series of presentations that combine science topics and popular culture in a fun way. The Libraries co-sponsor the talks with the Chemistry Department each spring semester. As a science major, this particular peer guide had the right knowledge to help develop the online bibliography for the series and to work closely with one of the science librarians. It was a great match to her interest because the SciPop Talks are educational and fun at the same time.

The strategy of matching interest with the assigned work leads to a peer guide invested in achieving a successful project. During the interviews, the student is told that they can use their experience as a peer guide to leverage more rewarding career experiences in the future. Figure 8.1 shows each of the peer guide's major area of study matched to the area of responsibility they were assigned in the program. The Libraries benefit from the marriage of interests or major to responsibilities because the quality of projects is better.

LIBRARIES NEED	MAJOR OF STUDENT
Outreach & Surveys	Pre-Health/Nursing
Event Planning	Hospitality
Sci POP Talks & Marketing Surveys	Business Finance/Environmental
Social Media	Public Relations/Advertising
Social Media Visuals	Graphic Design

Figure 8.1. Matching interests and majors of the peer guides to their assigned areas of responsibility.

Each hired peer guide receives an ASKus badge, to identify them in public, and begins reference assistance training with the instructional support associate. Under the UX team, the peer guides are no longer expected to perform roaming reference or work at the Reference Desk; however, when they are in the public areas of the Libraries, the peer guides are expected to help people locate a book or a resource. If they receive a more complicated question that they can't answer, the peer guide is expected to escort the patron to an ASKus service point.

For the remainder of the training, the peer guides read documents, including talking points and brochures about the Libraries, an office procedure manual, and a document outlining general expectations of all student employees that was developed by the Libraries' Dean's Office personnel. The expectations outlined in that document cover a range of topics, including time cards, office etiquette, dress codes, and emergency procedures. The last item they review is the Libraries website. My style of training combines instruction and demonstration. Even the most outgoing peer guide has to work up the courage to approach a stranger in the library and ask them to take a survey. Instructions didn't work alone for some tasks and I needed to model behavior that the peer guides were expected to follow.

Polo shirts were another addition to the program. In our first meeting as a group, all of the peer guides agreed that more identification and visibility of the program were needed. They were in favor of wearing a special polo shirt when they were in the public areas of the library, and one of them volunteered to research the options and present a selection of possible designs to the rest of the group. Consensus was reached on the color and design, and the polo shirts were ordered.

Outreach

Outreach for the UNL Libraries includes staffing booths at recruitment and orientation events sponsored by the UNL Admissions department. UNL recruitment days, known as Red Letter Days, include an hour-long information fair in which prospective students and their parents walk around a ballroom at the student union and visit with representatives of various UNL departments. A representative from the UNL Libraries is always in attendance, and from 2001–2014 that representative was either me or one of a small group of the most extroverted volunteers from the Libraries staff or faculty. The response from prospective students and their parents was mixed, even when we initiated conversations with people. The parents would stop to chat and seemed more interested in the Libraries than the prospective student. That changed when a peer guide was assigned to co-ordinate outreach and represent the Libraries at recruitment events. The first peer guide assigned to outreach started as a freshman and is now a sophomore. The peer guide had previous experience in a retail shop and her personality was positive and outgoing. She maintained the supplies, staffed the booth, and we worked together on crafting talking points about the UNL Libraries, including the construction of the Learning Commons.

The peer guide staffed sixteen Information Fairs/Red Letters Days during the fall and spring semesters. I accompanied the peer guide to the first Information Fair in order to train and observe her. She took the initiative to greet people, and more prospective students stopped to visit the booth and have a conversation. Our brochures were picked up by more people. Assigning a peer guide to do outreach by staffing our booth at various recruitment events created a great first impression and connection between prospective students and the UNL Libraries. Most important, more prospective students stopped by the Libraries table when a peer guide staffed the booth.

Social Media

The UNL Libraries has a presence in Facebook, Twitter, Instagram, and maintains a blog. I manage all of these accounts with the help of the peer guides.

A peer guide was assigned to help engage UNL students via each of our social media channels. The peer guide writes most of the posts, which I review and edit if needed. Hashtag creation is a collaborative effort and discussion. Peer guides also contribute ideas about what to post. They have opinions about favorite resources and what they know their classmates will want to use. Peer guides suggested promotion of specialized software and equipment offered by the Media Services Department and of specific study areas. All content is added into a content calendar spreadsheet to track and recycle some of the posts, especially those about services and resources, in the future.

The peer guide also proposes ways to increase our following or interactions. For example, a peer guide suggested writing the Libraries' Twitter or Instagram handle on popcorn bags. When the peer guides take the commercial popcorn popper into the library, they distribute the bags filled with hot fresh popcorn to students.

The peer guide assigned to social media does the majority of posts. The other peer guides contribute to the Libraries' social media accounts to a lesser degree. They might live tweet at an event (i.e. SciPop Talks) or post photos to Instagram. To ensure that all peer guides understand fully the responsibilities of representing the UNL Libraries' voice online, each of them signs a social media contract before they are given access to the accounts.

The social media contract outlines the responsibilities, expectations, the University brand, computer use regulations, and other parameters (See Appendix 8A). The contract provides a safety net for the Libraries. If the peer guide does not comply with the contract, their employment as a peer guide can be terminated. The UNL Libraries' social media contract is based on a contract developed by Tyler Thomas, the social media specialist and content creator working in UNL's central Communications Office. He developed it for use with other students assigned to campus social media. The contract was revised to match more closely the needs of the UNL Libraries.

At the start the 2015–16 academic year, a peer guide majoring in graphic design was hired to assist the full-time graphic designer in the UX Team and support our social media efforts with graphics. She has created graphics for each of the Libraries' workshops and events so that we can post something more than just a text announcement. The eye-catching graphics have improved the metrics of UNL Libraries' Facebook page. Before the PGP began, our Facebook "likes" had reached a plateau. The number of "likes" for our page has started to increase with the inclusion of visual content.

The Libraries' social media has benefited from the PGP with content that engages students, ideas that increase social media followers and engagement, and by providing the support to do social media during events.

Programs and Events

The UNL Libraries host and sponsor a variety of events that includes receptions, presentations, exhibits, workshops, and activities for students during finals. The peer guides have varying levels of involvement in events, from planning to set-up, and from hosting to evaluation.

In the fall of 2014, a student majoring in hospitality, restaurant, and tourism management was hired to assist with program planning on two major upcoming events, and to develop tools to sustain future planning as demand for programming and events increases. In order to keep the numerous events in a semester organized, the peer guide was assigned the task of developing an events checklist form and a template for an event timeline script. To create the checklist, the peer guide and I brainstormed and assembled a list of tasks based on both our previous program planning experiences. She added items to our list based on additional research. The checklist was used throughout the year to plan other programs and continued to be refined as needed. Some examples of tasks on the checklist include determine catering menu, reserve room, and other logistical details of implementing an event.

The template for the script timeline (See Appendix 8B) is used on the day of the event and outlines the sequences of tasks that need to be done in preparation before, during, and after the event itself. The hospitality peer guide created a script for our needs based on one from another institution. Our template includes a list of equipment needed, library staff and peer guides working the event, and a timeline sequence of the tasks and who is responsible for them.

Two major events were scheduled during the academic year along with many smaller events. The first major event was a reception for a new gallery and opening exhibit, which was attended by the chancellor of the University, faculty from several departments, donors, and alumni. I was able to delegate tasks to the hospitality peer guide due to the training and modeling of responsibilities she experienced. She handled all aspects of the event, including catering, rentals, flowers, and nametags. The hospitality peer guide worked with the other peer guides and employed them as greeters in the lobby to escort guests up to the second-floor gallery space. They were also on hand to give tours of the library upon request. The presence of peer guides in such a visible capacity at this donor event bolstered the event because the donors and alumni were reminded that students are the beneficiaries of their support to the UNL Libraries.

The second major event was our popular talk series, SciPop Talks, conceived by one of the science librarians and two chemistry faculty members. The talks feature topics that meld science and popular culture. Peer guides assisted with this event in two interesting ways: the creation of an online bibliography (Libguide) for the series and live-tweeting the presentation via the UNL Libraries Twitter feed.* Two of the four peer guides were science majors during the spring of 2015, and they collaborated on the creation of the online bibliography for each talk. They searched the Libraries' catalog and chose materials (books, games, videos) that could be listed in the bibliography and displayed at the talk. Some of the topics they searched included: fermented foods, radioactive properties of super heroes, and fire and explosions in films. Peer guides live tweeted interesting facts and points the speakers made during each presentation. The peer guides also responded to other members of the audience (online or in the room). The live-tweeting provides another way we can engage students in library programs.

Major events like those described above require significant planning, but there is also room for spontaneity in programming. At times the peer guides are asked to go into the public areas of the Libraries or other campus buildings and promote a service or resource to students. For example, two of the peer guides set up a table and laptop in the main library's lobby for a few hours to promote our print service to students. They engaged with students, demonstrated the steps to activate accounts, and gave them candy or a stress ball when it was completed. This type of event can be set up in a moment's notice within the libraries. We have used this type of promotion numerous times to inform students of our ASKus service, the upcoming learning commons, and the Big Red Ruckus event.

Surveys

Feedback from students that use the library, and even those students that do not, is an important part of understanding the user experience. This feedback guides the UX team's work. The peer guides help get feedback from students in two ways: first, by posting questions on a mobile white board and collecting the answers; and second, by asking students face-to-face to participate in a survey. One of the first questions the peer guides posted on a white board asked students to share the titles of their favorite books. Peer guides gathered the answers and created an online bibliography with the results. That bibliography has since been used as an acquisitions list for a popular fiction section added to the new learning commons.

---

* SciPop Libguide URL: http://unl.libguides.com/scipoptalks.

The UX team has also developed brief traditional surveys (printed or online) and assigned the peer guides to recruit students to take the surveys. The peer guides recruit both in the libraries and in other campus buildings. This experience usually yields a rapid collection of feedback from students and large samples of surveys. For the last two years, the peer guides have administered a survey on the recognition of the UNL Libraries' ASKus service brand. The peer guides are given directions on how to administer the survey by one of the UX team members. They take stress balls or pens that they can use to reward students for completing the survey. We record the number of surveys done at each location, and if we feel a location is not well represented, then we will send the peer guide back to that campus building to recruit more survey takers. None of the peer guides have given us negative feedback about the surveys or going out to recruit survey participants. The information yielded from these surveys has been valuable to the UX team in making changes to the Libraries website, services, or facility.

Challenges

The PGP has been a mix of challenges and successes for the Libraries and the peer guides. The challenges include hiring and training new peer guides on an annual basis and the number of qualified students to select from in the employment pool available.

It takes time and energy to hire, train, and supervise peer guides. Hiring involves time to search the student employment database for students with the right qualifications and availability. Next is time to schedule and hold interviews. Training involves other staff and their time. Hiring and training is done on an annual basis, and sometimes every semester, depending on the rotation of students. After training comes day-to-day supervision, planning, and communicating about projects. Prioritization, advance planning, and blocking time to mentor are critical factors that help me meet the time challenges required to successfully coordinate this program.

Finding the students with the type of majors or interests in the employment pool of available students can also be a challenge. Many UNL students seek employment with the UNL Libraries and the choices within the pool are very good for some of the needs we have in the PGP. There are many students with majors such as business, marketing, journalism, and English that could help with social media. However, when it comes to events and programs, there may be only one or two students with a hospitality major in our employment database. The student that was hired as the hospitality peer guide was referred to the PGP by one of the other peer guides. She assisted with events for one year as a peer guide and left for an internship. Since then, we have been unable to replace her. The Hospitality, Restaurant, and Tourism Management department requires its students to have a certain number of internships before graduation, which may be the reason why these students are not applying for jobs in the Libraries.

The demand for programs and events is increasing and we will work with the Hospitality, Restaurant, and Tourism Management department to set up an internship for this specific peer guide position to find many more qualified applicants.

Successes

The successes of the PGP have been numerous and include reaching out to more students, receiving valuable advice, ideas, and information from the peer guides, and success for the peer guide when the leadership skills and experience they gain propels them onto new opportunities.

The peer guides have helped the UNL Libraries reach more students through all the methods described in this chapter. More prospective students stop at our booth when it is staffed by a peer guide, and having the peer guides go out into the library with the popcorn machine and information to share with other students has been a big hit. Our increase in likes and followers on Facebook and Twitter demonstrate that we are reaching them online as well.

The challenge of hiring peer guides each year is counterbalanced by the fact that each new peer guide brings fresh energy and different ideas to the program. That is the case with the peer guides assisting with the social media during 2015–16. Peer guides share advice on the Libraries' marketing materials, programming ideas, or how the Libraries can support students during finals. Our peer guides represent the demographic we are trying to reach and serve, so their feedback is of great value.

Another sign of success for the program is when the peer guides use the experiences and skills they have gained in the program to leverage a new opportunity for themselves such as a prestigious internship. That was the case for three of the peer guides so far. In addition, the peer guides gain skills in leadership, marketing, interpersonal communication, and other soft skills.

Conclusions

Despite all of the hard work coordinating the PGP, I love mentoring these students. As a librarian and a marketer working in an academic environment, this program gives me an opportunity to turn the office into a classroom and mentor through real-life projects. At the same time, the peer guides gain leadership skills and experiences that they can use in the future. Benefits to the UNL Libraries include greater outreach potential, more publicity of our services and resources, and more feedback from other students. All of that ultimately shapes our strategic plans for the future.

Appendix 8A

N Social Media Contract – Peer Guides – 2015 University of Nebraska-Lincoln Libraries

Goal: Highlight appropriate Libraries experiences that would engage or peak interest from prospective undergraduate students. Through social media, the expectation is to share content regarding University of Nebraska-Lincoln Libraries services, events, and resources.

PROJECT REQUIREMENTS

- Social Media Platforms involved: Facebook, Twitter, Instagram
- Minimum of 5 posts total must be written on a weekly basis (includes all outlets), sporadically during the week
- Place your initial in the content calendar (excel sheet) once you have made your post
- Encouraged to post more during exciting events, social functions, etc.
- You will be posting on the University of Nebraska-Lincoln Libraries' accounts. Both the coordinator of the Libraries social media and your supervisor have the right to delete/change/add/edit any posts within each specific social media outlet. If at any time you disagree with the supervisor regarding the content of your posts, the supervisor's opinion/decision controls.

SOCIAL MEDIA ENGAGEMENT

- Must reply to any comments/feedback within a 24 hour window or notify your supervisor if you are unable
- Questions outside your knowledge should be forwarded to the Joan Barnes, unless provided in the "Stock Responses" Guide (located in the CommDev Drive)
- Any inappropriate comments, questions or concerns (such as references to drugs, alcohol, or tobacco, sexual activity, pornography, violence, threats, or harassment) must be reported to your supervisor before interacting with or deleting the post

UNIVERSITY COMMUNICATIONS

- You are an employee of the University of Nebraska-Lincoln, which means you must pay attention to branding. UNL has partnerships with Pepsi and Adidas. This means you cannot promote or feature other soda brands, sports brands or other universities the Libraries social media accounts. Any questions regarding branding should be directed to Joan Barnes.
- Refrain from posting anything with images or references to alcohol-use, tobacco-use, drug-use, sexual activity, pornography, violence, threats, harassment, or any illegal activity. Your audience involves minors.
- Be mindful that we are an open University and do not support one particular religion or political affiliation. Please use your best judgment.
- As a brand ambassador for the University of Nebraska-Lincoln, any work-related projects must be confidential and not shared with other institutions during your employment.

OTHER REQUIREMENTS & CONSIDERATIONS

- Social media is a 24-hour window into your world. Be mindful that many audiences may be following our online presence and may post on our outlets.
- All activities that you engage in have the potential to be posted publicly online by you or others. As a representative of the University Libraries via social media, any activity that is available publicly can affect your employment.
- Each peer guide is responsible for protecting the Libraries social media account usernames and passwords.
- If at any time, the coordinator of Libraries social media deems any post as something inappropriate or detrimental to the Libraries reputation, the Peer Guide must post a retraction and apology across all affected platforms within 24 hours. Such a post may result in disciplinary action up to and including termination of employment.
- Peer Guides cannot use the Libraries social media platforms for personal gain (i.e. additional pay, marketing own personal business ventures, exploiting other students, faculty, staff). If at any point, the Peer Guide uses the social media accounts in an inappropriate way, the supervisor has the right to determine appropriate consequences.

Signature _____   **Date** _____

Permission for use of contract granted. 2015.

Appendix 8B. Template Event Script

Name EVENT   Staffing: Name (Initials): Times

Date (start time—end time)   Name (Initials): Times

Name's Cell Number: ###-###-####

Items Needed (person responsible)

- ☐ Trashcan from 4th floor storage
  - o Skirted
- ☐ Podium from LIR (JB pick up am)
- ☐ Sound System (JB)
- ☐ Grey cart (CM)
- ☐ Alcohol permit sign (JB)

Day (Date) (Example Tuesday (3rd)

- ☐ Sign in room about event and closure

Day (Date)

Set up

#:## a.m. –##:## am

- ☐ AAA Rental arrives with tables, chairs, linens, plates, glassware, utensils

11:00 a.m.

- ☐ Put everything on grey cart (Initials of those responsible)
  - o Name tags, nametag printer, tablet, library tablecloths, signs, keys to study room & conference room, print of RSVP list, clear packing tape, remarks for podium

2:00 p.m.

- ☐ Close Room
- ☐ Room set up—podium/sound system/ and chairs at the north side of room.
  - o Number of chairs, tables, positions & locations
  - o Drawing available if possible
- ☐ Staff/students help move room
  - o Directions listed
- ☐ Conference Room set up
  - o Directions listed

3:00–3:30 p.m.
- ☐ Florist arrives
- ☐ Caterer arrives

5:00 p.m.
- ☐ Music Group arrives—three chairs for them
- ☐ Welcome table staffed (Initials of peer guides responsible)
- ☐ Greeting in Lobby (Initials of peer guides responsible)

Start of Event
5:30 p.m.
- ☐ 30-minute reception
- ☐ Music plays during reception
- ☐ Appetizers & drinks served

5:55 p.m.
- ☐ Give Chancellor 5-minute warning

6:00 p.m.
- ☐ Chancellor welcomes group & introduces Dean
- ☐ Library Dean speaks & introduces Program speaker
- ☐ Program Speaker—15-minute program

6:30 p.m.
- ☐ Reception continues
- ☐ Music plays during reception
- ☐ Appetizers & drinks served

Post Program
7:00 or 7:30 p.m.
- ☐ Put all of AAA's property in the dock

Friday 6th
  9:00–11:00 a.m.
- ☐ Put room back (staff & students)
- ☐ AAA Pick Up

Notes

1. Brie Betz, Stephanie Willen Brown, Deb Barberi and Jeanne M. Langendorfer, "Marketing Library Database Services to End Users: Peer-to-Peer Outreach Using the Student Ambassador Program (SAm)," *The Serials Librarian: From the Printed Page to the Digital Age* 56, no. 1–4, (2009): 250–254, doi: 10.1080/03615260802687088.
2. Julie L. Miller, "The Library Student Liaison Program at Eastern Washington University: A Model for Student Engagement," *College & Undergraduate Libraries* 18, no. 1 (2011): 1–15, doi: 10.1080/10691316.2011.550500.
3. Michelle S. Millet and Clint Chamberlain, "Word-of-Mouth Marketing Using Peer Tutors," *The Serials Librarian: From the Printed Page to the Digital Age* 53, no. 3 (2007): 95–105, doi: 10.1300/J123v53n03_07.
4. Michelle Twait, "Peer-to-Peer Outreach and Promotion," in *Innovative Solutions for Building Community in Academic Libraries*, ed. M.A. Hansen and S. Bonnard, (Hershey, PA: IGA Global, 2015), 97–116, doi: 10.4018/978-1-4666-8392-1.ch006.
5. University of Nebraska–Lincoln, Institutional Research & Planning, *Nebraska Just the Facts 2014–2015*, (Lincoln, NE; University of Nebraska–Lincoln, 2014), 5, 14–15.
6. Jeanetta Drueke, face-to-face conversation, December 1, 2015.
7. Signe Boudreau, face-to-face conversation, December 9, 2015.

Bibliography

Betz, Brie, Stephanie Willen Brown, Deb Barberi and Jeanne M. Langendorfer. "Marketing Library Database Services to End Users: Peer-to-Peer Outreach Using the Student Ambassador Program (SAm)." *The Serials Librarian: From the Printed Page to the Digital Age* 56, no. 1–4, (2009): 250–254, doi: 10.1080/03615260802687088.

Miller, Julie L. "The Library Student Liaison Program at Eastern Washington University: A Model for Student Engagement." *College & Undergraduate Libraries* 18, no. 1 (2011): 1–15, doi: 10.1080/10691316.2011.550500.

Millet, Michelle S. and Clint Chamberlain. "Word-of-Mouth Marketing Using Peer Tutors." *The Serials Librarian: From the Printed Page to the Digital Age* 53, no. 3 (2007): 95–105, doi: 10.1300/J123v53n03_07.

Twait, Michelle. "Peer-to-Peer Outreach and Promotion," in *Innovative Solutions for Building Community in Academic Libraries*, ed. M.A. Hansen and S. Bonnard. Hershey, PA: IGA Global, 2015. doi: 10.4018/978-1-4666-8392-1.ch006.

University of Nebraska–Lincoln, Institutional Research & Planning, *Nebraska Just the Facts 2014–2015*. Lincoln, NE; University of Nebraska–Lincoln, 2014.

CHAPTER 9[*]

GETTING ON THE INSIDE:
Developing a Discipline-Based Student Ambassador Program

April Hines, Tiffany Baglier, and Ben Walker

It Started with an Essay

In spring 2012, the Education Library, one of seven branches of the University of Florida (UF) George A. Smathers Libraries, was seeking more effective methods for reaching students within the twenty-six degree programs they serve in the UF College of Education (COE). The College's degree offerings are quite diverse and range from mental health counseling and higher education administration to educational technology and early childhood education. Student enrollment includes more than 1,800 full-time students on campus and nearly 3,000 distance-learning students; the COE's even mix of pre-professional practitioners and graduate researchers presents a unique set of challenges when it comes to devising effective outreach strategies for so many different user groups.

Students were somewhat aware of the library's physical offerings as a study spot and meeting location, but seemed to know less about the valuable subject-specific resources and services available. Traditional outreach methods, such as instruction sessions, presentations at student events, posts on social media, email announcements, and posters, had been met with limited success, but library events were still poorly attended, and resources (electronic and print) continued to be underutilized. Conversations with students often ended with "I wish I knew about this sooner!" or "I didn't know you had that!" and gate counts continued to drop.

Coincidentally, that same semester, the library human resources department held a scholarship essay contest for student employees, posing the question, "If you had to design an outreach program for students, how would you get the word out in a way that would make the largest impact?" The winning essay, written by a COE undergraduate student, outlined a program that would "train library student ambassadors to represent each library on campus, with the primary goal of using the libraries' resources to educate and enhance the college experience."[1]

Inspired by the student's vision, Education Library staff—two librarians and two paraprofessionals—saw an ambassador program as the perfect opportunity to connect with students in a more meaningful way while extending their reach. Perhaps this could be the missing link that bridged the gap between the COE student population and the library. Who better to know what students want and need than the students themselves? Library staff made the decision to pilot a student ambassador program on a small scale at the Education Library, rather than across the entire library system, because of their specific yet diverse patron base.

Before the initial planning stages began, Education Library staff met with representatives from COE student organizations to collect feedback on how a library student ambassador program could best contribute to student success. How did *they* envision the development of such a program? The student leaders made several recommendations, which included developing working relationships between student organization officers and the library ambassadors. They believed offering students a paid stipend for their service would be the ideal compensation for participation. A $500 amount for the honorarium, to be awarded after a two-semester service period, was suggested because they reasoned it was high enough to be an incentive and to instill a sense of accountability, but not so high as to attract those without genuine interest in the program.

Ambassador vs. Liaison

To determine if similar programs existed in other academic libraries, and the extent of those programs, a review of the library literature was conducted for mentions of library student ambassadors or liaisons. Examples were not plentiful, but a few stood out as possible models to emulate, such as the University of Connecticut, whose ambassadors were hired by the database vendor Elsevier to promote Scopus and Web of Science to graduate students.[2] Elsevier provided student stipends, training, and marketing materials. Student ambassadors marketed the instruction sessions and presented citation-searching techniques (showcasing Elsevier products along with other library resources) to their graduate student peers. Eastern Washington University employed one part-time undergraduate student who reported to the associate dean of libraries and served as the official liaison between library administration and the student body.[3] The student liaison maintained the library's social networking sites, conducted student surveys, and implemented library events. Another promising example was Missouri University, whose team of student ambassadors were recruited through an online application process and volunteered five to ten hours per month.[4] Ambassadors visited classrooms to promote library services, gave library tours, and staffed tables at new student orientation. They also attended alumni and donor events. While no one program stood out as a perfect fit, Education Library staff saw elements from each that would work nicely with their unique patron base, and that they could easily incorporate into their own pilot project.

After evaluating their needs, talking to the COE student leaders, and looking at other university ambassador programs, library and otherwise, the Education Library came to the conclusion that the ideal program would be a hybrid between an ambassador role and a liaison role. Traditional university ambassador programs usually consist of undergraduate student volunteers who serve as "the face" of a group or institution and are connected to a development office. They attend alumni dinners, represent at college events, offer tours, etc. Liaison programs, on the other hand, are usually paid positions that require training on resources and services, are more academic in nature, and facilitate communication between students and organizational staff. While library staff did want students who would be "the face" of the Education Library and promote its value at events throughout the college, they also wanted students who would act as liaisons among their specific academic department, their fellow students, and library staff. They wanted students they could train to be knowledgeable about Education Library resources and services, and act as their eyes and ears throughout the college.

Securing Funding: The Mini-Grant Process

Once the overall structure of the program was determined, Education Library staff realized they needed a funding source for advertising and student honorariums. Since this would be a pilot project, grant funding was considered a possible solution. The UF Libraries have an internal mini-grant program that allows faculty and staff to apply for awards of up to $5,000 to fund original project ideas. The program is designed to encourage creativity and innovation within the libraries. Education Library staff submitted a proposal with a brief overview of the student ambassador program, a discussion of why such a program was important, a timeline, and a plan for measuring ongoing impact. In the initial phases of the grant application process, the UF Libraries mini-grant committee came back to the project team with a few questions, the primary one being, "How are these activities different from an embedded or liaison-librarian?"

The project team assured the committee that the library student ambassadors would not be expected to be as well-versed in all of the intricacies of the library as an embedded librarian, but instead would act more as walking advertisements for the library's resources and services. For example, an ambassador would refer a student to a librarian for a research consultation instead of conducting an in-depth research consultation themselves. The team outlined more specifically what they envisioned the ambassadors doing, such as mentioning course reserves to their professors, evaluating and providing feedback on new resources, giving input on relevant topics for library workshops, and assisting with social media. After the committee's initial concerns were addressed, the Education Library was notified that their mini-grant proposal was accepted.

We Want You: Recruitment and Hiring

As soon as funding was secured for ambassador honorariums and marketing and promotional materials, Education Library staff began the advertising and recruitment process. They put up posters and flyers in the Education Library, around the COE, the student union, and other libraries on campus. They also advertised in the UF student newspaper, the library's

Facebook page, the COE's Facebook page, and on several email listservs. The library even experimented with paid Facebook advertising, targeting the specific demographic they were after (UF COE students living in Gainesville), but the results were less than favorable with only two clicks on the digital ad over a ten-day period. Fortunately, Facebook charges per click, so the library was only out $1.30 for minimal effort. Surprisingly, face-to-face advertising proved to be the most effective, with students reporting they heard about the program either through staff tabling in the COE's courtyard or presenting at student organization meetings. The second most effective method was signage posted around the building.

The application process was designed to be simple and easy to administer. First, the position description was posted on the Education Library website, with a link to the online application created in Google Forms. The entry-level requirements, determined after receiving feedback from the COE student organizations, were the following:

- Must be an upperclassman (junior or above) or graduate student
- Must be a College of Education major or minor
- Must be able to serve for two consecutive semesters (Fall 2012–Spring 2013)
- Must be available to work on campus for up to thirty hours per semester

Additionally, the team developed the following preferred qualifications:

- Public speaking experience
- Currently participating in student organizations or college events

Finally, the application included an essay question. The essay is an opportunity to learn more about the applicants' communication abilities, and introduces more personality into the application materials. Applicants were asked to describe what services, programs, or resources would be included in their ideal academic library. The essays, as hoped, allowed the applicants to display their creativity and motivation.

Once the positions closed, there were a total of ten applicants. Almost invariably, these applications came in close to deadline. Although the pool was not overwhelming, the team felt it was adequate to make decisions and select the best candidates. The applicants were mostly College of Education majors with only one student pursuing an Education minor.

After reviewing the applications, nine applicants were interviewed. Interview questions were standardized, and the project team questioned each student about their reasons for applying, their current involvement with college and campus activities, their familiarity with the library (and especially their first impressions of the library), and any ideas they had about improving the library. It was important to choose people that represented as many programs as possible to increase the library's reach. Library staff selected students from school psychology, educational technology, bilingual education (ESOL), Pro-Teach (elementary education–pre-service teachers) and higher education, for a total of four graduate students and one undergraduate senior.

Training, Scheduling, and Communication

Education Library staff decided against a training boot camp (one to two days of "everything you need to know about the library") anticipating that the information would be less overwhelming and more likely to be retained if it was parsed throughout the service period. The ambassadors initially participated in weekly one-hour meetings with at least half of the session dedicated to learning about a particular library resource, such as the library's discovery tool, citation managers, interlibrary loan, the library homepage, online catalog, course reserves, various education-specific databases, and research guides.

The training sessions transitioned into biweekly meetings once the ambassadors completed "basic training" and had a firm understanding of the library's major resources and services. The team then tested a "flipped classroom" approach: ambassadors were sent tutorials and training videos and asked to explore a particular resource on their own before each meeting. They were told they would be sharing what they discovered with their fellow ambassadors. This approach caused the students to become much more engaged with the content than during the initial training sessions. It was especially telling for library staff to see through fresh eyes how students approached/interpreted some of their top resources. The ambassadors pointed out search features they found confusing and highlighted additional benefits of resources that never occurred to library staff.

In the first semester, scheduling ambassador meetings was not very challenging. It was early enough in the school year that the students weren't overly committed. In the spring semester, however, there were only a few meetings where all five ambassadors were present. Their schedules were much more complicated, and three separate scheduling attempts went out before finding a time that "kind of" worked for everyone. There was always something that interfered at the last minute—award ceremonies, conferences, family in town, etc.—which made it increasingly difficult to properly disseminate information and collaborate. Library staff had to meet with some ambassadors one-on-one for training purposes, which became time consuming.

The ambassadors and project team initially communicated via email, but quickly moved to a Facebook group for easier communication and collaboration. Library staff posted weekly assignments, reminders, and meeting times, and solicited feedback by uploading documents and posting polls. Although the initial plan was for ambassadors to use the Facebook group to collaborate on their own, most communication was a direct response to the project team's posts.

One major development in communication happened when the team changed the format of the face-to-face meetings. In the fall semester, meetings were held in a classroom setting and library staff usually presented information. The ambassadors sat in a row and there wasn't much collaboration. The students were distracted by laptops, devices, and school work. In the spring semester, however, the team moved the meetings into a group study room and saw a major shift in engagement and collaboration. Sitting around a small round table caused students to interact with each other in a more meaningful way. (see Image 9.1) Meetings became student driven and focused. Ambassadors liked this arrangement much better. "Before, it felt like we were in class," one student commented.

Image 9.1. Library ambassadors enhance collaboration after moving meetings to a group study room.

Assignment Logs and Outreach Activities

In each meeting, the ambassadors were given an assignment. For example, "Get ten education students or faculty to 'like' our Facebook page by the next meeting," or "Create a Refworks account and import two articles about library outreach and marketing." The students were given logs so they could record all interactions on behalf of the library. Some examples of log entries included:

- "I talked to classmates about suggestions for the library, and they want more copies of current young adult books. For example, one of them said they wanted to borrow *Looking for Alaska*, but she never gets it."
- "I helped a student narrow down their search for data they needed for an inquiry project. I showed them how to narrow by publication date, peer-reviewed article, and language."

Even though the ambassadors had the logs from the beginning of the service period, they were only completed and submitted once library staff started requiring weekly deadlines. Ambassadors still needed reminders and had to be prompted to provide more details in their logs. Instead of "shared library resources with friends," ambassadors were asked to provide information such as who they talked to, what they shared, and how they shared it, and what was the reaction or response.

While certain assignments submitted in the weekly logs were performed by all five of the library ambassadors, each ambassador submitted activities unique to her and the group she served. One ambassador was a Chinese international graduate student in English for speakers of other languages (ESOL) education who worked with her ESOL classmates to identify needs specific to their coursework. Noticing her classmates were unaware of the libraries' discovery tool, OneSearch, and realizing how they could use it to save research time, the ESOL ambassador reached out to demonstrate how OneSearch could assist them. Another task the ESOL ambassador logged was speaking with COE international students about the libraries' Testing and Education Reference Center database, a resource that provides test preparation materials for the Test of English as a Foreign Language (TOEFL). Understanding how important passing the TOEFL is for non-English speaking foreign students, the ESOL ambassador made it a mission to inform students about this relevant resource, which not only assists international students in preparing for the TOEFL, but also saves them money. The ESOL ambassador recognized the importance of a teaching practice space for ESOL students and identified the Education Library's group study room as a place to meet student needs. The ambassador brought her classmates to the Education Library's group study room to record a teaching demonstration and practice with its SMART Board. The ESOL ambassador explained that student unfamiliarity with the Education Library's physical space, even when some of her classmates had attended the university for years, prompted her to introduce classmates to the library's rooms.

Another ambassador was a doctoral student in educational technology and an instructional designer for the COE's e-learning department. The educational technology ambassador emailed teaching assistants and adjunct instructors in her department regarding library study room reservations, research guides, the library catalog, databases, library workshops, training sessions, and librarian consultations. While attending the Future of Education Technology (FETC) 2013 conference, the educational technology ambassador used this opportunity to identify future education distance students and inform them of Education Library resources and services, extending the library's reach beyond the campus. One important contribution of the educational technology ambassador was facilitating a feedback session with the educational technology faculty and the head of the Education Library, who was able to provide information regarding library grant programs and updated projects.

One ambassador was a graduate student in student personnel in higher education. This student brought classmates into the Education Library to point out the new bookshelf and the resources she thought would be helpful. She also helped her classmates with journal access. After hearing students in her program complain about access to *The Chronicle of Higher Education*, she inquired about the title and relayed back to students that print access to the journal had been canceled, but electronic access was available. The ambassador also saw a classmate struggling to find resources, personally took the student into the library, and introduced the student to a librarian for research assistance. After the reference session, the referred student had plenty of resources and told several students in her cohort to visit the library when research help was needed. Additionally, this ambassador scheduled a workshop for undergraduates in the library's classroom. This brought first-year students into the Education Library, probably for their first time.

Another ambassador was an undergraduate student in elementary education. Since the ambassador was familiar with the Education Library's website and the resources available there, she was able to direct a peer to the library's curriculum guides page when the student needed a lesson plan for an important interview. As one of the more outgoing library ambassadors, she tabled for the Education Library during the COE's annual Education Career Night at the university's Career Resource Center, reaching out to students about library workshops and research resources. Knowing how useful RefWorks can be for papers, this ambassador also referred education students to workshops on the topic. And finally, this ambassador approached faculty to ask that class textbooks be placed on course reserve at the Education Library, making it easier for students to access required materials.

Another ambassador was a school psychology graduate student. This ambassador hung posters at the university's children's hospital where she interned, promoting the library's International Children's Book Day event to the children's families and staff at the hospital, and also invited friends through Facebook to join the festivities. Recognizing that a fellow grad student was having problems accessing materials, the ambassador walked the student through the process of requesting an article through interlibrary loan, a service the student was previously unaware of. This ambassador also talked to faculty, sharing the Education Library's streaming videos for this subject area and how course reserves could be useful for future classes. Additionally, she disbursed library workshop flyers in student mailboxes, helped a student with free scanning at the Education Library, and suggested to her faculty members that they set up course specific library instruction sessions with education librarians.

Shaping Library Content and Collections

About half way through the library ambassadors' service period, library staff noticed logs becoming repetitive. For example, "told professor about course reserves" or "sharing 'x' information on social media." The Education Library staff decided to "shake things up" and asked ambassadors to explore the library research guides for their discipline, since all were previously unaware these guides existed. They were asked to solicit feedback from their instructors and fellow students regarding the research guides.

The exercise was a success, with two ambassadors suggesting edits to four research guides, one student facilitating a discussion about research guides with faculty in her area, another suggesting the creation of a new research guide for a growing topic in her field. Also, a list of key resources recommended by faculty were sent to Education Library staff to be added to existing guides.

Near the end of the program, ambassadors were asked to gather material purchase suggestions from their faculty and peers by a deadline. The ambassadors appeared excited at this opportunity to represent and give back to their departments. One student said she had a folder of professional development items she wanted to read and it had never occurred to her that these titles could be suggested to the library for purchase. Another ambassador met with faculty, combed through books on faculty shelves, and asked for recommendations from others within her program. Her efforts provided valuable purchase lists from at least three faculty members in her department.

An Event of Their Own

To jump-start creativity and increase collaboration among the ambassadors, Education Library staff tasked the students with providing an outreach event idea they could plan and execute on their own. The ambassadors were asked to each post two ideas for an event on the group's Facebook page within a set time period. A variety of creative and innovative ideas emerged; however, many were very ambitious, large scale projects that could not be accomplished in the two months allotted.

After the ambassadors met to discuss their initial ideas with library staff guidance, they decided to set up a Finals Survival Center in the library during the two highest gate-count days of the semester, the Monday and Tuesday of the term's last week of classes. The center would have coffee, snacks, finals survival kits with common office supplies and earplugs, library tote bags, and water bottles (see Image 9.2). This event served a need, since the Education Library is located in the COE complex, which is on the outskirts of campus and is isolated from easy access to food and drink. The ambassadors designed their own "Finals at the Education Library" brochure listing exam week library hours, study tips, citation information, where to get food or "refuel," and general library information.

Image 9.2. Library ambassadors hand out coffee, snacks, study supplies, and brochures at their Finals Survival Center.

The event was a success, with the gate count increasing those two days by 140 people more than the previous year. Patron comments included, "Is this for us? This is great!" "Free water bottles! Shut Up!" and "We need to come to this library more often!"

Evaluation

Upon completion of the second semester of the library ambassador program, Education Library staff set up a meeting with the students to debrief and evaluate the program. Library staff wanted feedback about the ambassadors' experiences and to find out what worked, what did not, and what could be done differently to enhance the program.

One of the first questions Education Library staff asked was who ambassadors thought most benefited from the program—the ambassador, the library, or the students within the College of Education? Each Education Library ambassador responded that the ambassadors benefited the most. They gained in-depth knowledge of library resources and services. Fellow students were perceived to have indirectly benefited from this program as information was shared, but it was the intimate involvement with library staff and the program that was most beneficial.

Next, Education Library staff wanted to know what incentives could be offered to attract future ambassadors if funding was unavailable. One student thought promoting the ambassador program as a leadership opportunity and résumé-builder would work since College of Education students need letters of recommendation, and a letter from library faculty would satisfy this. Another ambassador responded that the program provides a great opportunity to form relationships with faculty and students within the college, both professionally and socially. Yet another ambassador thought positions could be designed to focus on specific areas, or have specific roles, such as social media ambassador, ambassador in charge of content development, displays coordinator, etc. Students wanting or needing experience in those areas would be more attracted to these positions.

Another question Education Library staff thought was important to ask was if the ambassadors were not graduating or leaving, would they be willing to reapply to be an ambassador again and why? Unanimously, ambassadors responded with a "yes." Each of them enjoyed working with the library's staff, learning about what the library had to offer, and sharing information with their peers. The comment that made Education Library staff smile most was when ambassadors told them they now saw librarians as people too.

Education Library staff also wanted to know what ambassadors were surprised to learn throughout the experience. Ambassadors responded with the amount of resources the library provides; they thought of the library as a place for books, and learning about all of the electronic resources was a pleasant and useful surprise. Another surprising fact for ambassadors was that students had a say in submitting purchase suggestions, requesting materials be placed on course reserve, and designing research guides. They never anticipated having such a strong role in library operations.

Finally, Education Library staff asked ambassadors to name one thing to change in the library that would cost nothing and could be accomplished over the summer term. They suggested rearranging the library's furniture, since it would require minimal effort and zero cost while changing the look and feel of the library dramatically. Also, it was suggested that library tables be moved to create long rectangles instead of just seating six people, where one might feel uncomfortable joining the table if others are already present. Providing the longer tables would encourage students to interact with each other as a community, which is exactly what happened once the change was made. (see Image 9.3)

Image 9.3. Ambassadors suggested placing study tables together to increase student interaction while making efficient use of space.

Lessons Learned—Moving Forward

While the students made many valuable contributions, the Education Library was unable to continue its ambassador program beyond the pilot. Lack of funding, staffing changes, time constraints, and a need to redesign all led to a decision to revisit at a future date. However, lessons learned by the project team led to a better understanding of what changes need to happen to create an even stronger program in the future. (see Figure 9.1)

One of the main challenges the program presented was the amount of direction and guidance needed and wanted by the ambassadors; they repeatedly told Education Library staff that they wanted benchmarks. The program was started with hopes that the students, especially the graduate students, would provide their own motivation, collaborate together without prompting, and bring ideas to the staff, but this never happened. Surprisingly, the most productive and conscientious student was the undergraduate. Results were not received until Education Library staff provided specific tasks and deadlines to ambassadors. Creativity and innovation spawned from the assignments, but the ambassadors frequently needed help to get started. In moving forward with the ambassador program, a more structured, deadline-driven design would offset this challenge and create an environment to meet student needs. Setting up an online guide for the program at the beginning of the year with expectations clearly outlined, weekly assignments pre-generated, and having a training guide with tutorials, videos, and resources for reference would provide the structure students need and want. Also, the Education Library ambassadors were exclusively led by the project team, a model that was very time-consuming for staff and less engaging for the students. Appointing officers (chair, co-chair) and allowing students to self-direct within an already determined set of guidelines, would place library staff in a more ideal advisory role.

LESSONS LEARNED FOR A SUCCESSFUL STUDENT AMBASSADOR PROGRAM

- ☐ Recruit students who are looking to gain experience and are not overly committed. Lack of availability can become a major hurdle.
- ☐ Make time expectations clear on application materials, during the interview, and throughout the training process. Require ambassadors block off 2–4 hours per week.
- ☐ Create a training guide with tutorials, videos, and links for a "flipped classroom" approach where ambassadors explore resources beforehand and share with the group during face-to-face meetings.
- ☐ Allow students to appoint officers (chair, co-chair) and self-direct within already established guidelines.
- ☐ Hold physical meetings in an area more conducive to group work, such as a study room or conference room—not a classroom.
- ☐ Set up an online guide with pre-generated assignments and deadlines. Students appreciate benchmarks!
- ☐ Allow ambassadors to take on individual roles based on their talents and interests (social media contributor, displays coordinator, event planner etc.).
- ☐ Promote the ambassador program as a leadership and networking opportunity, as well as a resume builder—especially if honorarium funding is unavailable.
- ☐ Use an effective means of communication, like a Facebook group to post updates, link to training materials, and upload documents and photos.

Figure 9.1. Lessons learned for a successful student ambassador program.

Another major challenge for the program was time. The ambassadors hired were involved in several organizations, excelled academically, worked, and interned. These students were chosen for their extensive reach, their work ethic, and their enthusiasm. However, Education Library staff did not realize the scheduling dilemma this would create. Trying to schedule face-to-face meetings during a time when all ambassadors were available was nearly impossible and proved a difficult challenge when planning outreach events. One way to overcome this challenge would be to make time expectations clear on application materials, during the interviews, and during training, requiring ambassadors to block off two to four hours per week for the program. Also, hiring students looking to be more involved and gain experience, instead of students who are already extensively involved, would help create time availability.

Evolution of Library Student Ambassador Programs at UF, 2012 to Present

While the program no longer exists at the Education Library, its development inspired successful manifestations in other branch libraries at the University of Florida. A second ambassador program was created just after the Education Library's at the main humanities and social sciences library on campus—Library West. This ambassador program still exists today and is more traditional in nature. Started by students interested in assisting the library, founding members of this group met with Education Library staff to find out more about what worked and what didn't work with the initial program. Students are self-governed with officer positions, student-led and organized, and focus on assisting the library through event planning, advising, fund raising, and assessment. Ambassadors can be seen at donor events, organizing student relaxation activities during finals week, tabling at library events, and meeting with library faculty. It is a group of students who value the library and wish to donate time to increase awareness of library facilities and collections.

The program most similar to the Education Library's started in August 2015 at the university's Marston Science Library. This program functions similarly, with training on library services, resources, and information regarding how to direct patron requests. Like the Education Library's program, Marston struggles with ambassadors attending meetings and staff needing to direct activities. This young program may undergo interesting developments as they attempt to create a more self-directed student liaison model that doesn't require a great deal of guidance and monitoring from library staff.

Conclusion

This collection of programs all began with a student essay, an internal grant proposal, and student interest. Academic libraries need to connect with students in new ways, creating knowledgeable ambassadors that can reach peers in ways librarians cannot. The University of Florida sought to bridge this gap in the 2012–2013 academic year through the creation of the Education Library Student Ambassador Program. As a pilot, this program succeeded. While it was time intensive and used funds as a stipend, it did provide a return on investment. Education Library social media exposure grew and traffic at the Education Library increased during the September to April time period from the previous year's gate count. Activity logs support this assessment where ambassadors escorted students into the Education Library who previously had not stepped foot into the building. Longstanding relationships were established with COE faculty, program directors, and student organizations. While some ambassadors graduated and are no longer on campus, each ambassador has a better understanding of what librarians do for a university and how students cannot only benefit from the services and resources provided, but also play a vital role in the library's success. These students left with a vested interest in the role of libraries and librarians, and continue to advocate and spread the word among their communities beyond the University of Florida.

Notes

1. Laura Browning, "Providing Outreach through Library Student Ambassadors" (essay contest submission, University of Florida Libraries, 2012).
2. Jeanne Langendorfer, Stephanie Willen Brown, and Brie Betz, "Marketing Library Database Services to End Users: Peer-to-peer Outreach Using the Student Ambassador Program (SAM)," *Serials Librarian* 56, no. 1–4 (2009): 250–254.
3. Julie Miller, "The Library Student Liaison Program at Eastern Washington University: A Model for Student Engagement," *College & Undergraduate Libraries* 18, no. 1 (2011): 1–15.
4. "MU libraries student ambassadors," Missouri University, last modified December 2015, http://library.missouri.edu/about/studentambassadors/.

Bibliography

Browning, Laura. "Providing Outreach through Library Student Ambassadors." Essay Contest Submission, University of Florida Libraries, 2012.

Langendorfer, Jeanne, Stephanie Willen Brown, and Brie Betz. "Marketing Library Database Services to End Users: Peer-to-Peer Outreach Using the Student Ambassador Program (SAM)." Serials Librarian 56, no. 1–4 (2009): 250–254.

Miller, Julie. "The Library Student Liaison Program at Eastern Washington University: A Model for Student Engagement." *College & Undergraduate Libraries* 18, no. 1 (2011): 1–15.

Missouri University "MU libraries student ambassadors." Last modified December 2015. http://library.missouri.edu/about/studentambassadors/.

CHAPTER 10*

IMPLEMENTING A PEER SUPPORT PROGRAM FOR INTERNATIONAL STUDENTS:
A Case Study at McGill University Library

Tara Mawhinney and Jennifer Congyan Zhao

Introduction

International students face many challenges when adapting to campus life in a new country due to their language difficulties, cultural differences, and distinct learning behaviors. Some of these challenges are related to their limited library use and information literacy competencies. One way to address the needs of international students is through peer learning, which is considered to be an effective pedagogy because it recognizes and highlights the significant impact of social interactions on an individual's learning.[1] Although some academic libraries have developed peer support initiatives to enhance the student experience, very few target international students in particular.

McGill University has a large population of international students, especially in engineering programs. The library is exploring innovative ways of reaching out to this user community through a peer support program entitled Multilingual Services for Engineering Students (MSES), which aims to promote use of the library's services and resources, and foster information literacy competencies among international students in engineering. The library has recruited two international student library ambassadors, who are currently enrolled in engineering programs, and encourages them to share their library knowledge with their peers. Their specific tasks consist of:

- Promoting the library to international students in various ways, including through social media
- Providing in-person and online library assistance
- Creating library instructional documentation in the ambassadors' native languages
- Facilitating library tours and/or workshops in English and their native languages.

The ambassadors have participated in a series of ongoing training sessions about library services and resources, as well as how to use them in a research context. This chapter presents a case study of the MSES program, outlining ambassador tasks, training, assessment strategies, and recommendations for implementing such a service. While the current program explores non-traditional ways of incorporating student input in developing library initiatives that target international students, it is also building a model that can be used to enhance library services for all students.

Purpose of Program and Background

McGill University is a large research university in Montreal, Canada. In the 2015 fall semester, it enrolled 39,988 full-time and part-time students,[2] approximately one quarter of whom (10,206, 25.5 percent) come from 158 countries outside of Canada[3] and more than half of whom do not have English as their native language.[4] Furthermore, the number of international students on campus has grown rapidly at a rate of 39.9 percent[5] over the past five years. According to the latest enrolment statistics, McGill's Faculty of Engineering enrolled 1,669 international students, accounting for 36 percent of all engineering students.[6] While international students benefit from studying abroad and generate revenue for the host institution and the local community, they face significant challenges when adapting to campus life in a new country. One of these challenges is their lack of awareness of the resources and services provided by the library in the host university.[7] In order to increase use of the library among these students, McGill University Library is piloting a peer support program for international engineering students in the 2015–16 academic year.

The MSES program is aligned with the library's strategic intention of growing the library as a user-centered organization, since it seeks to better promote and enhance services to international students, a growing demographic at McGill. It received funding as one of the library's Innovation in Services proposals and is also partly funded by the university's Work Study program, which subsidizes on-campus positions for students based on financial need. The MSES program was initiated in the fall 2015 semester by two engineering liaison librarians in the Schulich Library of Science and Engineering, the second largest branch library at McGill University, supporting physical sciences, life sciences, and engineering with a wide variety of library services and resources. Schulich Library has been successfully involving students in its daily operations, including shelving and loans services, assistance with library workshops, School of Information Studies' student practicums, and student posts to the library's blog. While there have been efforts by librarians to reach out to international students at Schulich Library, the MSES program represents the first time the library is involving international students in enhancing the library experience of their peers with similar backgrounds.

Literature Review

Peer Initiatives Addressing Library and Research Needs

Peer-to-peer learning models are considered to be effective[8] in that they promote group work, critical thinking, and skills in communication, self-management, and peer assessment.[9] In addition to basic assistance with shelving and circulation desks, academic libraries have begun to employ student workers to offer a wider range of services to their peers through reference assistance,[10] tutoring,[11] mentoring,[12] instruction,[13] and marketing.[14] Academic libraries also employ students to provide services in non-traditional reference formats, such as virtual reference service[15] and roving reference,[16] and at non-traditional service points, such as overseas branch libraries,[17] residence halls,[18] dormitory computer labs and academic service centers,[19] and campus cultural centers.[20] While some libraries hire students directly,[21] others train students already employed by other units on campus, such as the office of academic affairs, to serve as advocates for the library.[22] Further tasks reported in the literature include having students be ambassadors at fundraising events,[23] write blog posts,[24] and organize focus groups[25] for the library.

Benefits of a Peer Model

The existing literature identifies many benefits of a peer-based approach for users of the service, for student workers, and for libraries themselves. In terms of benefits to users, peer assistance leads to an increased awareness of scholarly resources.[26] Many students prefer to seek out peer mentors rather than librarians for "support and guidance specifically relating to research and information retrieval,"[27] and students may gain a better understanding of material when it is taught by their peers rather than by librarians.[28] The benefits to student workers include increased skills in information literacy and critical evaluation,[29] research,[30] teaching,[31] organization,[32] and problem-solving.[33] Libraries themselves can benefit from:

- Enhanced reach through increased number of instruction sessions,[34] increased number of service points and hours,[35] and greater outreach to non-traditional audiences (e.g. reaching professionals in practice settings).[36]
- Possible increase in demand for services, since the literature reports that students are more comfortable asking questions to other students than to a librarian.[37]
- Cost savings, which was a motivation for the implementation of such models in some libraries.[38]
- Better relationships between the library and its constituents[39] and with other units on campus, such as cultural centers[40] and learning centers.[41]
- Increased knowledge of existing library staff. Being involved in training and supervising student peers is an opportunity for librarians and library support staff to develop their own skills and knowledge. Not only do library staff increase their knowledge of library-related information, they may also gain an increased awareness of minority needs[42] and a better understanding of student behavior.[43]
- Increased library advocacy among students. Studies show that students trained to provide library and information services may become advocates for the library.[44]

That users of the service, student workers, and libraries themselves can benefit in so many ways suggests that such peer initiatives have an important place in future library planning and are worth exploring.

Although many researchers in the library literature examine the challenges faced by international students, identifying that the information needs of international students are significant and/or reporting on initiatives to improve library services for international students,[45] little has been reported on the application of peer learning in libraries related specifically to international students. The limited body of literature documents that minority and/or international students have been employed by libraries and other campus units to provide reference, outreach, and instruction services for their peers, and help build native language collections.[46] This case study on the McGill Library MSES program builds on the literature relating to library peer initiatives for international students. It creates a model that expands on the existing use of peer initiatives in libraries to address the specific library and research needs of international students. Additionally, this case study contributes to the literature by providing an example of using social media to facilitate peer learning for international students in libraries. Libraries are beginning to explore using Facebook to facilitate peer-to-peer learning. For example, a recent paper by van Beynen and Swenson reports that students at their university used this venue to ask general library-related information of their peers, and that it is a good venue for students to ask and respond to each other's questions.[47] Next, we will outline the MSES's objectives and methods for reaching out to the international student community.

McGill Library's Peer Support Program: Multilingual Services for Engineering Students (MSES)

The project's objectives are to enhance international engineering students' awareness and use of library resources and services by promoting the library's existing services to this target audience and to increase the types of services offered to these students through a peer assistance approach. To achieve these goals, two international student library ambassadors were hired at the beginning of the fall 2015 semester. One ambassador is a native Chinese-speaking doctoral student from the Electrical and Computer Engineering program and the other is a native Arabic-speaking second-year undergraduate student from the Mechanical Engineering program. During the pilot project phase of fall 2015 and winter 2016, the ambassadors are assisting to promote the library's resources and services to engineering international students and helping to deliver reference and instruction services to this body of students. Supervisors designed a work plan to structure the ambassadors' activities and monitor their progress (see Figure 10.1).

Week	Activities	Deliverables (due by the end of the week)
Begins Nov. 8	*With supervisors (Tara and Jennifer)* ☐ Discuss scheduling until the end of fall semester (30 min.) ☐ Discuss weekly work plan, log report, time sheets, social media channel task (30 min.) ☐ Orientation, tour of Schulich Library, and introduction to Schulich Library and staff (60 min.) *Independently* ☐ Set up a Google shared excel sheet for social media channels for McGill international students (2 hours, ideally do this task together) ☐ Read Getting Started slides and write 4 or more questions about the library (60 minutes)	☐ Weekly log report (with details about how the 6 hours were spent)

Figure 10.1. Sample work plan.

Outreach

Ambassador Tasks

The library ambassadors carry out many duties related to library outreach. In collaboration with the two librarian supervisors, they were tasked with naming the program. We selected Multilingual Services for Engineering Students (MSES) as the name with the goal of making this service as inclusive as possible. While our program targets international students in engineering, we did not wish to prevent native English-speaking students from receiving assistance from the ambassadors. Furthermore, there is a large portion of native French-speaking students from the local community. Though they are in their province of origin, they are often new to an English-speaking environment and may have library and information-related questions, making them a target population for this program as well. Additionally, there is a relatively large number of immigrant children on campus. Although they are not categorized as international students, they may have been in Canada for only a short period and many are still accustomed to communicating in their native language. By delivering services in two of the highest ranked, non-native English languages on campus, as well as in French (services provided by one of the library ambassadors and existing library staff members) and in English, we hope that students will be comfortable seeking out assistance from the library regardless of their linguistic background.

We designed a Facebook page for this project (see Image 10.1). We chose Facebook as a way to reach out to international students because it is so widely used among students. The two library ambassadors were asked to identify international student groups at McGill University and note what social media channels they employ to communicate with their members. Interestingly, all the student groups have a Facebook page, thus confirming that using Facebook would likely be an effective medium for reaching students. The ambassadors have now reached out to these groups and encouraged them to "like" and "share" the MSES Facebook content and have their members do likewise. The library ambassadors also promote library events using this channel and send targeted messages to specific international student groups (such as to the McGill Chinese Graduate Students Association) in their native languages when appropriate.

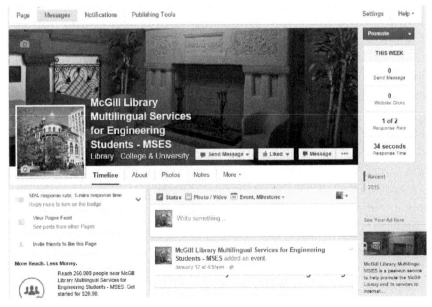

Image 10.1. The MSES Facebook page.

Together with the two librarians, the ambassadors created a library web page called Multilingual Library Services, where essential library services are listed. The library ambassadors translated this page into their native languages—Mandarin Chinese and Arabic. They also translated and recorded the "Welcome to the McGill Library" video. These web pages and videos were launched in the winter 2016 semester and advertised via the MSES and general McGill Library Facebook pages. The two librarians also coordinated the work of other librarian colleagues who are native speakers of French and Spanish to provide translations of this web page and the "Welcome" video. Additionally, the library ambassadors are recruiting student volunteers to translate these materials into other languages in the hope that the MSES program can not only enrich the library's web content, but also provide a means for students to participate in the program. Such content will be of benefit to many students, especially international students, and the creation process will likely be a rewarding experience for those who participate in the production as well.

In the winter 2016 semester, the library ambassadors began to promote this program to engineering departments, International Student Services, international student groups, and research groups in their respective departments—the Department of Electrical and Computer Engineering and the Department of Mechanical Engineering. They are helping to build strong communication channels between the library and these two departments in particular by marketing this program and library resources/services internally. The library ambassadors drafted the announcement message, created a poster for this program (see Image 10.2), and forwarded the message, including the poster, to the student listservs in all engineering programs. They also displayed the poster in strategic places on campus, including the public display screens in both the library and the engineering buildings. One of the ambassadors is also a leader of several student groups, which provides him with additional venues for promoting the MSES program.

Image 10.2. The MSES poster.

Outreach Training

As Deese-Roberts and Keating suggest, a good basis for peer support programs is sound training.[48] Therefore, one important element of our project was providing sufficient training for the library ambassadors so that they would be well positioned to promote library services and resources effectively. The two liaison librarians who are coordinating the program delivered training on library services as well as various aspects of outreach, including traditional channels used by McGill's liaison librarians and emerging social media. In addition, the ambassadors had the opportunity to benefit from the different skill sets of staff employed by McGill Library. They received training from the library's communications officer on the social media channels, including Facebook, Twitter, and blogs, which are used in the library, and strategies to identify social medial channels that are used by various student groups on campus. They also learned useful tips for promoting events using social media. At the request of the ambassadors, they had additional training with the communications officer to learn the basics of poster design using Photoshop in advance of creating the poster to advertise the MSES program. When recording the "Welcome" video, the library ambassadors benefited from the expertise of library staff specialized in recording and editing library videos. When designing, developing, and translating the Multilingual Library Services webpage, the library ambassadors were trained on Drupal, the open source web management system used by the library and the university. They were also trained on using the Schulich Library of Science and Engineering blog, the *Turret*, to write posts about this program as well as relevant library and information resources that would benefit international students in engineering.

Outreach Assessment

Assessment of the program as a whole generates ideas for improving the project and is required in order to seek funding to sustain the project in the future. Efficacy of outreach efforts is assessed using the following metrics:

- Number of likes, connected groups, and friends on the MSES Facebook page
- Number of visits to the Multilingual Library Services pages assessed using Google Analytics
- Number of views on the library's YouTube channel of videos in different languages
- Number of visits to the blog posts written by the library ambassadors

The impact on library use as a result of outreach initiatives, such as the Facebook page, promotional posters located in the library, on library and campus display screens, and emails promoting the program via departmental and student association listservs, is difficult to measure directly. However, we plan to indirectly assess the success of these activities by conducting a survey among international students to determine if and how they heard about MSES, and their awareness of library services in general.

Reference and Instruction

Ambassador Tasks

Another primary role of the library ambassadors is to assist in providing reference and instruction. In addition to the existing liaison librarian model, whereby students can contact the liaison librarian assigned to their department with any library or information-related question, the ambassadors are trained to be alternative first-tier reference service providers, ready to assist in known-item searching and provide information about library services and resources. They are encouraged to refer more difficult questions related to specific research topics to the designated liaison librarian. In the winter 2016 semester, the library ambassadors began delivering reference services to their peers in various ways. They answer questions received via the MSES email account and on the MSES Facebook page, and offer scheduled hours of virtual reference service (chat reference) through the MSES Facebook page in English, Chinese, Arabic, and French. Additionally, at the beginning of the winter term, they gave scheduled library tours in their respective native languages and delivered a presentation to incoming international students on basic library services at the International Student Services orientation day. They also offer in-person assistance to students upon request. These services are offered both inside and outside the library, seeking to expand the library's "service-point[s] from a fixed library location to a roaming network of service providers"[49] to address student questions in a more timely and convenient manner. Though some librarians offer office hours in departments, they rarely get the opportunity to attend classes, labs, and cafeterias as the student ambassadors frequently do. As a result, the library ambassadors are a means to extend library services beyond the library's walls.

Reference and Instruction Training

In preparation for assisting their peers with library and information-related questions, the ambassadors received extensive training on library resources, including specialized workshops on engineering databases such as Compendex, engineering ebooks, and the library's 3D printing services. In addition to library resources, they were also trained on strategies for conducting a reference interview in order to be better positioned to understand a user's information need and provide assistance. Part of their training includes learning when it is appropriate to refer a question rather than attempt to answer it without having the required skills or information to do so, as well as how to refer to the appropriate person within the library or another unit on campus. Their training has not been restricted to the beginning of their time as ambassadors, but rather is an ongoing process that spans the entire two semesters.

Reference and Instruction Assessment

To monitor library ambassadors' reference service delivered via email, chat, and in person, we created a question log to track questions that they receive and answers that they provide. The data that we are gathering include:

- Date
- Day and time of service
- Ambassador's name
- Question
- Answer
- Source used to answer the question
- Student level
- Service duration
- Method of assistance
- Question category
- Notes

Sample questions include:

- How do I access McGill Library electronic resources from off-campus?
- How do I place a hold request for a book at another McGill Library branch?
- What is the latest time I can borrow books from the library?

At the end of the pilot project, we will conduct a thorough analysis of the question log, including a distribution of questions by date, day, and hour, and categories of questions. In addition, we are using this log to monitor the quality of the ambassadors' reference assistance by regularly reviewing the accuracy of answers. For questions received through virtual reference, we have the added information provided by the actual reference transcript. These transcripts can be a way of providing ongoing training to the ambassadors.

We will also conduct a survey and/or interviews with students to determine the satisfaction and comfort level of those who have used the reference services provided by the library ambassadors. We have asked the ambassadors to gather students' contact information every time they provide assistance, including student name, email, department, and study level. The ambassadors submit the question log and contact information to the supervisors separately to ensure that students' names are not tied directly to the questions they asked, thus serving to protect the students' confidentiality. Like the question log, the survey and interview data will be gathered for future analysis. We are also collecting attendance information and participant feedback forms from the ambassador-led library tours.

Feedback from the Ambassadors

Not only is this program assessed for the gains achieved through library ambassadors' efforts in outreach and delivering reference and instruction, we are also assessing the input provided by the library ambassadors. As discussed in the literature review, students who deliver peer assistance benefit from the experience. Preliminary evidence from this case study suggests this is also true for the McGill Library ambassadors. The ambassadors are expected to write bimonthly reports, which help the supervisors to assess the knowledge and skills the ambassadors have gained and provide the supervisors with suggestions for improvements to the program (see Appendix 10A for the report template). The reports document the ambassadors' experiences and provide the opportunity to reflect on their skill development in the areas of library research, awareness of library services and systems, customer service, organization, promotion, communication, translation, teaching, and teamwork. A brief analysis of the first set of bimonthly reports indicates that ambassadors have acquired greater awareness of the library's resources and services, as well as enhanced skills related to promotion, translation, communication, organization, and teamwork. A thorough analysis will be conducted when the pilot project is completed with the goal of assessing the value of this project as a whole and generating suggestions for improvements in the future.

Conclusion

The peer support program that we have piloted at McGill Library has been a fantastic learning opportunity for the ambassadors and supervising librarians alike. Benefits have included increased library outreach to international students and improved understanding by librarians of international student information needs. Recommendations from our experience are as follows:

Before you begin:

- Start out small with a pilot project targeting a specific clientele. That way, you can learn and make changes before you expand the program.

- Get buy-in from all relevant stakeholders within and beyond your library, which will facilitate project planning. The project can be an opportunity to build collaborations with other units on campus such as international student services, the writing center, the office for academic affairs, and/or specific first-year writing or humanities courses. Explore what options you have on your campus.
- Start as early as possible; the interview and hiring process may take longer than you think.
- Plan ahead for assessment. If you want to be able to assess the program, it will be important to have thought about how you plan to do so ahead of time. For example, if you intend to survey or interview users, you can gather their contact information at the time they make use of the service.

Throughout the project:

- Use and motivate students to help develop the library ambassador's role.[50] The program should benefit the ambassadors themselves, so be sure to ask the students what they want to learn. You may find that they want to learn skills you had not thought of, like gaining experience teaching or doing graphic design. Also, spread out the training instead of having it only at the beginning.
- Have a written work plan to guide the project and update it regularly. This will keep you and the library ambassadors on track and clarify work expectations.
- Make sure to prioritize student tasks. There may be many things you want the ambassadors to complete by the end of the project and it will be important to identify the most important ones. Also, some of the tasks will be more time-sensitive than others (e.g. documentation or events that need to be ready for the start of a new semester), so schedule accordingly. Assign the ambassadors tasks to be accomplished early on in their employment to give them and the supervisors a feeling of accomplishment.
- Use your library's staff resources, including colleagues such as communications officers, graphic designers, or web designers as resources. Collaborating beyond the supervising team of librarians for this project has been a growing experience for everyone. Part of your job as a supervisor can be to facilitate those connections.
- Be flexible with student schedules. Keep in mind that students

have other priorities, such as their course work and exams. However, bear in mind that they may be able to devote more hours in weeks when school demands are less intense.

- Monitor and check in with students regularly. Sometimes there will be differences between what you expect and what the students deliver, so it is better to clear up any misconceptions related to work tasks as soon as they arise.

Future plans for the peer support program include expanding the service beyond engineering to all international students on campus. It is our hope that the experience documented in this case study can be adapted by other university libraries to reach out to international students, and that similar peer assistance approaches can be used to enhance library services for all students.

Appendix 10A. Bimonthly Report

Please reflect on your experience as a library ambassador by answering the following questions. Please provide a one-two paragraph answer for each question with your specific experiences.

1. Please discuss training you have completed and what you have learned from it.
2. What has been your experience in developing the following skills as a result of being an ambassador?

Awareness of library services and systems	
Library research skills (searching for, evaluating, synthesizing, and citing information)	
Customer service skills	
Organizational skills	
Teaching and presentation skills	
Promotional skills	
Communication skills (including both oral and written)	
Translation skills	
Technical skills (including using software—Camtasia, Drupal, Photoshop, EndNote, Facebook, etc.)	
Teamwork skills	
Other	

3. What benefits have you derived from being an ambassador (e.g. improved position as a student leader, more easily accomplishing your schoolwork, more comfortable seeking help within the library or other units on campus)?
4. How comfortable were you asking questions in the library before you started working as an ambassador and how comfortable are you now?
5. What ways could the program be improved?

Notes

1. Keith J. Topping, "The Effectiveness of Peer Tutoring in Further and Higher Education: A Typology and Review of the Literature," *Higher Education* 32, no. 3 (1996): 321–345, http://link.springer.com/article/10.1007%2FBF00138870#.
2. McGill University Enrolment Services, Enrolment Reports, accessed December 20, 2015, www.mcgill.ca/es/registration-statistics.
3. McGill University Enrolment Services, Enrolment Report Fall 2015: Total (FT and PT) Visa Enrolments by Countries, accessed December 20, 2015, www.mcgill.ca/es/files/es/fall_2015_-_total_full-time_and_part-time_visa_enrolments_by_countries.pdf.
4. McGill University Enrolment Services, Enrolment Report Fall 2015: Total (FT and PT) Enrolments by Mother Tongue, accessed December 20, 2015, www.mcgill.ca/es/files/es/fall_2015_-_total_full-time_and_part-time_enrolments_by_mother_tongue.pdf.
5. McGill University Enrolment Services, Enrolment Report Fall 2015: Total (FT and PT) Visa Enrolments by Countries.
6. Kathleen Massey, University Registrar and Executive Director, McGill University Enrolment Services, email message to authors, December 9, 2015.
7. Yan Liao, Mary Finn, and Jun Lu, "Information-Seeking Behavior of International Graduate Students vs. American Graduate Students: A User Study at Virginia Tech 2005," *College and Research Libraries* 68, no. 1 (2007): 23, http://dx.doi.org/10.5860/crl.68.1.5.
8. Topping, "The Effectiveness of Peer Tutoring," 321–345.
9. David Boud, Ruth Cohen, and Jane Sampson, *Peer Learning in Higher Education: Learning from & with Each Other* (London: Kogan Page, 2001), 8–9.
10. Allison I. Faix et al., "Peer Reference Redefined: New Uses for Undergraduate Students," *Reference Services Review* 38, no. 1 (2010): 90–107, doi.org/10.1108/00907321011020752; Allison Faix, "Peer Reference Revisited: Evolution of a Peer-Reference Model," *Reference Services Review* 42, no. 2 (2014): 305–319, http://dx.doi.org/10.1108/RSR-07-2013-0039.
11. Susan Deese-Roberts and Kathleen Keating, *Library Instruction: A Peer Tutoring Model* (Englewood, Colo.: Libraries Unlimited, 2000); Ann Elizabeth Donahue, "Charting Success: Using Practical Measures to Assess Information Literacy Skills in the First-Year Writing Course," *Evidence Based Library & Information Practice* 10, no. 2 (2015): 45–62, https://ejournals.library.ualberta.ca/index.php/eblip/article/view/24183.
12. Tamsin Bolton, Tina Pugliese, and Jill Singleton-Jackson, "Advancing the Promotion of Information Literacy through Peer-Led Learning," *Communications in Information Literacy* 3, no. 1 (2009): 20–30; Wendy Holliday and Cynthia Nordgren, "Extending the Reach of Librarians: Library Peer Mentor Program at Utah State University," *College and Research Libraries* 66, no. 4 (2005): 282–284.
13. Brett B. Bodemer, "They CAN and They SHOULD: Undergraduates Providing Peer Reference and Instruction," *College and Research Libraries* 75, no. 2 (2014): 162–178, http://dx.doi.org/10.5860/crl12-411; Jana Ronan and Mimi Pappas, "Library Instruction Is a Two-Way Street: Students Receiving Course Credit for Peer Teaching," *Education Libraries* 25, no. 1 (2001): 19–24.

14. Michelle S. Millet and Clint Chamberlain, "Word-of-Mouth Marketing Using Peer Tutors," *The Serials Librarian* 53, no. 3 (2007): 95–105, http://dx.doi.org/10.1300/J123v53n03_07.
15. Faix, "Peer Reference Revisited," 312.
16. Lys Ann Reiners, Helen Williams, and Rachel Farrow, "PALs—Students Supporting Students at the University of Lincoln Library," *SCONUL Focus* 47 (2009): 31.
17. Kimberly Posin Chan et al., "Libraries across the Sea: Using a Virtual Presence and Skilled Student Assistants to Serve Students Abroad," *Journal of Library Administration* 55, no. 4 (2015): 278–301, http://dx.doi.org/10.1080/01930826.2015.1038921.
18. Bodemer, "They CAN and They SHOULD," 170.
19. Holliday and Nordgren, "Extending the Reach of Librarians," 284.
20. Elaina Norlin, "University Goes Back to Basics to Reach Minority Students," *American Libraries* 32, no. 7 (2001): 60–62.
21. Norlin, "University Goes Back to Basics," 60–62; Michael M. Smith and Leslie J. Reynolds, "The Street Team: An Unconventional Peer Program for Undergraduates," *Library Management* 29, no. 3 (2008): 145–158, doi.org/10.1108/01435120810855287.
22. Millet and Chamberlain, "Word-of-Mouth Marketing," 99.
23. Holliday and Nordgren, "Extending the Reach of Librarians," 284.
24. Christopher Chan and Dianne Cmor, "Blogging toward Information Literacy: Engaging Students and Facilitating Peer Learning," *Reference Services Review* 37, no. 4 (2009): 395–407, http://dx.doi.org/10.1108/00907320911007001.
25. Jamie Seeholzer, "Making It Their Own: Creating Meaningful Opportunities for Student Employees in Academic Library Services," *College and Undergraduate Libraries* 20, no. 2 (2013): 219, doi.org/10.1080/10691316.2013.789690.
26. Millet and Chamberlain, "Word-of-Mouth Marketing," 101.
27. Bolton, Pugliese, and Singleton-Jackson, "Advancing the Promotion of Information Literacy," 24.
28. Bodemer, "They CAN and They SHOULD," 174.
29. Bolton, Pugliese, and Singleton-Jackson, "Advancing the Promotion of Information Literacy," 24–25; Laura Sbaffi et al., "Nice Evidence Search: Student Peers' Views on Their Involvement as Trainers in Peer-Based Information Literacy Training," *Journal of Academic Librarianship* 41, no. 2 (2015): 203, doi.org/10.1016/j.acalib.2014.08.002.
30. Holliday and Nordgren, "Extending the Reach of Librarians," 283; Barbara MacAdam and Darlene P. Nichols, "Peer Information Counseling: An Academic Library Program for Minority Students," *Journal of Academic Librarianship* 15, no. 4 (1989): 207.
31. Holliday and Nordgren, "Extending the Reach of Librarians," 283.
32. Sbaffi et al., "Nice Evidence Search," 205.
33. Reiners, Williams, and Farrow, "PALs—Students Supporting Students," 33.
34. Bodemer, "They CAN and They SHOULD," 171; Sbaffi et al., "Nice Evidence Search," 202.
35. Faix, "Peer Reference Revisited," 312.
36. Sbaffi et al., "Nice Evidence Search," 205.
37. Smith and Reynolds, "The Street Team," 150.
38. Faix et al., "Peer Reference Redefined," 92; Seeholzer, "Making It Their Own," 222.
39. Reiners, Williams, and Farrow, "PALs—Students Supporting Students," 32; Doreen Harwood and Charlene McCormack, "Growing Our Own: Mentoring Undergraduate Students," *Journal of Business & Finance Librarianship* 13, no. 3 (2008): 214, http://dx.doi.org/10.1080/08963560802183195.

40. Norlin, "University Goes Back to Basics," 62; MacAdam and Nichols, "Peer Information Counseling," 208.
41. Deese-Roberts and Keating, *Library Instruction,* 60.
42. MacAdam and Nichols, "Peer Information Counseling," 208.
43. Reiners, Williams, and Farrow, "PALs—Students Supporting Students," 32.
44. Chris Langer and Hiromi Kubo, "From the Ground Up: Creating a Sustainable Library Outreach Program for International Students," *Journal of Library Administration* 55, no. 8 (2015): 605–621, doi.org/10.1080/01930826.2015.1085232; Sbaffi et al., "Nice Evidence Search," 204–205.
45. Pamela A. Jackson and Patrick Sullivan, *International Students and Academic Libraries: Initiatives for Success* (Chicago, Ill.: Association of College and Research Libraries, 2011); Liao, Finn, and Lu, "Information-Seeking Behavior," 5–25; Zhixian Yi, "International Student Perceptions of Information Needs and Use," *Journal of Academic Librarianship* 33, no. 6 (2007): 666–673, http://dx.doi.org/10.1016/j.acalib.2007.09.003; Yu-Hui Chen and Mary K. Van Ullen, "Helping International Students Succeed Academically through Research Process and Plagiarism Workshops," *College & Research Libraries* 72, no. 3 (2011): 209–235, http://dx.doi.org/10.5860/crl-117rl.
46. Norlin, "University Goes Back to Basics," 60–62; MacAdam and Nichols, "Peer Information Counseling," 204–209; Langer and Kubo, "From the Ground Up," 605–621; Dawn Amsberry and Loanne Snavely, "Engaging International Students in Academic Library Initiatives for their Peers," in *International Students and Academic Libraries: Initiatives for Success,* ed. Pamela A. Jackson and Patrick Sullivan (Chicago, Ill.: Association of College and Research Libraries, 2011), 69–82.
47. Kaya van Beynen and Camielle Swenson, "Exploring Peer-to-Peer Library Content and Engagement on a Student-Run Facebook Group," *College & Research Libraries* 77, no. 1 (2016): 46, doi.org/10.5860/crl.77.1.34.
48. Deese-Roberts and Keating, *Library Instruction,* 63.
49. Smith and Reynolds, "The Street Team," 150.
50. Reiners, Williams, and Farrow, "PALs—Students Supporting Students," 33; Holliday and Nordgren, "Extending the Reach of Librarians," 283.

Bibliography

Amsberry, Dawn, and Loanne Snavely. "Engaging International Students in Academic Library Initiatives for their Peers." In *International Students and Academic Libraries: Initiatives for Success,* edited by Pamela A. Jackson and Patrick Sullivan, 69–82. Chicago, Ill.: Association of College and Research Libraries, 2011.

Bodemer, Brett B. "They CAN and They SHOULD: Undergraduates Providing Peer Reference and Instruction." *College and Research Libraries* 75, no. 2 (2014): 162–178, http://dx.doi.org/10.5860/crl12-411.

Bolton, Tamsin, Tina Pugliese, and Jill Singleton-Jackson. "Advancing the Promotion of Information Literacy through Peer-Led Learning." *Communications in Information Literacy* 3, no. 1 (2009): 20–30.

Boud, David, Ruth Cohen, and Jane Sampson. *Peer Learning in Higher Education: Learning from & with Each Other.* London: Kogan Page, 2001.

Chan, Christopher and Dianne Cmor. "Blogging toward Information Literacy: Engaging Students and Facilitating Peer Learning." *Reference Services Review* 37, no. 4 (2009): 395–407, http://dx.doi.org/10.1108/00907320911007001.

Chan, Kimberly Posin, Jaimie Beth Colvin, Marc Vinyard, Claire Leach, Mary Ann Naumann, and Paul Stenis. "Libraries across the Sea: Using a Virtual Presence and Skilled Student Assistants to Serve Students Abroad." *Journal of Library Administration* 55, no. 4 (2015): 278–301, http://dx.doi.org/10.1080/01930826.2015.1038921.

Chen, Yu-Hui, and Mary K. Van Ullen. "Helping International Students Succeed Academically through Research Process and Plagiarism Workshops." *College & Research Libraries* 72, no. 3 (2011): 209–235. http://dx.doi.org/10.5860/crl-117rl.

Deese-Roberts, Susan, and Kathleen Keating. *Library Instruction: A Peer Tutoring Model.* Englewood, Colo.: Libraries Unlimited, 2000.

Donahue, Ann Elizabeth. "Charting Success: Using Practical Measures to Assess Information Literacy Skills in the First-Year Writing Course." *Evidence Based Library & Information Practice* 10, no. 2 (2015): 45–62. https://ejournals.library.ualberta.ca/index.php/eblip/article/view/24183.

Faix, Allison. "Peer Reference Revisited: Evolution of a Peer-Reference Model." *Reference Services Review* 42, no. 2 (2014): 305–319, http://dx.doi.org/10.1108/RSR-07-2013-0039.

Faix, Allison I., Margaret H. Bates, Lisa A. Hartman, Jennifer H. Hughes, Casey N. Schacher, Brooke J. Elliot, and Alexander D. Woods. "Peer Reference Redefined: New Uses for Undergraduate Students." *Reference Services Review* 38, no. 1 (2010): 90–107. doi.org/10.1108/00907321011020752.

Harwood, Doreen, and Charlene McCormack. "Growing Our Own: Mentoring Undergraduate Students." *Journal of Business & Finance Librarianship* 13, no. 3 (2008): 201–215, http://dx.doi.org/10.1080/08963560802183195.

Holliday, Wendy, and Cynthia Nordgren. "Extending the Reach of Librarians: Library Peer Mentor Program at Utah State University." *College and Research Libraries* 66, no. 4 (2005): 282–284.

Jackson, Pamela A., and Patrick Sullivan. *International Students and Academic Libraries: Initiatives for Success.* Chicago, Ill.: Association of College and Research Libraries, 2011.

Langer, Chris, and Hiromi Kubo. "From the Ground Up: Creating a Sustainable Library Outreach Program for International Students." *Journal of Library Administration* 55, no. 8 (2015): 605–621. doi.org/10.1080/01930826.2015.1085232.

Liao, Yan, Mary Finn, and Jun Lu. "Information-Seeking Behavior of International Graduate Students vs. American Graduate Students: A User Study at Virginia Tech 2005." *College and Research Libraries* 68, no. 1 (2007): 5–25, http://dx.doi.org/10.5860/crl.68.1.5.

MacAdam, Barbara, and Darlene P. Nichols. "Peer Information Counseling: An Academic Library Program for Minority Students." *Journal of Academic Librarianship* 15, no. 4 (1989): 204–209.

McGill University Enrolment Services. Enrolment Report Fall 2015: Total (FT and PT) Enrolments by Mother Tongue. Accessed December 20, 2015. www.mcgill.ca/es/files/es/fall_2015_-_total_full-time_and_part-time_enrolments_by_mother_tongue.pdf.

McGill University Enrolment Services. Enrolment Report Fall 2015: Total (FT and PT) Visa Enrolments by Countries. Accessed December 20, 2015. www.mcgill.ca/es/files/es/fall_2015_-_total_full-time_and_part-time_visa_enrolments_by_countries.pdf

McGill University Enrolment Services. Enrolment Reports. Accessed December 20, 2015. www.mcgill.ca/es/registration-statistics.

Millet, Michelle S., and Clint Chamberlain. "Word-of-Mouth Marketing Using Peer Tutors." *The Serials Librarian* 53, no. 3 (2007): 95–105, http://dx.doi.org/10.1300/J123v53n03_07.

Norlin, Elaina. "University Goes Back to Basics to Reach Minority Students." *American Libraries* 32, no. 7 (2001): 60–62.

Reiners, Lys Ann, Helen Williams, and Rachel Farrow. "PALs—Students Supporting Students at the University of Lincoln Library." *SCONUL Focus* 47 (2009): 31–33.

Ronan, Jana, and Mimi Pappas. "Library Instruction Is a Two-Way Street: Students Receiving Course Credit for Peer Teaching." *Education Libraries* 25, no. 1 (2001): 19–24.

Sbaffi, Laura, Frances Johnson, Jillian Griffiths, Jennifer Rowley, and Anne Weist. "Nice Evidence Search: Student Peers' Views on Their Involvement as Trainers in Peer-Based Information Literacy Training." *Journal of Academic Librarianship* 41, no. 2 (2015): 201–206. doi.org/10.1016/j.acalib.2014.08.002.

Seeholzer, Jamie. "Making It Their Own: Creating Meaningful Opportunities for Student Employees in Academic Library Services." *College and Undergraduate Libraries* 20, no. 2 (2013): 215–223. doi.org/10.1080/10691316.2013.789690.

Smith, Michael M., and Leslie J. Reynolds. "The Street Team: An Unconventional Peer Program for Undergraduates." *Library Management* 29, no. 3 (2008): 145–158. doi.org/10.1108/01435120810855287.

Topping, Keith J. "The Effectiveness of Peer Tutoring in Further and Higher Education: A Typology and Review of the Literature." *Higher Education* 32, no. 3 (1996): 321–345. http://link.springer.com/article/10.1007%2FBF00138870.

van Beynen, Kaya, and Camielle Swenson. "Exploring Peer-to-Peer Library Content and Engagement on a Student-Run Facebook Group." *College & Research Libraries* 77, no. 1 (2016): 34–50. doi.org/10.5860/crl.77.1.34.

Yi, Zhixian. "International Student Perceptions of Information Needs and Use." *Journal of Academic Librarianship* 33, no. 6 (2007): 666–673, http://dx.doi.org/10.1016/j.acalib.2007.09.003.

Part 4

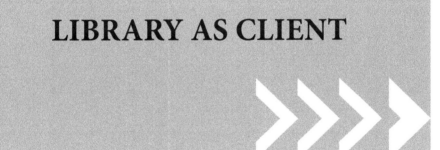

LIBRARY AS CLIENT

CHAPTER 11

KEEP IT LOCAL:
Tapping Student Expertise to Build Better Libraries

Luke Leither

Introduction

Some projects are born and grow out of the most unexpected places. De-sign-Model-Build, a collaborative project at the University of Utah between a librarian and a faculty member in its School of Architecture, emerged from one of these small and fortuitous places. The ongoing collaboration is an example of how a routine event at a university can be employed as a learning opportunity for students and faculty alike. The initially unfunded but ambitious passion project has now grown into a fully supported, multi-million-dollar initiative.

This chapter outlines a student-centered partnership that began with a small library renovation proposal. This project, despite its humble beginnings, has served to strengthen professional relationships, improve learning outcomes for students, and produce a new library addition that has been shaped by student design and leadership. In fact, it is the student participation that inspired donors and administrators to make the dream a reality.

Who We Are
The K.W. Dumke Fine Arts & Architecture Library at the University of

Utah is located on level 2 of the J. Willard Marriott Library, the main library on campus. The Dumke Library is one of the few remaining independent collections in the library system, maintaining its own dedicated space and staff. Visual and performing arts, music, architecture, and city planning are the departments that regularly make use of our resources. However, we consult with anyone interested in creative thinking and do outreach to most departments on campus.

We support our patrons in the usual ways—collection development, teaching, research consultations, etc.—but have also begun to make concerted efforts to develop programs and infrastructure that draw in practitioners from the creative fields. Artists and architects have traditionally been the most elusive portion of our patron population, mainly because it is not immediately clear to them how the library serves their needs.[1] This is, in part, a communication and outreach problem. However, we also have come to see more clearly that we need to provide the space, expertise, and resources that practitioners need to be successful in their endeavors. It was with these issues in mind that the idea for a library renovation was developed and Design-Model-Build came into being.

Our Space

The Dumke Library sits one level below the east entrance of the Marriott Library. During an extensive renovation and addition in 1996, architects added additional square footage below ground level, while adding a light well for subterranean floors to receive natural light throughout the year. Our library is perched on the edge of this light well, with a large, unused patio on our east and north sides (Image 11.1). The patio connects by an outside stair to a courtyard below on level 1, but travel is currently restricted between the two levels by a metal security gate that was put in place during the renovation. Consequently, nearly all of this extensive space is off limits to our users, despite its cool and shaded climate during warmer months.

In the spring of 2014 we created a proposal to assess the feasibility and costs associated with granting patron access to the patio. Initial meetings with administration and code officials made it clear that simply opening the doors and moving some chairs and tables outside was not a reasonable suggestion. Doors would have to be replaced to grant emergency egress, floor surfaces would have to be leveled and refinished to accommodate furniture, and pigeons and their droppings would have to be removed.

Image 11.1. Photograph of the eastern patio and lower courtyard.

The unexpected cost and complexity of opening this space demanded that we focus our ideas and develop a plan. If we intended to ask for thousands of dollars to significantly remodel our library, then we wanted to build something that effectively served the needs of our community. We needed a strong vision for what we wanted and a convincing reason for why it was necessary.

Design-Model-Build

We convinced library colleagues and university administration to allow the project to move forward by strategically aligning our goals with theirs. We studied vision statements and speeches to draw out important themes and then reported back, highlighting how we would advance our collective missions simultaneously. Several themes emerged, but promoting student success was the most important and natural from the beginning.

Early on in the project, library administration had given us a small stipend to hire an architect to perform a site study for the patio and to draw up a basic construction budget. However, given that our lofty ambitions went well beyond the basic upgrades, we needed to find smart, motivated people to help us see the possibilities and develop a design. A partnership with the School of Architecture seemed like a wonderful way to jump-start the project while providing students a one-of-a-kind, engaged-learning experience.

We took the project to Erin Carraher, a faculty member in the School of Architecture, in the summer of 2014. Collaboratively we developed a plan to recruit young architecture students for help with design while exposing them to all the challenges and considerations of a real building project. Fortunately for us, Erin and several other faculty members in the architecture program are experts in a form of Community Engaged Learning called Design-Build.* The University of Utah's program, called Design-BuildBluff, sends graduate students into a Navajo community in southern Utah to design and build structures in collaboration with the residents there. The students and faculty involved have built unique buildings, often with recycled or repurposed materials, like those we were interested in for our own project. Erin's extensive expertise paired with a unique building project right on campus was likely to provide our students with an experience that would stay with them throughout their careers.

What Do Our Students and Faculty Need?

Our first step in developing a project for our students was to learn what kind of spaces we needed to create. To do this, we looked at local and national trends in higher education, and made several useful observations. For example, in the last few years, administrators, faculty, and staff at the University of Utah have made concerted efforts to insert creativity and transdisciplinary collaboration into the curriculum. This movement is part of a nationwide trend, commonly called the Creative Campus, that stems from research suggesting creativity and divergent thinking can and should be incorporated into higher education.[2] Some studies have begun to show

---

*For examples of real-world DesignBuild projects from the perspective of the instructors who started them see Steve Badanes et al., "Teaching by Example," interview by David Sokol, *Architectural Record* 186, no. 10 (October 2008):120. For two excellent articles discussing Design-Build education, see V. B. Canizaro, "Design-Build in Architectural Education: Motivations, Practices, Challenges, Successes and Failures,"*Archnet-IJAR: International Journal of Architectural Research* 6, no. 3 (2012) and Jonathan Foote, "Design-Build :: Build-Design,"*Journal of Architectural Education* 65, no. 2 (2012).

that students in the sciences will seek out a second major or additional classes in the arts to augment their coursework.[3] These students recognize they will be more successful academically and professionally if they are able to call upon alternative modes of thinking and perceiving in their everyday lives.

Furthermore, in higher education there has been an increasing amount of interest and experimentation in community-engaged learning, essentially synonymous with service or experiential learning. It is a teaching and learning strategy that incorporates community service and hands-on lessons to enhance the educational experience.[4] Programs that prioritize this teaching style seek to inspire students to become outstanding global citizens who understand and confront the challenges that exist in their communities.[5]

Faculty and students are demanding more collaborative research and learning environments, and university campuses have struggled to effectively support these expectations. However, many libraries are already well situated to accommodate demands for open and flexible spaces, and are accustomed to supporting multifaceted research programs. The discipline-agnostic nature of university libraries makes them a perfect place to come together and experiment. Thus, we have recently seen maker spaces, gaming labs, data visualization centers, and flexible collaboration spaces proliferate in academic libraries across the country.

For the Dumke Library staff, the creative campus movement has been especially exciting, considering our specialized collections and creative users. We have the resources and relationships that are necessary to act as a catalyst for such a movement, and found ourselves needing more square footage to explore the growing number of opportunities all around us. The unused patio seemed like the only and obvious choice for an expansion that could meet the needs of our students and their ongoing creative initiatives. After assessing these needs and our own ideals, we set the following as priorities in our formal proposal to renovate: opening space for the exhibition of creative works, an emphasis on sustainability, and flexible design for a diverse user population.

Exhibition Spaces

From the beginning of our visioning process we wanted to develop a venue to display three-dimensional work that would closely mimic a professional exhibition environment. The interior of the Marriott Library has many places to display two-dimensional work, along with an exhibitions advisory committee that approves shows and helps with installation and curation. However, locations for three-dimensional objects are quite limited.

Additionally, as mentioned above, it is an ongoing challenge to convince studio art students to come in and use the library. While there are many explanations for this, one reason may be that artists learn from looking at and participating in exhibitions. They need to see what their peers are creating and how diverse the creative landscape is. They also need to see that the library recognizes their artwork as a product of academic exploration, equivalent to an academic paper or report. Thus, the library can support them in their endeavors by becoming an active participant in the research, creation, and exhibition of creative work.

Building exhibition space would allow our patrons to see the creative output of our community and also provide an excellent training ground for artists. Furthermore, facilitating "Signature Experiences," like those that would be provided by this new art space, is one of the seven university priorities outlined in the inaugural address of our president, David Pershing.[6] The Fine Arts & Architecture exhibition space would embrace the creative campus ideal, would provide an opportunity for student-engaged learning, and also serve to directly support the mission of the University of Utah.

Sustainability

Sustainability, a second university priority set by President Pershing, was another area of focus we identified for our project.[7] The patio itself is a natural-light area that would require zero artificial lighting for study during the day. Sustainable materials could be prioritized for new tables, chairs, and other necessary additions. Native plants and a living wall system could beautify the area, creating an inviting ambiance and also provide some acoustic dampening for the predominately concrete infrastructure. We felt that setting this as a priority would help to educate our community on sustainable practices and simultaneously reflect the values of the university.

Flexibility

Finally, flexibility was a key priority for us as we began to consider how the space might be used. We wanted to provide an open venue for innovative art shows, impromptu lectures, performance pieces, events, quiet and group study, and any new opportunities that would come in time. This meant that remodeling of the space needed to account for our wide range of programmatic ambitions.

All of our goals required a design that was thoughtful, creative, and unique to the University of Utah. We felt confident that our architecture students would be up to the task and would stick with us no matter the challenges. Our collaboration is now in its third phase and has lasted nearly two years. The successes that we have enjoyed have come through some effective planning, but also a great deal of flexibility and willingness to course correct when things didn't go as expected. Some of these adjustments will be highlighted as we now discuss the three phases of the project.

Phase I

For Phase I of Design-Model-Build, we tasked Professor Carraher's first-year architecture studio class with the design, modeling, and fabrication of furnishings for a combined study and art exhibition space on the level 2 patio. Furnishings were to include tables and chairs for study, permanent and moveable pedestals for public art, and moveable living walls for low-light plants.

Together we laid out a framework to complete this project successfully and to evaluate our efforts as we went along. Using some money we had solicited from the university and the library, we hired two professional fabricators as consultants to the students. The consultants were there throughout the semester to guide the students' thinking as they tried to make the leap from designs on paper to the real-world fabrication of objects on a large scale.

By the beginning of the fall in 2014, we had developed the following plan to carry us through the semester:

1. **Design Research:** Students will study from print and digital library resources provided by the Fine Arts & Architecture Library. The resources will focus on sustainable design, public art display, institutional design, and furniture design.
2. **Design Concept:** Students will design using Rhinoceros 3D software licensed by the Marriott Library.
   a. Designs to be evaluated by the instructor and the librarian. Several will be selected to move to Phase 3.

3. **Design Development:** Student groups will develop and build full-scale prototypes for their proposals in consultation with professional fabricators. Fabricators have already been selected and hired based on previous experience with museum installations and product fabrication.
   a. *Mid-review:* designs will be evaluated by the fabricator for feasibility, by architecture jurors for design intent, and by the library professionals for client needs.
   b. *Final review:* a formal review to give students feedback regarding designs. Selected designs to move on to Phase 4.
4. **Design Documentation:** Selected designs will be printed in the 3D printer and combined with presentation boards for display.
   a. Models will be used by library selection group (Luke Leither, Greg Hatch, Ian Godfrey, and Catherine Soehner) for final approval.
5. **Fabrication and Evaluation:** Approved designs will go to the fabricator under instructor and student supervision.
   a. Completed designs to be evaluated through a student satisfaction survey.

While we planned to adhere as strictly as possible to this program, things inevitably changed and adjustments were made along the way. For example, in the beginning we broke the class of around forty students into eight groups, all working independently under the supervision of the architecture faculty and consultants. We planned to reduce the number of designs down to four after the final review, but ended up seeing so much potential in all eight that we allowed everyone to build models and continue their work. We also found that most of the groups preferred to construct models using wood and metal rather than using the 3D printers, sticking as closely as possible to the materials that they would select for the fabricated objects.

It was exciting to lead the project as designs evolved with the growing expertise and skill of the students. Representatives from the library were profoundly engaged throughout the process. Two librarians, our facilities director, and our Associate Dean of Research and User Services offered feedback at each review. Additionally, we made ourselves available to offer guidance in using our collections and the vast array of technology that is accessible through the library.

By the end of the semester, designs were staggering in their ingenuity as well as their diversity. Students created flowing canopies that established "rooms" within the patio, they invented a "plug-and-play" living-wall system from which you could pull individual plants when they needed to be replaced or repotted, and they devised ingenious flooring and zoning systems that would encourage visitors to naturally move through the space and view the art on display (Images 11.2 & 11.3). Our ideas about what was possible for our renovation changed completely and for the better by the end of this first phase.

Image 11.2. Scale model of the upper patio created by students Otto Stefan, Adam Hayes, Mike Soderberg, Jason Robb, Oi Lam Poon.

Image 11.3. Plug-and-play wall system by students Otto Stefan, Adam Hayes, Mike Soderberg, Jason Robb, Oi Lam Poon.

However, successful designs were not the only—nor even the most important—outcomes of this collaboration. The students' education was our highest priority, and we wanted to be sure this experience was as valuable for them as we thought it would be. We chose to measure this by administering an anonymous course survey at the beginning and end of the semester. We then compared the results to see how responses changed over time. Using a 1–5 Likert Scale, we asked students to rate their confidence in multiple areas, including use of 3D modeling software, use of 3D printing technologies, use of Marriott Library resources, and their confidence in understanding and meeting the needs of real-world customers. We also asked open-ended questions to hear about the project in the students' own words. After we compiled results, we found that both sets of measures were overwhelmingly positive. Based on their survey responses, the students finished the semester more confident in their skills and abilities. Responses like this were the norm: "I've learned about what all is needed and required to meet real project standards, such as budgeting for materials, learning new programs, meeting the needs of a space through creative design, and how to be interactive with your client."[8]

Fundraising

While the students were developing their design concepts, the library team worked on securing funding. Not only did we need funds to proceed with the renovation, but we also needed money to pay for the students' prototypes and other costs associated with running the course. Library administration was extremely supportive of our efforts, but did not have funding for anything beyond what they had already provided. We eventually managed to cover the Design-Model-Build costs through a teaching grant awarded by the university. We then were able to pursue the larger renovation funds with the help of our development director. Almost immediately a donor approached us who loved the vision for the project as well as the built-in student engagement. By the end of 2014, the donor had agreed to support our efforts and was generous beyond what we could have ever hoped for.

The private donation significantly altered the trajectory of the renovation and the student collaboration. The gift allowed us to expand and incorporate the entire courtyard on level 1, more than doubling the size of the original plan. With this expanded footprint, we reconsidered the patio space on level 2, eventually deciding to partially enclose the north end to make it usable throughout the year. All of these changes occurred during the last month of fall semester as the students were finalizing their patio designs. There was not enough time for them to adjust their work to include the lower level, and so we allowed them to proceed with the original concept without interruption. We finished the semester proud of the work our students created and excited by where we were heading in the future.

Phase II

The significant changes to the size and scope of the project forced us to rethink much of what we had done through December 2014. Until then, we had been operating on almost no budget and without the guarantee that our dream of a renovation would ever occur. However, with the finances together and a larger, multi-level space to consider, we had a significant amount of design work to do that demanded the services of a licensed architecture firm. We knew this could continue to be a great opportunity for students, but it was necessary to adjust our goals to meet the changing needs of the project.

For the 2015 spring semester we continued our collaboration with Professor Carraher and the School of Architecture by hiring eight students to work with us as research assistants. Professor Carraher supervised the students' work while the library team acted as employers and advisors. We wanted these students to continue to drive the project and shape the library into something they would use and be proud of. We wanted them to have the experience of working with us as clients, working with the architecture firm as colleagues, and working with each other as collaborators. Finally, we wanted to change the scenario from a theoretical learning exercise to a paid position that would reflect the impact their work would have on the eventual renovation.

Students were invited to apply for the assistantship positions in January 2015. The successful applicants were to be tasked with the design, documentation, and prototyping of all furniture and art display systems for the renovated space. They were to do this work in partnership with the architecture firm hired by the Marriott Library. We had dozens of applications and, in the end, selected five applicants from the previous semester's class. We also chose to accept one upper-level architecture student, one urban ecology student, and one industrial design student. We felt that these new additions would add fresh eyes and perspective to the work that had already been done. We ended up with a great team (Image 11.4).

Image 11.4. Top Row: Otto Stefan, Brooke Keene, Michael Hoehn, Katja Lund, Luke Leither, Elizabeth Poulsen, Scott Thorne. Bottom Row: Sara Xu, Greg Hatch, Genie Bey, Erin Carraher.

Like the previous phase of the project, Phase II began with a semester-length program that Erin organized based on her professional experience and our feedback. The following is a brief summary:

1. **Scope Definition + Assignments** (weeks 1–2)
   a. Introduction to the new scope of the project and new expectations.
   b. Each student will assume a leading role, depending on his or her strengths/interests.
2. **Review + Research** (weeks 3–5)
   a. Review the work of the previous semester and select strong elements to carry forward into new designs.
   b. Perform site analysis, user-group studies, and materials investigation.
3. **Design + Prototyping** (weeks 6–8)
   a. Small groups will begin designing for assigned elements of the patio and courtyard. Communication between groups will be key.
   b. Perform graphic and physical presentations that address the specific requirements of the project.
4. **Refinement + Model Construction** (weeks 10–12)
   a. In collaboration with a professional fabricator, refined designs and models will be constructed.

   b. Final designs to be delivered to client.
5. **Finalized documentation + Presentation** (weeks 13–14)
   a. Finalized documentation, budget, and prototypes delivered
        to the library client.

Once again, from the very beginning our carefully laid plans were upset by circumstances beyond our control. One problem that persisted throughout the semester was an ongoing administrative delay in hiring an architecture firm. Our plan counted on a partnership with the architects, both for the students' educational experience and also to guarantee a unified design aesthetic. Unfortunately, it became clear early on that this would not be possible and so we proceeded without them, giving our students carte blanche to design as they pleased.

Throughout the semester we met with students weekly and provided as much feedback as possible. We participated in two lengthy charrettes to brainstorm new possibilities. Meanwhile, the students also met with stakeholders around the campus and developed several user archetypes that they used to make design decisions. For example, one archetype detailed a student who habitually sought out isolated places in the library for quiet study and reflection. This student didn't enjoy feeling crowded by others and needed a quiet environment to get their work done. In response to this, our designers created "low-energy zones" with seating and workspaces to accommodate such needs.

Image 11.5. Rendering of a level 1 "low-energy zone" by students Genie Bey, Michael Hoehn, Brooke Keene, Katja Lund, Elizabeth Poulsen, Otto Stefan, Scott Thorne, Sara Xu.

By the end of the semester, the students had developed a tightly programmed space with diversity and creativity throughout. On the west end of level 1, designated high-activity zones contained permanent seating for group study and socializing. Activity levels dropped as one moved through the space, and there were more individual seating options and opportunities to view art on the far end. As seen in Image 11.6, the entire corner of the L-shaped courtyard was covered by an innovative canopy system that would provide shade, a place to hang artwork, and an opportunity for growing vines to proliferate. Along with the growing vines, a living wall system populated with native plants was built into the multi-story walls (Image 11.7). The upper-level patio mirrored the energy zones of level 1, but had more moveable furniture and display units, making it possible to clear the area for a class or event (Image 11.8). Finally, the students created an additional wall structure that incorporated material samples for research purposes and bar-height workstations as a seating alternative (Image 11.9).

Image 11.6. Rendering of lower courtyard by students Genie Bey, Michael Hoehn, Brooke Keene, Katja Lund, Elizabeth Poulsen, Otto Stefan, Scott Thorne, Sara Xu.

LIBRARY TERRACE TEAM
LOWER LEVEL VERTICAL GARDEN
SPRING 2015

ASARUM EUROPAEUM

ASARUM SPLENDENS

ATHYRIUM GHOST FERN

CAREX DIVULSA

CAREX PENSYLVANICA

DRYOPTERIS MARGINALIS

GALIUM ODORATUM

HOSTA PLANTAIN LILY

LIRIOPE MUSCARI

MILIUM EFFUSUM

20'

40'

Image 11.7. Suggested planting scheme for living wall system by Genie Bey, Michael Hoehn, Brooke Keene, Katja Lund, Elizabeth Poulsen, Otto Stefan, Scott Thorne, Sara Xu.

Image 11.8. Rendering of upper patio with all furnishings designed by students Genie Bey, Michael Hoehn, Brooke Keene, Katja Lund, Elizabeth Poulsen, Otto Stefan, Scott Thorne, Sara Xu.

Image 11.9. Rendering of upper patio with material sample wall designed by students Genie Bey, Michael Hoehn, Brooke Keene, Katja Lund, Elizabeth Poulsen, Otto Stefan, Scott Thorne, Sara Xu.

The students presented their designs to library administration and staff, and were honored with a small reception at the end of the semester. Parents and friends were invited to attend, and everyone was impressed with the thoughtful, refined work that had been accomplished in a few short months. The students also delivered shop-ready drawings and sent them off to our fabricator for full-scale prototypes to be made.

Phase III

We are currently in the final phase of our project. The university hired an architect in the beginning of summer 2015, and the firm was presented with the entirety of the student work. They were asked to consider and incorporate as much as possible as they moved forward with their own design process. The students have also had the opportunity to meet directly with the lead architect, who took part in a charrette to better understand their perspectives.

The furniture prototypes are nearly finished and all of the student design work has been documented and archived. The furniture prototypes will be put on display in the library and open to feedback from the community when they are delivered. The feedback will be incorporated into our final decisions for purchasing furnishings and display systems.

Lessons Learned

Over the course of this project there have been many lessons learned that any reader could generalize and apply to their own work. Below are suggestions based on our experience:

- Be an effective and prolific communicator. This project had many people involved and everyone had a personal stake in its progress. This is especially true for the students, who worked so hard and shared their best creative selves. It was easy to forget that not everyone was privy to changes in priority or even major shifts in direction. It takes a deliberate and regular effort to maintain good communication, and it is worth the work.

- Expect change and prepare people for it. This doesn't mean one shouldn't have a plan; on the contrary, the plans we made helped keep us on track and organized despite the changes that seemed to happen on a daily basis. However, preparing your team to anticipate and adapt to change is training that will serve them for every project they work on afterward.

- Know that collaboration is hard, but worth it. There were times during Design-Model-Build that all of the coordination, the unexpected challenges, the endless explanations and proposals, all seemed like too much. Yet, we provided our students with a unique experience, we built lasting professional relationships, and we will end up with a library space that was tailor-made by and for our students. This was difficult work worth doing.

- The key to student involvement is through their teaching faculty. Students are busy and distracted, and it is often difficult to bring them in on their own time. However, collaborating with their instructors incentivizes them and doesn't cut into their impossible schedules. It also acknowledges the expertise of their faculty and creates good relationships among departments.

- Presentation matters, so don't overlook it. There is no doubt that a significant reason our fundraising effort was so successful was because we were ready to discuss our project with a polished and focused presentation. We had visuals that brought our ideas to life and a clear direction that was backed by experience and data. Donors and administrators alike instantly responded and understood where we wanted to go, and then wanted to go there with us. Carefully selected images will help tell your story, so make the extra effort in creating a beautiful and engaging presentation.

Next Steps

The next big step for us is to begin construction. As of this writing, the first round of design schematics is being assessed by the code officials and university designers. Once approved, budget finalization and construction planning will begin. We hope to break ground in June 2016 and finish by the end of the year. Based on experience, we can hope it all proceeds as planned and then be ready to adjust if necessary.

We are beginning to think through how the space might be used and how we can prepare our community for its opening. As noted in the early pages of this chapter, one of the original goals was to provide students and faculty a venue to share their creative work. Running such a venue requires planning and engagement from various partners across campus. Fortunately, we have included faculty members from architecture and the studio arts in the design meetings. We also have recently partnered with sculpture and art history faculty in hosting events in the library. We hope to extend partnerships like these to take advantage of the space in unexpected and exciting ways.

Performances, film screenings, and university events are additional programming possibilities we are anticipating and planning for. We imagine a gathering place where our community members can share ideas, express themselves, and celebrate their successes and achievements. To that end, we have set aside money and space to incorporate a projection screen and audio system. Additionally, there are multiple locations designed to encourage gatherings and lectures for groups of all kinds. Programming policy still needs to be written, but will naturally be influenced by student need and leadership.

Finally, we want people to know how and why this incredible resource came to be. We want the university to look at the successful collaboration in Design-Model-Build and begin to see the campus as a sandbox for student learning. The university community contains all of the motivation and talent we could ever need to address the challenges that arise on a daily basis. We need to make the extra effort to provide our students and faculty the opportunity to address these challenges, rather than looking elsewhere. This, ultimately, was the final and farthest-reaching goal of our project. Let's share the responsibility of building a better library and university with our students. We think they can handle it, and we'll all be better for it if we do.

Notes

1. For excellent literature reviews and additional explorations on this subject see Hannah Bennett, "Bringing the Studio into the Library: Addressing the Research Needs of Studio Art and Architecture Students," *Art Documentation: Journal of the Art Libraries Society of North America* 25, no. 1 (2006) and Kasia Leousis, "Outreach to Artists: Supporting the Development of a Research Culture for Master of Fine Arts Students," *Art Documentation: Journal of the Art Libraries Society of North America* 32, no. 1 (2013).
2. Elizabeth Lingo and Steven Tepper, "The Creative Campus: Time for a 'C' Change," *The Chronicle of Higher Education*, last modified October 10, 2010, accessed February 14, 2015, http://chronicle.com/article/The-Creative-Campus-Time-for/124860/.
3. Richard Pitt and Steven Tepper, *Double Majors: Influences, Identities, & Impacts*, Curb Center Report (Nashville, TN: Vanderbilt University, 2012), 39.
4. There are many fine resources related to the study and execution of Community Engaged Learning. For a selected bibliography on the subject see Lynn M. Wallace, "A Librarian's Guide to Service-Learning," *Academy of Management Learning & Education* 4, no. 3 (2005). For an in-depth exploration see David A. Kolb, *Experiential Learning: Experience as the Source of Learning and Development*, 2nd ed. (Upper Saddle River, NJ: Pearson Education, 2015). The university's Bennion Community Service Center has led the organization in its efforts to study and expand this style of instruction. To explore the superlative work and academic study being done through the Bennion center see "Mission and Values," Lowell Bennion Community Service Center, accessed January 2, 2015, http://bennioncenter.org/about/index.php.
5. The concept of Service Learning has a fascinating history. For two excellent books that highlight pioneers in the field see Lee Benson, Ira Harkavy, and John Puckett, *Dewey's Dream: Universities and Democracies in an Age of Education Reform, Civil Society, Public Schools, and Democratic Citizenship* (Philadelphia, PA: Temple University Press, 2007) and L. Jackson Newell, *The Electric Edge of Academe: The Saga of Lucien L. Nunn and Deep Springs College* (Salt Lake City, UT: University of Utah Press, 2015).
6. David Pershing, "President Pershing's Agenda for the U: The Inaugural Address," audio file, University of Utah, 2012, accessed February 14, 2015, http://admin.utah .edu/office_of_the_president/inauguration-recap.
7. Ibid.
8. Anonymous Student, "Course Evaluation" (unpublished raw data, University of Utah, 2014).

Bibliography

Badanes, Steve, Thomas Dutton, David Lewis, and Hank Louis. "Teaching by Example." Interview by David Sokol. *Architectural Record* 186, no. 10 (October 2008): 120.

Bennett, Hannah. "Bringing the Studio into the Library: Addressing the Research Needs of Studio Art and Architecture Students." *Art Documentation: Journal of the Art Libraries Society of North America* 25, no. 1 (2006): 38–42.

Benson, Lee, Ira Harkavy, and John Puckett. *Dewey's Dream: Universities and Democracies in an Age of Education Reform, Civil Society, Public Schools, and Democratic Citizenship.* Philadelphia, PA: Temple University Press, 2007.

Canizaro, V. B. "Design-Build in Architectural Education: Motivations, Practices, Challenges, Successes and Failures." *Archnet-IJAR: International Journal of Architectural Research* 6, no. 3 (2012): 20–36.

Colegrove, Tod. "Editorial Board Thoughts: Libraries as Makerspace?" *Information Technology & Libraries* 32, no. 1 (March 2013): 2–5.

"Course Evaluation." Unpublished raw data, University of Utah, 2014.

Foote, Jonathan. "Design-Build :: Build-Design." *Journal of Architectural Education* 65, no. 2 (2012): 52–58.

Kolb, David A. *Experiential Learning: Experience as the Source of Learning and Development.* 2nd ed. Upper Saddle River, NJ: Pearson Education, 2015.

Leousis, Kasia. "Outreach to Artists: Supporting the Development of a Research Culture for Master of Fine Arts Students." *Art Documentation: Journal of the Art Libraries Society of North America* 32, no. 1 (2013): 127–37.

Lingo, Elizabeth, and Steven Tepper. "The Creative Campus: Time for a 'C' Change." *The Chronicle of Higher Education.* Last modified October 10, 2010. Accessed February 14, 2015. http://chronicle.com/article/The-Creative-Campus-Time-for/124860/.

Newell, L. Jackson. *The Electric Edge of Academe: The Saga of Lucien L. Nunn and Deep Springs College.* Salt Lake City, UT: University of Utah Press, 2015.

Pershing, David. "President Pershing's Agenda for the U: The Inaugural Address." Audio file. University of Utah. 2012. Accessed February 14, 2015. http://admin.utah.edu/office_of_the_president/inauguration-recap.

Pitt, Richard, and Steven Tepper. *Double Majors: Influences, Identities, & Impacts.* Curb Center Report. Nashville, TN: Vanderbilt University, 2012.

Wallace, Lynn M. "A Librarian's Guide to Service-Learning." *Academy of Management Learning & Education* 4, no. 3 (2005): 385–90.

CHAPTER 12

APPLIED LEARNING AND THE ACADEMIC LIBRARY:
Creating Opportunities for Students to Lead

Anne Pemberton, Laura Wiegand, and Christopher Rhodes

Introduction

Applied learning, "a pedagogical model that places students in experiences requiring them to integrate theories, ideas, and skills they have learned in new contexts, thereby extending their learning,"[1] is one of the hallmarks at the University of North Carolina Wilmington (UNCW). In 2013, UNCW implemented its Quality Enhancement Plan (QEP) for accreditation review. The plan focuses on applied learning. UNCW, like many other universities, has strengthened its applied learning focus because of its correlation to student success.

Applied learning (of which experiential-learning, service-learning, and active-learning are components) has been linked to enhanced learning outcomes, student retention, job placement, and other positive impacts on students. Research indicates that applied learning increases students' personal engagement in learning, creating more meaningful learning experiences and opening other doors for students to grow professionally and personally.[2]

Kuh et al. studied the relationship between student engagement and student success, finding that there was a statistically significant correlation between academic persistence for first-year students and their level of engagement.[3] They concluded that universities that offer comprehensive programs designed to increase engagement, such as service learning opportunities, can impact grades and retention rates positively. Other studies confirm that multiple opportunities for students to engage in applied learning provide the most value, citing benefits of job placement and personal growth,[4] in addition to the positive outcomes for student retention.[5] This is a widely accepted conclusion backed up by meta-analyses of studies, such as the one conducted by Cielo et al., which find that service learning programs are linked to improved student outcomes in five areas, including "attitudes toward self, attitudes toward school and learning, civic engagement, social skills, and academic performance."[6]

High-impact practices, such as internships, service learning, and study abroad, have been linked in nationwide studies to student success, especially among traditionally underserved populations.[7] Other universities and schools have committed to a systematic emphasis on applied learning, such as SUNY Potsdam, which recently invested in a Center for Applied Learning.[8] Institutions, such as George Mason and Evergreen, frequently cited as examples of schools that facilitate student success, all integrate multiple opportunities for service, experiential, and applied learning across the curriculum and throughout the university.[9]

UNCW, and many other schools, have found ways to provide academic, financial, and administrative support to programs that seek to create applied learning opportunities for students.[10] The UNCW program that supports applied learning across the university is called "ETEAL" (Experiencing Transformative Education through Applied Learning).* It provides resources such as funding, training, mentoring, and advertising of opportunities for faculty and students.[11] Because of its relationship to student success, applied learning is not only encouraged and supported, it is also a required component of every student's academic career at UNCW. In the general education curriculum (called

---

* See ETEAL: An Overview at http://uncw.edu/eteal/overview/index.html.

"University Studies") students are required to complete "Explorations Beyond the Classroom Experience,"[12] which vary among students, but at their core, these are applied learning opportunities. Some students choose to complete faculty-mentored research projects, study abroad programs, internships, or service learning projects. While students are only required to complete one applied learning experience, most students choose to engage in applied learning through several avenues. An applied learning experience might be completed in a single class project or an entire semester overseas. The experiences vary, but the goal is the same.

With an undergraduate enrollment of just over 13,000 students and a graduate population of 1,700, UNCW offers fifty-five bachelor's degree programs in forty-nine majors, forty-two master's degree programs, and two doctoral degree programs. William Madison Randall Library is the main library for the campus with one small branch library (the Curriculum Materials Center) housed in the Education Building. There are currently twenty-two librarians and twenty-four staff working full-time, many of whom are engaged in creating applied learning experiences. Not only do students benefit from the participation and completion of these opportunities, the library as a whole benefits, and it provides excellent opportunities for students to lead the library.

Randall Library has facilitated and engaged students in applied learning opportunities in different ways over the last several years. Staff and librarians assist faculty and students in applied learning opportunities, create opportunities for students across the campus, and showcase the outputs of these experiences. This chapter seeks to describe the rationale behind the library's involvement in these initiatives, give some specific examples of opportunities created by or assisted by the library, and provide guidance on best practices for libraries wishing to engage in applied learning in similar ways. The authors of this chapter have served as leads for many student applied learning projects for the library and have been involved with applied learning at UNCW in a number of ways. Authors previously served as an applied learning fellow at the university,[13] collaborated with campus partners to create an online applied learning gallery highlighting exemplary projects at the university,[14] and led in the creation of several successful applied learning initiatives in which students participate.

A Culture of Student Leadership through Applied Learning

Randall Library is a highly student-focused organization with student success at the forefront of decision-making and operations. Staff and librarians are dedicated to ensuring students achieve their academic goals. The library is committed to providing an environment, services, and resources that are responsive to student needs. Applied learning has long been one of the methods utilized by Randall Library to engage students in activities that expand their experiential learning opportunities while providing the library with both input about student needs and products that meet them.

As is the case in most academic libraries, librarians are often involved directly with students' research through information literacy instruction, research help desk assistance, or individual consultations with students. In some cases, students may be working on a traditional research paper or presentation. In other cases, students may be gathering research for a directed independent study, a thesis, or in preparation for an internship. In any case, librarians have traditionally had a role in helping students apply the skills they have learned in the classroom to the research product. This has proved to be beneficial for both the library and the student. The student gains research skills and new knowledge about research resources while the library, and specifically the librarian involved, gains insight into students' interests and research behaviors. Students are not usually aware that by providing such input they help transform the services, collections, and spaces the library offers. All librarians at Randall Library are required to work at the Research Help Desk, no matter the position they hold. This is an example of the commitment the library has to student success, and to learning about students and the research endeavors they pursue. In addition to these traditional means of engaging students in applied learning, Randall Library has been able to facilitate student leadership roles along the way.

Expanding Student Leadership through Applied Learning Opportunities

Given Randall Library's role as the center for academic research on campus, students may use the library's unique position as a platform for leadership in applied learning:

1. Students may create library products, with the library serving in the role of "client" for applied learning projects.
2. The entire student body may lead and shape the future of the library through cross-campus collaborations for applied learning initiatives.
3. Students may voice their own ideas using our central location, which fosters conversations related to other campus applied learning projects and to showcase project outcomes.

Randall Library as Client

For applied learning projects that are tied to class assignments, the role of the library has been that of the "client." The library as a client is, in essence, contracting the services of the student(s) to produce a solution to an identified need. Such solutions may include reports, usability studies, artwork, videos, graphic design, websites, or marketing materials. The collaboration of library faculty and staff with students in two courses ("Typography" and "Introduction to Professional Writing") provide two examples of the library serving as client.

Changes made to Randall Library's second floor were a direct outcome of an applied learning project and a prime example of student work leading the library, in this case demonstrated visually to everyone who visits this floor of the library. In contrast with the first floor, where collaborative work and talking is welcomed, the second floor is for silent study. Based on student feedback, library staff recognized that visual cues to indicate that the floor is a quiet floor were needed and sought to launch a student-led "Quiet Campaign."

To achieve this, the library partnered with "Typography," a class in the UNCW Department of Art & Art History, and pitched the project as an applied learning opportunity. With the understanding that environmental graphic design exists at the intersection of communication design (design through visual storytelling) and the built environment (design through architecture), typography students were given the following client statement:

> Randall Library's goal is to promote quiet on the second
> floor, not through signs or redundant "shhh" symbols,
> but through visual cues that immediately illustrate to

our users the feeling of calm, tranquility, and silence. It is our hope to create the following: a learning environment that inspires study; a space for individual activities; a comfortable and inviting location; and a go-to area for learning. Our experience proves that too many signs can result in creating clutter and do not serve the purpose for which they are intended.

Along with this statement and a series of prompt questions ("What does quiet look like?" "What does it sound like?" "What is the relationship between seeing and hearing (visual and acoustic experience)?" "How can you create a design that will respond to and work within the existing visual environment?"), students were asked to design their own solutions, which were to be visual, noticeable, cost-effective, reproducible, nonpermanent, beautiful, sustainable, and functional.

Each student developed a concept paper that included mocked-up photos of the library along with their design idea, a rationale statement, a list of typefaces they would utilize, recommended materials, ideal color selections, and other necessary information about how their design could be fabricated. The concept papers served a dual purpose: first, they provided the library with a proposed design for the specific space; and second, they challenged the student to draw upon the skills learned in the typography course and apply them to a real world situation.

From the twelve student concepts, the library selected elements from four and partnered with a local vendor to have the designs fabricated into adhesive vinyl images adhered to columns and walls on the library's second floor. The campaign was considered a success by the faculty instructor, the students, and the library faculty and staff involved. Students applied their skills and, in turn, the library received a viable product, created by students, which is still in use (See Images 12.1 and 12.2). Students have responded well to the outcomes of "The Quiet Campaign;" the second floor is noticeably quieter with students enforcing quiet among themselves. The only signage or marketing indicating that the second floor is for quiet study are the graphics from the applied learning project, yet it is well-known in the student body that quiet is taken seriously on the library's second floor.

Image 12.1 and 12.2. Images of Quiet Campaign outputs.

For several years, the library has also partnered in applied learning experiences with "Introduction to Professional Writing," a class in the UNCW English Department. This course gives students an introduction to professional writing, including audience analysis and visual thinking. The format of the final product for the course is different from semester to semester and from instructor to instructor. Examples of products created by students in this course include: brochures that outline a particular service point in Randall Library; videos that introduce other UNCW students to various services or locations in Randall Library; usability study reports that analyze and provide feedback for various library websites; and posters that provide instructions on library technology (e.g. microform reader instructions). In each instance, the course instructor has contacted a librarian and described the focus of the course. The instructor and the librarian(s) work together to identify an area in need of student input or a product best created by students. This theme is worked into a practical class project for that semester. After this initial discussion, the librarian is invited to come speak with the students and provide necessary background information. Then the project is turned over to the students and they are asked to take the lead. If they need feedback, additional information, or review of drafts, the librarian(s) are available. At the end of the semester, the students present and share the outcomes of their projects to the librarian(s), and the librarian(s) provides feedback on the students' work, including information about how it will be used (e.g., if a video will be included on the library's website).

The fall 2015 semester's project was to provide usability reports on Randall Library's "BUILD Tutorial" (Beginning Undergraduate Information Literacy Development).[*] Based on Notre Dame's "Pot of Gold,"[†] this tutorial was launched in fall 2015, and all students enrolled in the university's required First Year Seminar were expected to complete it. The library needed students to provide feedback and make suggestions about the tutorial, and the students enrolled in "Introduction to Professional Writing" needed to complete a usability project. Students applied concepts learned throughout the semester to the usability process. Working in small groups, students went through the tutorial in its entirety and wrote a final report with recommendations, all of which were reasonable, thoughtful, and useful. Students suggested that the graphics be updated to look more modern, to shorten particular sections, and to change the tutorial navigation. These recommendations, and others, are in the process of being implemented, and the tutorial will be better because of this applied learning experience and students' leadership. The student suggestions are shaping the future development of this tutorial, which will likely be used for years to come.

Creating Leadership Opportunities through Cross-Campus Collaborations

The best example of creating student leadership opportunities through cross-campus collaboration is Randall Library's annual Flash Fiction contest. The Flash Fiction contest is a creative writing contest, open to all UNCW students. It aims to stimulate a conversation among participants about a current library issue and to encourage student leadership. Flash Fiction puts students in charge as they write, illustrate, and copyedit stories

---

[*] For more about BUILD: Beginning Undergraduate Information Literacy Development see http://library.uncw.edu/build/.

[†] See the Pot of Gold Information Literacy Tutorial at https://library.nd.edu/instruction/potofgold/.

before assembling them all into a high-quality anthology for distribution throughout the campus and beyond. Flash Fiction places Randall Library at the center of a student learning initiative that connects different academic branches of the university through a common endeavor linking creating writing, art, and publishing. Through the Flash Fiction Contest, students get hands-on experience in graphic design with the Department of Art & Art History and in publishing with the Department of Creative Writing's Publishing Laboratory. At the library, after the contest details are set, planning begins on a book reception and party that will be student led from beginning to end with readings, discussions about process, and a display of the winning stories and illustrations.

Early in the spring semester, the library chooses a relevant theme. Once the contest is announced, participants are given five days to write a 500-word (or less) piece of fiction on the theme, which mentions Randall Library. Cash prizes are offered for the top three winners, but the real honor is getting published. Once the stories are collected, the entries are whittled down by a group of judges who choose the top three stories and select a number of runners up.

Graphic design students create illustrations to accompany the stories, with the library acting as client and mediator. Graduate students in the Publishing Laboratory are responsible for putting together the Flash Fiction anthology (including cover art, copyediting, book design, etc.). Library representatives provide mentoring to the students working in the Publishing Lab and manage the content details, but the outcome is very much student-driven.

The final element of the annual Flash Fiction contest is a book reception and party, where the fruits of the applied learning labor are celebrated and shared among the students. At the event, the professionally published books are handed out, student writers read their winning stories, illustrators talk about the challenges involved in designing for fiction, and book publishers-to-be lecture on books as craft. Flash Fiction has become a popular, fun, engaging experience, and student participants have commented on feeling a sense of accomplishment upon completion. It provides students with an opportunity to apply their skills, produce tangible outcomes in the library and on campus, and gives the library an opportunity to work with students directly.

More Than Four Walls: A Showcase of Applied Learning and Leadership

Randall Library is not just a laboratory where applied learning initiatives can ignite and develop, it also serves as a place for showcasing applied learning byproducts and fostering conversations about the importance of student learning through hands-on experience. Randall Library provides opportunities for students to spotlight applied learning for their faculty, other students, parents, and the community. The library has several areas for exhibits and programming, so it is a natural meeting space for UNCW academic departments to display and celebrate student-initiated projects such as the Flash Fiction contest. In addition, the library hosts twice yearly poster sessions for the UNCW Wentworth Fellows' and the Undergraduate Research and Creativity Showcase, which feature students as leaders in research at the institution. The Wentworth Fellowship was established in 2001 to enable a select number of students to travel to sites, nationally or abroad, associated with literary authors and texts. The Undergraduate Research and Creativity Showcase, which highlights innovative student research and creative scholarly activity, is on display for the entire campus and community, exhibiting upward of seventy-five student posters. Undergraduate research and study abroad are both core categories of applied learning supported at UNCW. During the times of the year when these projects are on display, areas of Randall Library overflow as student research becomes a focal point. The poster sessions are widely attended by the campus community and provide students facetime with faculty from around campus, often including the university's upper administration. This is an unparalleled opportunity for students to discuss their research with the people who lead UNCW, and it allows Randall Library staff and faculty to experience firsthand how their day to day work informs student success.

In the fall of 2015, the student work once again appeared front and center at the library as the largest gallery space in the library showcased "Dubtown Skates: Skateboarding Culture and Applied Learning at UNCW." In this exhibit, skateboard designs from students enrolled in the Art & Art History Department course, "Two-Dimensional Design," highlighted what they learned about the fundamentals of art through a hands-on project judged by a local business owner. To draw attention to the exhibit, the student artists, the instructor, and the owner of a local surf and skateboard shop came together to discuss the project, the art, and the rich skateboard culture on the UNCW campus in a panel discussion event hosted by the library. The event attracted a wide range of users to Randall Library, including members of the community, and allowed the library to show off its public art from local artists. This was a unique opportunity for students interested in both art and skateboarding to lead the campus community in a discussion about the intersection of the two. Individuals who had never set foot in the library were drawn to this exhibit and potentially created new library users.

Image 12.3. Image of "Dubtown Skates" panel along with skateboard deck art.

The library has also been a partner for providing virtual spaces that showcase student work and facilitate discussions. Students expressed a need for such spaces, so the library created them. Given the library's experience with digital collections, online exhibits, and web technologies, this was a natural partnership between students and the library. The desire to showcase students' applied learning projects drove a library initiative to create the "Applied Learning Gallery."[15] The library partnered with other academic units to create this space, which allows students to describe, in their own words, their completed applied learning projects and to share these projects with prospective employers, graduate schools, and others.

In addition to providing a space to showcase exemplary applied learning projects, this website was also designed to connect the various partners who participate in and support applied learning, both across the university and in the community. It is set up to serve as a selective archive of examples, helping both faculty and students to identify types of projects that have been completed in the past, and to provide them with ideas for future projects. Library faculty and staff expertise was employed to create and maintain a website for users to search and browse projects. Students can upload and describe their projects themselves, and administrators can review and publish submissions. Without student leadership, this showcase might never had been created. The library served as the technical developer, graphic designer, project co-lead, and web hosting service for the site. While providing support for this particular online space may seem outside of the normal scope for a library, this collaboration depicts the library as a valuable partner in campus applied learning initiatives, and gives students a space where they can talk about applied learning on their own terms.

Best Practices

The first step in encouraging student leadership through applied learning is to identify campus partnerships, including instructors interested in adding a service or experiential learning component to their classes, or programs that produce outcomes that could be displayed or integrated into library programing. These partnerships may stem from pre-professional programs where students are seeking opportunities to apply their learning, or from campus services such as the Career Center or Undergraduate Research Centers, which actively support student activity related to applied learning.

To be a successful client for class assignment and projects, the library should work with the instructor to set clear, achievable goals for the project, and to provide sufficient background information and supporting materials. Library faculty and staff found it helpful to provide background information and an explanation of the identified need in a variety of formats, such as a written client statement, a video introduction, links to information, a classroom visit (or synchronous meeting time) both at the introductory stage and, if possible, a follow-up visit at the first draft stage.

It is important to remember that unlike when contracting with a professional service, the outcome is dictated by the needs of the assignment and instructor, as well as the skills and limitations of the students. This is a pedagogical activity with the goal of enhancing student learning, and not with the goal of giving the library a solution that they can use out of the box. It is also important to be aware of the limitations of classroom time. The outcomes sought by the library should be realistic and based on the amount of time in the class dedicated to the project. During the duration of the project, the client (the library) should be available to promptly answer student requests for clarification if they arise. If time permits, the client may want to give feedback at the draft stage so that the students know if they are on the right track. The outcomes of the project should be shared with the client, ideally in presentation style or a final project report, including any associated products in electronic format. Finally, the client should provide feedback or, even more effective, demonstrate real-world use of selected work to the students. Assessing and acknowledging student work is an important part of applied learning, otherwise the student is not informed of the practical outcome of their work nor informed about improvements that could be made to their skillset.

When students are given the opportunity for creativity, the results can be completely unexpected. However, it can be difficult for libraries to relinquish preconceived ideas of what the outcome should be or look like. Be prepared from the outset to accept (and encourage!) creativity. If the product must conform to certain standards, make sure to explain these at the outset. Try not to let past practices (e.g., "Our brochures are always in this format!") dictate the outcomes; instead, be ready for surprising interpretations of your instructions.

For a more formal overview of best practices, consult the National Society for Experiential Education's "Eight Principles for Experiential Learning."[16] They state that "Intention, Preparedness and Planning, Authenticity, Reflection, Orientation and Training, Monitoring and Continuous Improvement, Assessment and Evaluation, Acknowledgement" should be incorporated into all applied learning. Even when serving as a client, understanding these best practices can help the library be a better partner to faculty and instructors, and facilitate successful applied learning and leadership.

When creating cross-campus applied learning opportunities, such as the Flash Fiction contest previously described, best practices include effective communication with the other collaborators, agreeing upon outcomes at the outset, and determining ahead of time who will take the lead on different parts of the project. It is important for each group to outline individual expectations from the beginning, bearing in mind that the goal of applied learning is to produce student outcomes. Various collaborators should focus on the activities and outcomes that meet the students' needs, not necessarily the needs of the department or campus unit. From the students' point of view, to reduce confusion it is also important that it is clear who the lead is, what their expectations are, and with whom the student should be communicating. Certainly, students are leaders in these opportunities, but even leaders need boundaries and guidance. In some instances, the library has found that it is best if the students report only with their assigned instructor and that any cross-departmental correspondence occur only between campus staff members.

As discussed above, one of the easiest ways of supporting applied learning is by offering the library facility or virtual space to foster conversations and showcase outcomes of applied learning. This can be through gallery space to display artwork, projects, or virtual online galleries of project outcomes. In these situations, the library should treat the students with the same professional respect that they would treat any user or group who was occupying the space for an exhibit or program by providing adequate space, signage, and marketing. This also means that students, like any other professional person or group, should be expected to meet deadlines and follow rules and decorum of the building or virtual space. Creating and hosting a programming event for the campus or community around the students' work is another way to extend the reach of the students' work and provide potential networking opportunities.

Benefits of Participating in Applied Learning

The benefits of supporting applied learning in the library include products created at no cost, opportunities to educate the students about the client (library), and occasions to network with project stakeholders (campus partners, faculty, etc.).[17] Randall Library has received tangible products, such as signage, displays, marketing products, and assessment (including usability reports), as a result of these projects.

Being a client for applied learning projects has also allowed the library to share issues and concerns with students, faculty, and other campus partners, who gain a deeper understanding of the academic library. Conversely, by interacting with students beyond the research help desk, library faculty and staff can keep current with each population of students, learning more about students' interests, perceptions, and the academic environment, and encouraging them to take an active leadership role in changing their library. In addition, faculty, instructors, and other campus units view the library as a partner in student success outside of the standard role of providing library materials and information literacy instruction and assistance. Through collaboration, the library also learns about faculty interests and teaching practices.

Finally, many universities have identified applied learning as a strategic priority in their campus planning. It is crucial that the library demonstrate its value to the campus community. Aligning the library's initiatives with a university strategic goal demonstrates the library's value and relevance to the institution. Other libraries may wish to follow suit and determine if applied learning is important to their institutions and to create opportunities for the library to facilitate applied learning. Depending on the programs in place at the institution, there may also be funding opportunities to support applied learning initiatives, either for the students involved or for the library. At UNCW, the applied learning opportunities provided by the library are seen as a service to the university, and the campus has recognized this in tangible ways. For example, Randall Library received seed money from the campus for an Honors papers digitization project because hosting student projects was a priority to the university.

Conclusion and Future Plans

Library faculty and staff have discussed other avenues for participation in applied learning with a focus on facilitating student leadership. UNCW is currently investigating a campus-wide e-portfolio requirement and the library can likely be involved in this effort. Also, perhaps students can provide needed input. The university's institutional repository (IR), administered by the library, is yet another arena for students to provide leadership to the library in order to best showcase applied learning to the campus. While initially focused on including faculty publications only, the IR has recently been expanded to include student work.

Additionally, opportunities such as the Flash Fiction Contest will be continually expanded and improved. Plans for the 2016 contest include a connection to a UNCW Student Art Invitational curated by the faculty of the Department of Art & Art History and juried by members of the community. The reception and book party will double as an art opening, where the library and university community can celebrate the physical manifestation of student work and skills, and provide a showcase for student initiative and leadership.

The library's involvement in applied learning continues to expand and continues to be a useful and gratifying experience for students and library faculty and staff. Randall Library is proud of the work it has done to serve as a client, create opportunities for applied learning, and showcase applied learning experiences. Other academic libraries could benefit from exploring these opportunities at their institutions. Working with campus instructors and students to engage the library in the learning process is beneficial for all involved, and serves to place students in valuable leadership roles in the academic library.

Notes

1.   "What Is Applied Learning?" University of North Carolina Wilmington, last accessed April 7, 2016, http://www.uncw.edu/eteal/overview/AppliedLearning.html.
2.   Michele Wolff and Shannon M Tinney, "Service-Learning & College Student Success," *Academic Exchange Quarterly* (Spring 2006): 57–61.
3.   George Kuh, Ty Cruce, Rick Shoup, and Jillian Kinzie, "Unmasking the Effects of Student Engagement on First-Year College Grades and Persistence," *The Journal of Higher Education* 79, no. 5 (2008): 540–563.
4.   Jeffrey Coker and Desiree J. Porter, "Maximizing Experiential Learning for Student Success," *Change: The Magazine of Higher Learning* 47, no. 1 (2015): 66–72.
5.   Meaghan Mundy and Janet Eyler, "Service-Learning & Retention: Promising Possibilities, Potential Partnerships" (Report No. ED482320), last accessed April 7, 2016, http://eric.ed.gov/?id=ED482320. 2002.
6.   Christine Celio, Joseph Durlak, and Allison Dymnicki, "A Meta-Analysis of the Impact of Service Learning on Students," *Journal of Experiential Education* 34, no. 2 (2011): 164–181.
7.   Ashley Finley and Tia Brown McNair, *Assessing Underserved Students' Engagement in High-Impact Practices.* (Washington, DC: Association of American Colleges and Universities, 2013).
8.   "Center for Applied Learning," The State University of New York at Potsdam, last accessed April 7, 2016. http://www.potsdam.edu/academics/appliedlearning/.
9.   George Kuh, Jillian Kinzie, John Schuh, and Elizabeth Whitt, *Student Success in College: Creating Conditions That Matter.* (San Francisco: Jossey-Bass, 2010).
10. Tom Ehrlich, "Service-Learning in Undergraduate Education: Where Is It Going?" *Carnegie Perspectives*, July 2005, last accessed April 7, 2016, http://files.eric.ed.gov/fulltext/ED498997.pdf. 2005.

11. Jacquelyn Lee, Kristen DeVall, Jess Boersman, Jimmy Reeves, and Melanie Forehand, "Cultivating Community Engagement through Applied Learning: A Transformative Campus-Wide Model," Presentation at the Pathways to Achieving Civic Engagement (PACE) Conference, University of North Carolina Wilmington, Wilmington, NC, February 5, 2014.
12. "University Studies," University of North Carolina Wilmington, last accessed April 7, 2016, http://uncw.edu/universitystudies/.
13. "ETEAL for Faculty and Staff," University of North Carolina Wilmington, last accessed April 7, 2016, http://uncw.edu/eteal/overview/Faculty.html.
14. "Applied Learning Gallery," University of North Carolina Wilmington, last accessed April 7, 2016, https://randall3.uncw.edu/applied_learning/.
15. "Applied Learning Gallery." University of North Carolina Wilmington, last accessed April 7, 2016, https://randall3.uncw.edu/applied_learning/.
16. "Eight Principles of Good Practice for All Experiential Learning Activities," National Society for Experiential Education, last accessed April 7, 2016, http://www.nsee.org/8 -principles.
17. Leora Waldner and Debra Hunter, "Client-Based Courses: Variations in Service Learning," *Journal of Public Affairs Education* 14, no. 2 (2008): 219–23.

Bibliography

Celio, Christine, Joseph Durlak, and Allison Dymnicki. "A Meta-Analysis of the Impact of Service Learning on Students." *Journal of Experiential Education* 34, no. 2 (2011): 164–181.

Coker, Jeffrey and Desiree J Porter. "Maximizing Experiential Learning for Student Success." *Change: The Magazine of Higher Learning* 47, no. 1 (2015): 66–72.

Ehrlich, Tom. "Service-Learning In Undergraduate Education: Where Is It Going?" *Carnegie Perspectives*, July 2005. Last accessed April 7, 2016. http://files.eric.ed.gov/fulltext/ED498997.pdf.

Finley, Ashley and Tia Brown McNair. *Assessing Underserved Students' Engagement in High-Impact Practices.* Washington, DC: Association of American Colleges and Universities, 2013.

Hesburgh Library, University of Notre Dame. "Pot of Gold Information Literacy Tutorial." Last accessed April 7, 2016. https://library.nd.edu/instruction/potofgold/.

Kuh, George, Ty Cruce, Rick Shoup, and Jillian Kinzie. "Unmasking the Effects of Student Engagement on First-Year College Grades and Persistence." *The Journal of Higher Education* 79, no. 5 (2008): 540–563.

Kuh, George, Jillian Kinzie, John Schuh, and Elizabeth Whitt. *Student Success in College: Creating Conditions That Matter.* San Francisco: Jossey-Bass, 2010.

Lee, Jacquelyn, Kristen DeVall, Jess Boersman, Jimmy Reeves, and Melanie Forehand. "Cultivating Community Engagement through Applied Learning: A Transformative Campus-Wide Model." Presentation at the Pathways to Achieving Civic Engagement (PACE) Conference, University of North Carolina Wilmington, Wilmington, NC, February 5, 2014.

Mundy, Meaghan and Janet Eyler. "Service-Learning & Retention: Promising Possibilities, Potential Partnerships" (Report No. ED482320). Last accessed April 7, 2016. http://eric.ed.gov/?id=ED482320. 2002.

National Society for Experiential Education. "Eight Principles of Good Practice for All Experiential Learning Activities." Last accessed April 7, 2016. http://www.nsee.org/8-principles.

The State University of New York at Potsdam. "Center for Applied Learning." Last accessed April 7, 2016. http://www.potsdam.edu/academics/appliedlearning/.

University of North Carolina Wilmington. "Applied Learning Gallery." Last accessed April 7, 2016. https://randall3.uncw.edu/applied_learning/.

University of North Carolina Wilmington. "ETEAL: An Overview." Last accessed April 7, 2016. http://uncw.edu/eteal/overview/index.html.

University of North Carolina Wilmington. "ETEAL for Faculty and Staff." Last accessed April 7, 2016. http://uncw.edu/eteal/overview/Faculty.html.

University of North Carolina Wilmington. "University Studies." Last accessed April 7, 2016. http://uncw.edu/universitystudies/.

University of North Carolina Wilmington "What Is Applied Learning?" Last accessed April 7, 2016. http://www.uncw.edu/eteal/overview/AppliedLearning.html.

Waldner, Leora and Debra Hunter. "Client-Based Courses: Variations in Service Learning." *Journal of Public Affairs Education* 14, no. 2 (2008): 219–23.

William Madison Randall Library, University of North Carolina Wilmington. "BUILD: Beginning Undergraduate Information Literacy Development." Last accessed April 7, 2016. http://library.uncw.edu/build/.

Wolff, Michele and Shannon Tinney. "Service-Learning & College Student Success." *Academic Exchange Quarterly*, (Spring 2006): 57–61.

Part 5

STUDENT GROUPS AS LIBRARY LEADERS

CHAPTER 13

MOBILIZING STUDENT LEADERS TO ENHANCE A FIRST-YEAR COHORT PROGRAM

Marybeth McCartin, Nicole E. Brown, and Paula Feid

Introduction

This chapter provides a case study describing New York University librarians' experience leveraging a pre-existing group of student leaders involved in a school-wide, first-year experience program, which was informed by a focus on high-impact practices in higher educational environments. In 2012, the NYU College of Arts and Science (CAS) implemented the College Cohort Program (CCP) to build community, increase retention, facilitate academic success, and develop student leaders. The program's commitment to peer leadership is evidenced by the deployment of selected upper-division students, called "college leaders," to co-lead each cohort group. We describe the CCP program and explore how we mobilized these student leaders to design, develop, and deliver large-scale library instruction to meet the affective and cognitive learning goals for this program.

Background and History

Institutional Context

New York University is a large, urban, research institution located in Greenwich Village in New York City, and spanning the globe with campuses in Abu Dhabi and Shanghai, and eleven smaller study abroad sites around the world. NYU enrolls more than 25,000 undergraduate students. Nearly one-third (29 percent) of the undergraduate student body is enrolled in NYU's College of Arts and Science (CAS), where each fall approximately 1,500 first-year students arrive.[1]

Elmer Holmes Bobst Library is the main library of a 5.9 million-volume system comprised of eleven libraries. Bobst Library is an expansive space, and it is busy: close to 3,000 seats are spread over twelve floors, and 10,000 visitors enter the building every day when school is in session.[2] NYU's collection includes more than 200,000 thousand serial titles, and over 5 million microforms, and provides access to thousands of electronic resources.[3]

Our research instruction program is robust, with many workshops offered every semester. Our department, Undergraduate Instructional Services, leads course-integrated library instruction for freshmen and sophomores, while more than thirty-five subject specialist librarians teach the majority of upper-division undergraduate and graduate-level library instruction. Given the size of the University, the Undergraduate Instructional Services department is relatively small, with four librarians. For this reason, large-scale sustainable instructional programming requires a partnership approach. In 2012, we seized an opportunity to become a partner with the CAS College Cohort Program.

The College Cohort Program

In the spring of 2012, NYU's dean of libraries asked us (the core library instructional team at the time), to attend an exploratory meeting with our administrator colleagues in the College of Arts and Science to discuss a school-wide program that they were in planning to launch in the fall. The College Cohort Program (CCP) would place every incoming CAS student in a cohort group with the intention of building community, increasing retention, facilitating academic success, and developing student leaders. Student life, academic inquiry, and service would be the organizing principles.

At the same time, CAS was unveiling a new curricular requirement: each student would be required to enroll in one of ninety Freshman Seminars, which would be "small, discussion-based courses taught by the University's top professors, who are leading thinkers in their fields."[4]

CAS administrators explained their plan to scale the program: each cohort would be comprised of the students enrolled in two seminars who share an academic advisor. The cohorts would be co-led by the advisor and an upper-division student called a "college leader." Cohorts would meet biweekly throughout the first semester to focus on topics such as study skills, time management, and diversity in the college learning environment. Grading would be pass/fail.

In fall 2012, the College of Arts and Science officially launched the CCP with the mission to provide "all CAS first-year students the opportunity to build a small community within CAS that is diverse in intellectual range, serves as a crucible for debate and scholarship, and fosters a welcoming and supportive home."[5] Since then, every fall brings forty-four cohort sections of thirty-six students each. There are seven meetings throughout fall semester that expose students to the same content in the same sequence, for example:

- Cohort Meeting 1: *Welcome and Introduction to CCP*
- Cohort Meeting 2: *Understanding the Liberal Arts*
- Cohort Meeting 3: *Research Readiness*
- Cohort Meeting 4: *Midterm Preparation & Pre-Registration Advising*
- Cohort Meeting 5: *Arts and Culture in NYC*
- Cohort Meeting 6: *NYU and the World*
- Cohort Meeting 7: *Winding Down the Semester*

CAS administrators asked us to create and lead the *Research Readiness* sessions. We always wondered what would happen if every freshman within a school received library instruction—and now it was happening. How could we create a genuine partnership?

From Broad Context to Mutual Benefits

In a recent mixed-methods study on collaboration across campus allies and partners, Booth showed that "curricular collaborations between librarians and faculty/staff coordinators of first-year and other academic programs can increase the efficacy and relevance of library instruction by facilitating shared outcomes and a 'unified front' of skills assessment and messaging around information literacy competencies and expectations."[6] In this spirit, alongside a renewed focus on high-impact educational practices and the social-emotional aspects of learning, we set out to work with the CCP.

The CCP at NYU exemplifies a national trend to engage in educational practices that are proven to impact student success. Like most student affairs professionals, our administrator colleagues in CAS are influenced by Astin's work on student involvement, which underscores the role of peers as "the single most potent source of influence on growth and development during the undergraduate years."[7] Astin argues that peers impact every aspect of student development—from cognitive to affective, and psychological to behavioral. By creating the college leader role, the CCP sought to maximize this impact.

Connecting with High-Impact Educational Practices

To understand the goals and benefits of the CCP, it is important to explore the underlying theories that guided its development; one such theory is high-impact educational practices (HIPs). Identified in work led by Kuh, high-impact educational practices are teaching and learning practices that "have been widely tested and have been shown to be beneficial for college students from many backgrounds."[8] HIPs include such things as first year seminars, common intellectual experiences, and learning communities.

The CCP is a clear example of several high-impact practices in action, making it a logical partner for the library. It is a first-year experience program that links with a seminar and uses a learning community model. The curriculum further incorporates HIPs, such as diversity and service learning, through cohort meeting topics and activities. Academic librarians have long impacted student success by teaching information literacy to students across the disciplines, but intentionally integrating our work with high-impact practices can optimize our instructional efforts. High-impact practices are "excellent opportunities for embedding information literacy" because they "often include active, contextual pedagogies, span the college experience, and engage students in the learning process."[9] Indeed, many libraries are already active in high-impact educational practices. A recent study explored academic libraries and student retention by surveying library deans at more than 200 public universities. Results showed that library leaders "tend to view their library as being involved with many high-impact practices," and that "information literacy instruction was a primary theme for first-year seminars, learning communities (among high alignment libraries), writing-intensive courses, and capstone courses and projects."[10]

Addressing the Affective Domain

Engaging with peers is a key component of affective development during college. Deploying college leaders in a learning community positions the CCP to impact student learning beyond the traditional cognitive domain. From a student affairs perspective, Astin identified "student-student interaction" as a practice that produces positive affective results.[11] He asserts that "how the students *approach* the general education (and how the faculty actually *deliver* the curriculum) is far more important than the formal curricular content and structure…suggesting that one of the crucial factors in the educational development of the undergraduate is the degree to which the student is actively engaged or *involved* in the undergraduate experience."[12]

In the library literature, Schroeder and Cahoy identified the importance of addressing students' "attitudes, emotions, interests, motivation, self-efficacy, and values."[13] They built on Kuhlthau's mid-eighties work on the role of feelings in the library research process[14] and Mellon's finding that first-year students associated the library with fear and anxiety that got in the way of their learning.[15]

Mellon found that students perceive peers as competent library users and fear that asking questions could expose their own inadequacy.[16] Thirty years after its publication, this finding still resonates in students' tendency to preface their questions with, "I should already know this, but…" Mellon identified "the size of the library; not knowing where things were; not knowing what to do; and not knowing how to begin the research process"[17] as key sources of library anxiety. The research around the affective domain made us optimistic about leveraging college leaders to help freshmen normalize their feelings of being overwhelmed by our imposing building, large collection, and the mystique of conducting research in an academic library.

The *ACRL Framework for Information Literacy* also emphasizes this dimension of learning through the inclusion of "dispositions," which "describe ways in which to address the affective, attitudinal, or valuing dimension of learning."[18] Our CCP *Research Readiness* lesson plan most closely maps to the "Research as Inquiry" frame, which calls for students to acknowledge the open-ended and exploratory nature of research, value intellectual curiosity, and demonstrate intellectual humility.

Why Mobilize College Leaders?

The CAS College Leader Program leverages peer learning and the affective domain by developing peer mentors to help first-year students transition socially and academically to life at NYU. Coping with forty-four cohort sections and 1,500 students is a significant human resource challenge, and these student leaders provide a solution. College leaders spend extensive face-time with students in their cohorts, becoming consistent figures in the lives of first-year CAS students. Their peer status makes them relatable and approachable.

College leaders undergo substantial training and development to build their leadership capacity. Each year, CAS administrators appoint three experienced college leaders as college captains who co-lead training sessions, hold monthly meetings, and conduct periodic check-ins with college leaders. Over the semester, college leaders work with their academic advisor partner to plan and co-facilitate each seventy-five-minute bi-weekly session, including *Research Readiness*, which takes place in early October. This preparation and training puts college leaders in a position to contribute meaningfully to *Research Readiness*. Collaborating with a vetted, trained, and collegial group of student leaders has proved to be a strategic advantage, and their contributions have been critical to scaling our CCP instructional efforts.

Pilot Year: College Leaders in the Background

In 2012, the pilot year, college leaders had a small role in the *Research Readiness* session but were not involved in planning. Instead, we worked with CCP administrators to develop the session. One administrator, who had recently finished a doctoral program, proposed that the session focus on JSTOR and EndNote. The other believed that demonstrating as many databases as possible was critical. Our idea, on the other hand, was to contextualize the academic library and emphasize its role in today's information landscape.

What seemed like a conflict became an opportunity to unpack and examine our perspectives together. The administrators shared that EndNote, JSTOR, and other specific databases were invaluable to them as graduate students, and they were eager introduce these resources at the earliest stage possible. We shared our hesitation about teaching specific databases and tools that address no immediate information need. We expressed concern about repetitive library instruction in the freshman year, explaining that many CAS freshmen attend a library research workshop with their *Writing the Essay* class or freshman seminar. These courses include research assignments, providing a better venue for introducing specific databases and tools. By differentiating instruction, we hoped to avoid a chorus of "We already did this in CCP!" Lastly, we shared an analysis of our instruction feedback surveys: the data showed that students remained fuzzy and apprehensive about navigating the physical library. Having clarified our perspectives, the discussion circled back to the overarching goal of the College Cohort Program—to cultivate academic success by building a supportive community—and we resolved to design the session around this goal.

The *Research Readiness* lesson plan included a conceptual element about the nature of scholarly communication and a practical component, with student teams exploring different service points and spaces in Bobst Library. We reached out to our subject specialist colleagues for help leading the forty-four sections and provided them with training and a ready-to-use lesson plan. The session opened with a ten-minute mini-lecture about the university as a community of scholars with the library at its hub, connecting people to knowledge and facilitating scholarly conversation. Students were encouraged to think of themselves as the newest members of our scholarly community and to envision joining the scholarly conversation—tiptoeing in with their first research assignment, and deepening their engagement as they proceed through their undergraduate years. Next, we divided the thirty-six students into groups of four. Each group scoped out two library locations (e.g., a section of the stacks, Reference, Circulation, Special Collections, the Research Commons) and answered a few questions about how the space supports the library's function as a nexus of scholarship. When the groups came back to the classroom, each presented their findings.

The role of the college leaders was to corral the students into groups and distribute location assignments. Along with the advisor, college leaders checked in with the students in various locations and made sure they returned to the classroom within the time limit. The college leaders also provided the last word of the session, testifying to their "favorite thing" about the library—be it a choice study space, go-to database, or a redeeming Ask-a-Librarian experience.

Feedback about Pilot Research Readiness Session

At the end of the fall semester, we invited library instructors to a thank-you reception and debrief. We captured their responses to "What went well?" and "What didn't go so well?" Several library instructors were pleased to talk about the scholarly communication cycle and welcome cohort students into our reciprocal learning community. Others questioned whether the students grasped this concept and its relevance. Some instructors felt that the mini-lecture was hard to deliver because it was so tightly timed and scripted to accommodate a packed lesson plan. Some found it difficult to coax student teams to report out about the library spaces they visited. In discussing college leaders' contributions to the session, library instructors were unanimous in their praise, citing the positive influence that they had on student participation. One librarian said, "It was great when the college leader and advisor chimed in about their library experiences and offered tips."

CAS advisors' feedback indicated that the *Research Readiness* session helped develop students' knowledge about the library's services, collections, and spaces. One advisor remarked, "...I think that it was useful for them to see the different study spaces, with their different social expectations, and to understand how to get research assistance, et cetera." Another commented, "I think students want to learn about the resources and physical spaces of Bobst, so this is an important aspect of their freshman experience." Several recommended that the session place more emphasis on the availability of databases. Overall, advisors' responses to the session were mixed; they acknowledged the value of the session but saw room for improvement.

Feedback from college leaders emphasized that it was helpful for students to explore the physical library space. They especially enjoyed the "jigsaw" aspect in which student groups reported back to their classmates about different services and spaces. The college leaders used words and phrases such as "orient," "comfortable," and "find their bearings" to describe the strengths of the session. One college leader commented, "Overall, it was an amazing program but can be improved in a multitude of ways. It is a definite must for all incoming students." Echoing the concerns of the CAS academic advisors, the college leaders felt that this session should have included the library's digital resources.

In summing up the pilot year, we concluded that the college leaders were being underutilized and began envisioning a larger role for them, starting as early as the lesson planning stage. CCP administrators enthusiastically agreed and suggested that we work with the three college captains. This decision turned out to be a game-changer.

Second Year: College Leaders Increase Participation

We invited college captains to join us for regular meetings throughout the summer of 2013 to plan the next iteration of *Research Readiness*. They confirmed our sense that last year's mini-lecture about scholarly communication had not fully connected with students and suggested pivoting in a more practical direction. Agreeing with college leaders' pilot year feedback, the college captains thought the session should focus on exploring databases. They also felt that students should have the experience of searching the catalog and retrieving a book from the stacks. We articulated our concern about the futility of finding sources for the sake of it and pointed out that courses with research assignments are a better fit for that type of activity.

We reached a compromise and agreed to integrate a database searching experience. All agreed on the value of sending students out to explore and get comfortable navigating the library's physical space, so we kept this in the lesson plan. Seizing on the community-building goal of the CCP, we incorporated a team-building component to help strengthen student connections. This idea came from our experience designing professional development opportunities for teaching librarians that leverage sociocultural learning theories and center around social interaction. Sociocultural learning theories, commonly associated with Vygotsky, describe learning and development as embedded in social events and occurring as a learner interacts with other people and objects in the collaborative environment.[19] Making the *Research Readiness* session more social and less like a "class" seemed like a way to achieve desired outcomes while avoiding the pitfalls of the pilot year, namely students' disengagement during the mini-lecture and their reluctance to participate in the debrief following the activity.

With this in mind, we decided to devote most of the session to a friendly competition in which student teams would seek out several library locations, take a team "selfie" at each spot, then return to share their photos and findings with the class. We selected the locations and wrote corresponding clues. The tech-savvy college captains worked out a solution for uploading team selfies so the librarian and college leader could judge the photos in real time and announce the "winners" when students returned to the classroom. To prepare, we conducted a practice run at the fall college leader training intensive, with the student leaders acting as cohort students. They responded enthusiastically to the plan.

The forty-four sections of *Research Readiness* took place over a two-week period in October 2013. After a brief introduction in the classroom, the librarian introduced the activity. The college leader grouped students into teams, had them designate a team smartphone, helped them create a Google Drive folder to share with the librarian, and provided technical troubleshooting. The library instructors handed each team a set of nine clues leading to various locations around the library. The locations were strategically chosen to cover spaces and services deemed essential for undergraduates. Along with the clues, teams were given a map of Bobst Library and an exact time to be back in the classroom. Clues ran the gamut, including realistic scenarios such as:

- You're hungry! Make your way to the Snack Lounge and take a photo of a delicious snack option.
- Lower Levels 1 & 2 are open twenty-four hours. Get your team together and strike an "it's 3 a.m. and we've been studying all night" pose.
- You have a group project and need to meet somewhere to talk it through. Go to South Side of the 5th Floor and take a picture of your team "working on" this project.

Some clues required students to use databases:

- Go to the Historical *New York Times* (link provided) and find an article from the 1930s about the World's Fair. Take a screenshot of the article you find.
- Go to *ProQuest Central* and search on Brooklyn Bridge. Refine your results to peer-reviewed journals and select an article. Upload a screenshot of the article and the "happy researchers" who found it.

Other clues provided students with the experience of finding books:

- Go to catalog to find the book *Gangland Gotham: New York's Notorious Mob Bosses*. Click through to the detailed description and take a screenshot showing the SUBJECTS covered in the book. (Tip: Subjects are useful for finding additional books!)
- You need a book about the history of cheese making. Most of the books seem to be between SF231-SF274. Go to this area of the stacks and capture a photo of books and call numbers in this section.

As teams followed the clues, they took selfies at each location and uploaded their photos. Back in the classroom, the librarian and college leader monitored the photos and selected a few of the most fun, original, and illuminating as winners. When students returned, they seemed to enjoy viewing the winning photos along with a selection of other uploads. College leaders concluded the session by sharing something they wished they had known about the library as a freshman.

Research Readiness library instructors reported that students found this year's lesson plan more engaging than the previous year. CAS administrators' 2013–2014 CCP assessment data showed that 57 percent of cohort students found the session helpful. We had expected higher percentages. It seemed that students found the activity fun, but not particularly constructive.

Third and Fourth Years: College Leaders Take the Lead

When planning began for the 2014–2015 iteration of *Research Readiness*, the new college captains had concrete ideas about redesigning the session. They acknowledged that students enjoyed the photo activity and had likely become more comfortable navigating the library, but felt that the session was too light on content and could have more academic impact. We agreed. The college captains proposed increasing the emphasis on databases. They also felt that there is a limit to what students can learn from exploring library spaces on their own. Without a knowledgeable guide, students were missing out on too much important information, and the college captains suggested that a library tour would be a more efficient and effective way to meet the objective.

Our tendency is to veer away from tours, pushing ourselves to design instruction that is more active and engaging. We disclosed this and shared our experience of tours falling flat with freshman audiences. Still, we understood why the college captains made the suggestion. It eventually occurred to us that having college leaders provide the tours could change the dynamic. We had seen college leaders build rapport with students in the classroom and decided to give it a try. A peer tour leader could provide insider tips and observations apt to hold students' attention. We shared our existing tour outline with the college captains and encouraged them to do a fresh take. Over the summer, they drafted their version, checking in with us for feedback along the way.

Looking for a way to introduce databases in the absence of an assignment, we reasoned that choosing a research topic is a universal challenge for first-year students and decided to design a related activity. Librarians at North Carolina State University (NCSU) produced a short, engaging YouTube video called *Picking Your Topic IS Research!*[20] that seemed a perfect introduction to the activity. We showed it to the college captains and they agreed. The video cleverly illustrates that choosing a topic is an iterative process of searching for information on an initial idea, then tweaking the idea based on the information available and what looks interesting, followed by further rounds of searching and refining. For the activity, we created an assignment prompting students to brainstorm a topic, apply the video's strategies in two databases, and document how their topic changed in the process. The session's title was expanded to *Research Readiness and Study Skills: What Every Freshman Needs to Know.* The learning outcomes were:

- Practice refining a topic and testing its viability for college-level academic research.
- Become familiar with two core multidisciplinary resources: *ProQuest Central* and *EBSCO Discovery Service.*
- Develop a knowledge base about key library spaces and services, including librarians' availability for research assistance.
- Prepare students with resources and study tips for their upcoming midterms.

The college captains were enthusiastic about this direction, and together we worked out the details of the lesson plan. College leaders were given their biggest role yet and we relied heavily on the college captains to train them. We introduced the *Research Readiness* lesson plan to college leaders at their fall training intensive, and the college captains led a dress rehearsal. They also followed up with college leaders to make sure that they practiced and timed the tour, encouraging them to inject their personality and library experiences into it.

The *Research Readiness* sessions occurred in October as usual. The session started out with all thirty-six students working on the assignment prompt and watching the NCSU video. For manageability, we then divided the students into two groups of eighteen. While the college leader took one group on a tour, the librarian stayed in the classroom to supervise the "focusing a topic" exercise. The groups swapped activities after thirty minutes. Everyone returned to the classroom for a wrap-up by the college leader.

College leaders reported having fun leading the tours and found the students to be appreciative and attentive. Library instructors observed that students were responsive and engaged during the classroom activity. CCP assessment data revealed that 80 percent of students found the *Research Readiness* session to be helpful—a marked improvement over previous years. CCP administrators, college leaders, and librarians concurred that we had found a winning formula, and we agreed to repeat this model for the 2015–2016 academic year. Figure 13.1 shows how the college leaders' involvement increased over time as they demonstrated their leadership capacity and the program matured.

Year 1	Year 2	Years 3 and 4
☐ Helped with classroom management	☐ Helped with classroom management	☐ Helped with classroom management
☐ Encouraged student participation	☐ Encouraged student participation	☐ Encouraged student participation
☐ Shared "What I wish I had known about the library as a freshman."	☐ Shared "What I wish I had known about the library as a freshman."	☐ Shared "What I wish I had known about the library as a freshman."
☐ • Provided assessment feedback	☐ College Captains collaborated on session content	☐ College Captains collaborated on session content
	☐ Worked with librarians to select "winning" photos	☐ College Captains worked with librarians to write scenario for "Picking a research topic"
	☐ Provided assessment feedback	☐ College Captains created a customized library tour
		☐ College Captains trained College Leaders to lead tours
		☐ Provided assessment feedback

Figure 13.1. Summary of college leader contributions by year.

Keys to Success for Mobilizing Student Leaders

Our experience with the College Cohort Program demonstrates that leveraging student leaders from a pre-existing campus program can help librarians take a more programmatic approach to library instruction. In our case study, CAS administration acknowledged the need for a library component in the planning stages of the CCP. However, we recognize that librarians may need to reach out to campus partners directly if they want to collaborate with large-scale efforts involving student leaders. Reflecting on our experience, the following principles emerged as keys to success that can be generalized to other institutional contexts.

- **Learn to speak the language of administrator colleagues.** Gaining fluency in the language used to describe high-impact educational practices and exploring the literature on retention and persistence can help instruction librarians connect with student affairs administrators. Advisors and other administrators often recruit and train student leaders to participate in their programs. Once you engage with them, use their language to identify mutual goals.

- **Create peer-driven experiential learning opportunities.** Over time, our *Research Readiness* sessions became more interactive and experiential, which made our teaching load easier to manage and more fun, while ensuring an environment conducive to learning. Our college leader collaborators helped us reality-test our ideas about library tours and ensured that our scenario for testing and tweaking a research topic was a genuine simulation of the freshman experience.

- **Listen to what you don't want to hear.** When the college captains first suggested that we give tours and demo a catalog search, we thought they were asking us to go back to an old model, and it was hard to hear the message behind what they were asking. After listening to their motivations, we were able to flip our thinking and leverage our knowledge of learning theory, peer-influence on the affective domain, and college student behavior to create a *Research Readiness* session that met our mutual goals.

- **Build in a process for continuous assessment.** For us, this meant depending on the college captains to provide us with direct feedback on our impact. Our CAS colleagues also shared their student and academic advisor survey feedback and it enabled us to see the strengths and weaknesses of all seven CCP sessions. Each year, we used these feedback mechanisms to inform and improve our lesson plan.

Conclusion

Student leaders are not trained information professionals, and their notions of what is possible can come across as naive. For this reason, clear communication and trust is essential. This extra effort means that working with student leaders can be a time-consuming process, especially in the early phases of collaboration. But the rewards are well worth the effort. Seeking out and forming partnerships with student leaders who are engaged in pre-existing student leadership programs on campus means working with a population that has been selected on established criteria. Finding such a group made the CAS Cohorts *Research Readiness* collaboration possible for us, while opening our eyes to similar opportunities on our campus.

Notes

1. NYU Office of Institutional Research, "Total Undergraduate Fact Sheet," accessed December 23, 2015, https://www.nyu.edu/ir/factbook/.
2. NYU Libraries, "About the Libraries," accessed December 23, 2015, http://library.nyu.edu/about/.
3. Ibid.
4. "College Cohort Program," accessed December 22, 2015, http://newstudents.cas.nyu.edu/page/cohort.
5. Ibid.
6. Char Booth et al., "Degrees of Impact: Analyzing the Effects of Progressive Librarian Course Collaborations on Student Performance," *College & Research Libraries* 76, no. 5 (July 2015): 636.
7. Alexander W. Astin, *What Matters in College?: Four Critical Years Revisited*, 1st ed, The Jossey-Bass Higher and Adult Education Series (San Francisco: Jossey-Bass, 1993), 39.
8. George D. Kuh, "High-Impact Educational Practices," Text, *Association of American Colleges & Universities*, (June 24, 2014), https://www.aacu.org/leap/hips.
9. Catherine Fraser Riehle and Sharon A. Weiner, "High-Impact Educational Practices: An Exploration of the Role of Information Literacy," *College & Undergraduate Libraries* 20, no. 2 (April 2013): 134, doi:10.1080/10691316.2013.789658.
10. Adam Murray, "Academic Libraries and High-Impact Practices for Student Retention: Library Deans' Perspectives," *Portal: Libraries and the Academy* 15, no. 3 (2015): 485.

11. Astin, 424.
12. Ibid., 425.
13. Robert Schroeder and Ellysa Stern Cahoy, "Valuing Information Literacy: Affective Learning and the ACRL Standards," *portal: Libraries and the Academy* 10, no. 2 (2010): 129.
14. Carol Collier Kuhlthau, "Developing a Model of the Library Search Process: Cognitive and Affective Aspects," *RQ* 28, no. 2 (1988): 232–42.
15. Constance A. Mellon, "Attitudes: The Forgotten Dimension in Library Instruction," *Library Journal* 113, no. 14 (1988): 138.
16. Ibid., 138.
17. Ibid., 138.
18. ACRL, "Framework for Information Literacy for Higher Education," 2015, http://www.ala.org/acrl/standards/ilframework.
19. L. S. Vygotsky and Michael Cole, *Mind in Society: The Development of Higher Psychological Processes* (Cambridge: Harvard University Press, 1978).
20. "Picking Your Topic IS Research," YouTube video, 3:10, posted by "libncu," May 1, 2014. https://www.youtube.com/watch?v=Q0B3Gjlu-1o.

Bibliography

ACRL. "Framework for Information Literacy for Higher Education," 2015. http://www.ala.org/acrl/standards/ilframework.

Astin, Alexander W. *What Matters in College?: Four Critical Years Revisited.* 1st ed. The Jossey-Bass Higher and Adult Education Series. San Francisco: Jossey-Bass, 1993.

Booth, Char, M. Sara Lowe, Natalie Tagge, and Sean Stone. "Degrees of Impact: Analyzing the Effects of Progressive Librarian Course Collaborations on Student Performance." *College & Research Libraries* 76, no. 5 (July 2015): 623–51. doi:10.5860/crl.76.5.623.

"College Cohort Program." Accessed December 29, 2016. http://newstudents.cas.nyu.edu/page/cohort.

Kuh, George D. "High-Impact Educational Practices." Text. *Association of American Colleges & Universities*, June 24, 2014. https://www.aacu.org/leap/hips.

Kuhlthau, Carol Collier, "Developing a Model of the Library Search Process: Cognitive and Affective Aspects." *Research Quarterly,* 28, no. 2 (Winter 1988): 232–242.

Mellon, Constance A. "Attitudes: The Forgotten Dimension in Library Instruction." *Library Journal* 113, no. 14 (9/1/1988 1988): 137–39.

Murray, Adam. "Academic Libraries and High-Impact Practices for Student Retention: Library Deans' Perspectives." *portal: Libraries and the Academy* 15, no. 3 (2015): 471–87. doi:10.1353/pla.2015.0027.

NYU Libraries. "About the Libraries." Accessed December 23, 2015. http://library.nyu.edu/about/.

NYU Office of Institutional Research. "Total Undergraduate Fact Sheet." Accessed December 23, 2015. https://www.nyu.edu/ir/factbook.

"Picking Your Topic IS Research," YouTube video, 3:10. Posted by "libncu," May 1, 2014. https://www.youtube.com/watch?v=Q0B3Gjlu-1o.

Riehle, Catherine Fraser, and Sharon A. Weiner. "High-Impact Educational Practices: An Exploration of the Role of Information Literacy." *College & Undergraduate Libraries* 20, no. 2 (April 2013): 127–43.

Schroeder, Robert, and Ellysa Stern Cahoy. "Valuing Information Literacy: Affective Learning and the ACRL Standards." *Portal: Libraries and the Academy* 10, no. 2 (2010): 127–46.

Vygotsky, L. S., and Michael Cole. *Mind in Society: The Development of Higher Psychological Processes*. Cambridge: Harvard University Press, 1978.

CHAPTER 14[*]

TWO-WAY STREET:
Ambassadors Sharing the Road

Adriana Gonzalez, Sara K. Kearns, Darchelle Martin, and Jason B. Reed

Creating a Student Ambassador Program

> Ambassadors are more than student volunteers that choose to dedicate their time toward the libraries; we are active and engaged members of the student body that believe that the libraries are worthy of time and investment. The ambassadors not only acknowledge the library as a crucial part of our campus, but we devote our time and talents toward increasing its value for all students and faculty. (Ambassador Interview)

The Kansas State University Libraries Student Ambassador group formed in fall 2013. This chapter documents the first three years of our program, focusing on the program's development: our impetus, establishing the foundation in our first year, shifting leadership from advisors to student officers in our second year, and student ambassadors defining their goals and objectives in our third year. We offer practical guidance and the philosophy informing our decisions throughout the narrative.

Kansas State University (K-State) is a public, land-grant institution with an enrollment of more than 24,000 students (approximately 20,000 undergraduate and 4,000 graduate students). K-State Libraries are staffed by approximately 100 tenure-track librarians, professional staff, and support staff. In the summer of 2013, Adriana Gonzalez, head of faculty and graduate services, Sara K. Kearns, head of undergraduate and community services, and Darchelle Martin, public relations officer, began to plan an ambassador program. While our objectives varied, partially due to the missions of the departments we represented, we identified three common goals for a program: outreach, feedback, and advocacy.

We researched library student groups at other institutions, scouring the professional literature and the Internet in order to better understand existing practices. Our review of more than twenty student groups from other libraries, all of which were described as advisory councils or boards at that time, revealed that our vision to have students serve in advisor and ambassador roles was relatively unique. Several sources confirmed the value of library student advisory boards for improving library services and relationships with students[1]. Deuink and Seiler's article[2] and book[3] describing Penn State Schuylkill Campus's library student advisory board as a student "friends of the library" model offered insights into students serving as ambassadors to the campus community. Acting as more than sounding boards, we envisioned our ambassadors also serving as advocates for the libraries to external audiences, including other students, faculty and staff, donors, and potential donors. We wanted our student group to be fully engaged with the libraries, and as future alumni, our most invested constituents.

While we found minimal evidence of this model in other libraries, we discovered that many K-State academic colleges had a student ambassador group. Reaching out to these groups was extremely helpful. We wondered if our expectations of student involvement would only be possible as a paid position; speaking with other advisors reassured us that students value volunteer service, too. We encouraged student employees of K-State Libraries to apply, but decided not to develop a model with ambassadors as employees because we wanted students to feel empowered to speak critically without feeling they were risking their jobs. We also noted that none of the ambassador programs on our campus operated as internship models. While some of our ambassadors have expressed an interest in librarianship as a profession (and one recent graduate is currently enrolled in library school), our ambassador program would not provide the pre-professional educational experience expected of an internship. We also learned that registering with K-State's Office of Student Activities and Services as an official student group offered many benefits, such as funding, training, the ability to create listservs and websites, and to participate in activities fairs.

We submitted a proposal to the libraries' leadership team, comprised of our administration and department heads. Because the student group would represent and advise the libraries, we needed to ensure support from within the libraries prior to starting a group. Our proposal outlined the essentials of our program, from recruitment through funding. Ambassadors would:

- Be selected through a two-step process of a written application and, if selected, an in-person interview
- Serve for two years or until graduation, whichever came first; those in good standing could serve beyond two years
- Meet once a month

We requested funds from the dean to cover refreshments for monthly meetings and polo shirts. The ambassadors would operate under the dean's purview, so would not have a separate budget. With approval from our library's leadership, the group was officially named Kansas State University Libraries Student Ambassadors and was charged to advocate for K-State Libraries and serve as representatives to guests, alumni, prospective students, and current students. Ambassadors would also advocate for the perspectives and needs of the student body. Our dean was so invested in the ambassadors that she committed to attending monthly meetings as her schedule permitted.

Recruitment and Membership

The success of our ambassador program relies on the caliber of the students who serve. Recruitment is one of our most time-intensive processes. The first year was most difficult because we recruited all new members with an untested process. We guessed at the size of our inaugural membership and borrowed from other campus groups to establish our recruitment process. Fortunately, our initial process proved to be successful and we have used it as our foundation, with some adjustments, in subsequent years.

We established from the beginning that the Ambassadors would be a diverse program. We define a diverse group as students of different backgrounds, race and ethnicity, gender, sexual orientation, year in school, and majors. Every year, the ambassadors have represented almost every college and included students in every year in school, from freshman through graduate students. The group always includes in-state, out-of-state, and international students, and students of diverse races and ethnicities. This diversity ensures that our ambassadors represent our student body.

We recruit, interview, and select our new class at the beginning of the fall semester so we can recruit freshman. We employ traditional marketing methods to advertise the program, including printed materials and social media. We promote the ambassadors at activities fairs, student orientations, and library events. Each of these methods was mentioned when we surveyed applicants about how they heard about the program. Asking professors and other advisors to send email (which we draft) directly to students has the largest impact. We promote the program as a chance for an organization or college to be represented and as a leadership opportunity for students. We also increase our pool by reaching out to colleges from which we receive few or no applicants, letting them know we want their college to be represented.

The advisors handled recruitment the first year; in subsequent years we work with the ambassador's recruitment/membership committee. This meant that recruitment served as our first foray into collaborative leadership. Three ambassadors serve on the recruitment committee each year, along with the advisors and the incoming chair of the ambassadors. One advisor begins planning the recruitment process with the committee in late summer. Diversity among the ambassadors remains a key objective, so we focus on contacting a variety of student groups and degree programs. Ambassadors reach out to students, while advisors reach out to faculty and staff. Interested students have two weeks from the start of the semester to submit a written application online. All members of the recruitment team review applications using the same rubric. Based on the written material, some applicants are invited for in-person interviews.

We schedule interviews for a weekend with an away football game. We include the interview date on promotional materials so applicants can save the date. Applicants sign up for slots online using Google Calendar. We allocate twenty minutes per candidate—ten minutes each with the recruitment committee and the advisors. We separate the interviews so that candidates start by talking to fellow students, hopefully alleviating the stress early ambassadors reported when meeting with advisors. In addition to the advisors and recruitment team, three ambassadors volunteer to serve as hosts (greeting candidates and escorting them to interviews) or to tabulate scores from the interview rubrics.

The interview day for the recruitment committee looks like:

1:00 p.m.	Recruitment committee, advisors, and hosts arrive and make final arrangements
1:30–3:00 p.m.	Interviews—rubrics are collected and tabulated after every interview
3:00–3:30 p.m.	Break
3:30–5:30 p.m.	Interviews
5:30–6:30 p.m.	Review applicants, select new ambassadors

The interview day for a candidate looks like:

2:25 p.m.	Arrive at library, greeted by host
2:30–2:40 p.m.	Interview with recruitment committee
2:40–2:50 p.m.	Interview with advisors

We select new ambassadors within an hour, using a method proposed by ambassadors: identify a pool that clearly meet all requirements and a pool that do not, and only discuss borderline applicants. The recruitment team and advisors look for applicants who can articulate why libraries are important to them. When reviewing applicants, the ambassadors and advisors contribute equally to the discussion. The hosts offer insight into the general social skills of applicants. Applicants are contacted within twenty-four hours with a letter either inviting them to join the ambassadors or thanking them for their interest and time.

One ambassador explained why she served on the recruitment committee (now known as the membership committee):

> I believe that library ambassadors are an instrumental part of the libraries here at K-State. Being a part of the membership committee allows me to serve the ambassador program by selecting new members and creating an experience all of the members can enjoy. And through serving the members, we serve the program and in turn the libraries. (Ambassador Interview)

While applying to be an ambassador is time-intensive, we continue to be impressed by the number of applicants:

- Year One: 43 applicants, 27 interviews, 23 ambassadors selected
- Year Two: 31 applicants, 20 interviews, 11 ambassadors selected
- Year Three: 33 applicants, 22 interviews, 11 ambassadors selected

A significant number of ambassadors stay with the program beyond the two-year commitment. At the end of our second year, ten of the fourteen ambassadors who completed their commitment chose to remain with the group, with others graduating or pursuing other opportunities. By year three, the number of ambassadors rose to thirty students. While this is a large group, requiring a significant time commitment from the advisors, as the program has matured, the ambassadors have assumed more of the organizational responsibilities.

Year One: Creating a Shared Foundation

In the first year of the ambassador program, ambassadors and advisors alike were learning what it meant to be library student ambassadors. The advisors communicated this to the ambassadors, even during the interview process, to explain why we did not always have an immediate answer to questions and to encourage the ambassadors to share ideas to improve the program. During the first year, the advisors took a more active leadership role than in subsequent years. We focused on training, establishing an organizational structure, and engaging the ambassadors in advocacy and outreach.

Once the ambassadors were selected, they attended a mandatory, two-night orientation to equip them to advocate and advise. The first night introduced ambassadors to the libraries' mission and work; the second night covered donor relations. During the introduction to the libraries, our dean welcomed the ambassadors and shared our vision of how they would support and advocate for the libraries. We conducted a "behind the scenes" tour of the main library, allowing ambassadors to learn about the variety of work necessary to run a library while exploring spaces not typically seen by the public. The tours definitely pique the ambassadors' interest, and the insights stay with them:

> I don't think that I would know how intricate our library was if it weren't for the ambassador program. I have

found out that there are a wide variety of types of librarians serving in various behind-the-scenes positions, I
have seen parts of the library that many students don't
know exist, and I have seen just how much effort the
library puts into meeting the needs of students. (Ambassador Interview)

A development officer from the university's Foundation provided soft-
skills training on approaching and interacting with donors. This component has been included in training every year since. While our ambassadors do not actively fundraise, we know from experience that donors like
to hear from students, so our ambassadors need to be knowledgeable and
comfortable interacting with donors.

Many ambassadors joined because they wanted to contribute to the
progress of the libraries. The advisors were already in position to inform
students of the libraries' questions and ideas. However, if the program
was solely directed by the advisors, we would lose the ambassadors' energy and initiatives. We believed that switching to a model of shared gov-
ernance that included student officers would embed student engagement
into the program. Therefore, we sought student officers to lead meetings,
develop programming, and raise student concerns. We held elections for
officers at our first meeting. Ambassadors stood for chair, chair-elect,
secretary, and Open House co-chairs. The first chair of the Ambassadors
was a graduate student with leadership experience who was comfortable
leading the meetings and drafting bylaws and a constitution. The new-
ness of the program meant we did not have precedent in terms of content or activities for the officers to follow, so the advisors more heavily
influenced meeting agendas and outreach opportunities than we would
in subsequent years.

The advisors engaged the ambassadors in a decision-making process
at the first meeting in order to reinforce the value we would place on their
contributions. We sought feedback on the use of study space during finals week and a finals event called Caffeine Fix, when the libraries provide
refreshments for three nights. Our libraries strive to maintain a balance
between quiet study space and group study space. Silent/quiet study space
is very limited, particularly during finals. The advisors shared this struggle
and the ambassadors brainstormed suggestions, two of which were imple-

mented. The energy level during the brainstorming was very high and the ambassadors demonstrated both creativity and thoughtfulness.

We agreed at the meeting to implement several of their suggestions, demonstrating the importance of ambassador input. Suggestions that could not be implemented became a learning opportunity for the ambassadors, helping them understand the constraints of the budget, facilities, and staffing resources. The advisors learned about significant barriers to studying in our main library, notably a lack of power outlets and unreliable Wi-Fi. We gained perspective on what students find disruptive, what they are willing to overlook, and the fluidity of student expectations for the library's physical spaces, particularly in terms of the time of day and time of the semester. Testing our assumptions and gathering feedback allowed us to more confidently experiment with services.

The ambassadors continue to provide invaluable feedback. Our dean brings high-impact issues to the ambassadors, including a student library fee proposal and a proposal to redesign our main floor. The transformation in the ambassadors, when they shift from seemingly passive listening to a flurry of questions and discussion points, is phenomenal. Due to the diversity of our ambassadors, they call upon backgrounds that include student government, experience with school bonds at their high schools, and knowledge of fees from different colleges on campus. This generates rich discussion and provides perspectives that we would not have known to ask about in a survey.

Finally, we identified venues for the ambassadors to act as our advocates. Ambassadors volunteered for events such as the Friends of the Libraries Annual Gala, Homecoming, Family Day, International Games Day, and Orientation and Enrollment. The ambassadors contributed ideas and insight to make every event more rewarding for all involved. For instance, the open house co-chairs worked with Darchelle Martin to organize entertaining activities for more than 1,000 attendees that promoted the libraries. Ambassadors relished engaging with faculty, donors, and alumni at the Gala, providing a much needed student presence at a key fundraiser for the libraries.

Year one was a year of learning for both the ambassadors and the advisors. The meetings created opportunities for the ambassadors to ask questions and learn about the libraries. We established precedents regarding soliciting and responding to ambassador feedback and understanding how the ambassadors engaged with students, the public, and donors. We introduced an environment of shared leadership, allowing the ambassadors to identify areas in which they could assume more leadership in the future. Most important, the ambassadors believed they made an impact. As an ambassador shared:

> I do feel like I have made a difference to the libraries and to K-State students. First of all, our continued feedback on the Wi-Fi in the building directly led to improvement of that service. Also helping at events like the Gala, where we are showing donors and alumni how much students care about the libraries, are very beneficial. I also just feel like my increased knowledge has helped me tell students in my classes and my friends about services the library has to offer. (Ambassador Interview)

Year Two: The Ambassadors Define Themselves

The ambassadors assumed more leadership of the program's development in our second year and became fixtures in our outreach efforts. The foundation we established the prior year allowed the advisors to continue bringing questions, ideas, and volunteer opportunities to the ambassadors. However, to be truly responsive to our students, the advisors needed to step aside so the ambassadors could establish goals reflecting their awareness of what students needed from the libraries. As long as the advisors and dean could solicit feedback from the ambassadors and count on participation in outreach events, we were content to accept their decisions.

We were fortunate that the chair and chair-elect also served as officers in our first year. The secretary, while a new officer, was part of the inaugural ambassadors cohort. We experienced change within the advisors as Jason Reed replaced Adriana Gonzalez. With experienced officers in position, the advisors moved into a more advisory role (e.g. answering questions about the budget, building and infrastructure, and IT limits). The officers took more direct leadership, particularly in guiding the group through the process of identifying their objectives as ambassadors.

Prior to a meeting in the early fall, each ambassador posted two goals for the year on our online message board. The executive committee and ad-

visors identified three significant themes from the submitted ideas: learning about/educating others about the libraries, ambassadors as a team, and
advocacy ideas. The officers distributed the thematically grouped ideas to
the ambassadors, including new ambassadors, prior to the next meeting so
they were prepared to discuss them. At the start of the meeting, we posted the ideas and themes on the walls. Each ambassador used color-coded
sticky dots to vote for or against ideas that they wanted to pursue. This
process developed consensus as the ambassadors chatted while voting, and
everyone could see trends develop. Our chair then led the ambassadors
through a discussion finalizing the goals.

While the ambassadors identified clear goals, the organizational structure of the group proved to be a roadblock. Announcements from the advisors were taking up the majority of the monthly meetings, not leaving
enough time for the ambassadors to work on their goals. Ultimately, the
ambassadors decided to form committees that would meet once a month
to handle the business of the group. There were several ideas how the committees would function, so the ambassadors asked the chair to review the
options and propose a committee structure that they would vote on for inclusion in the bylaws and constitution. The chair and the co-chair, with feedback from advisors and the secretary, drafted a proposal and a presentation.

Simultaneously, a smaller group of ambassadors developed a second
proposal to address ideas they felt the officers' proposal did not encompass.
Competing proposals were an opportunity for the group to discuss how
they envisioned their roles as ambassadors. The ambassadors also learned
how professional organizations use guidelines like Robert's Rules of Order
to regulate their meetings and manage changes to bylaws and organizational constitutions.

The officers' proposal outlined:
- Eight standing committees
- Ambassadors would serve on one committee, with the option to serve on more
- Committees would meet monthly, have a chair, and submit a monthly activity report
- The ambassador's proposal outlined:
- Two standing committees
- Ambassadors could propose new committees with the approval of the chair

- The chair would establish goals and subcommittees at the start of every year after gathering ideas from the ambassadors
- The chair-elect would assign ambassadors to subcommittees; the subcommittees would report to the chair-elect
- Every ambassador would serve on a subcommittee

The ambassadors' proposal also called for a treasurer, provided more detail about replacing officers, and added language for a vote of no confidence. For the May meeting, our chair presented the proposals alongside each other and the original text of the bylaws or the constitution (see Figure 14.1).

BY-LAWS: ARTICLE III (COMMITTEES)		
Original	**Proposal 1**	**Proposal 2**
Each group member will be expected to serve on a committee, either standing or special.	Each group member will be expected to serve on a committee, either standing or special.	Every member is expected to serve on a subcommittee, members are welcome to propose new committees for further exploration of an issue· The Chair must approve all new committees.
• Standing Committees: committees that oversee tasks or events that occur every year. The standing committees for this group are:	• Standing Committees: committees that oversee tasks or events that occur every year. The standing committees for this group are:	• Standing Committees: committees that oversee tasks or events that occur every year. The standing committees for this group are:
• Open House	– Events	• Open House
	– Incoming Students	• Recruitment
Special Committees: determined by the group's immediate needs. Special committees are appointed by the Chairperson. The Chair of the committee is appointed and will only serve as long as needed.	– Promotional	
	– Membership	Subcommittees: determined by the Chair at the start of each year, organized by the Chair-Elect. The Chairperson appoints subcommittees.
	– Building/Facilities	
	– Education	
	– Graduate Students	
	– Executive	
	Special Committees: Same as original	Special Committees: Same as original

Figure 14.1. Example of how proposed bylaw changes were presented along with original text.

The chair reviewed the proposals according to bylaw or constitution section. The ambassadors discussed each proposal following Robert's Rules of Order. Ultimately, the ambassadors voted to move forward with the standing committees, requiring each ambassador to serve on a committee, and the language about replacing officers (see Figure 14.2).

FINAL TEXT OF BY-LAWS	
By-Laws: Article I (Election of Positions	**By-Laws: Article III (Committees)**
Section 6-Position Replacement	Each group member will be expected to serve on a committee, either standing or special.
In the event that an officer needs to be replaced for any reason, the other officer and group advisors will determine who will make a suitable replacement and that person will be voted on by the other officers and advisors. In committee chamber, the new officer candidate will be presented to the group for assessment. Upon the absence of said person, a majority vote will dictate the support and election of a new candidate. Any observed nay votes will result in a nomination and discussion period. If a nomination is not selected within the allotted time increment, the discussion will be moved to an online ballot to be open a known amount of time.	Standing Committees: committees that oversee tasks or events that occur every year. The standing committees for this group are: Events Incoming Students Promotional Membership Building/Facilities Education Graduate Students Executive
In the event of a vote of no confidence an online ballot will be given to determine leadership. A majority vote is necessary for election.	

Figure 14.2. Text of the approved bylaws.

During the year, our officers sought guidance from a variety of groups in addition to the advisors. They relied heavily on each other, listened to the ideas and experiences of fellow ambassadors, and learned from other campus ambassador groups. By the end of the year, our officers demonstrated confidence in leading meetings and handling questions. The ambassadors were increasingly comfortable raising and addressing issues among themselves and looked to the officers first for clarification, then the advisors.

This was the first time many of the ambassadors had been part of a group creating itself, so there were growing pains and discussions about professionally expressing opinions and timely communication. As advisors, it was difficult at times to remain neutral and focus on mediating the discussion, but we were proud to see the group mature and the officers demonstrate leadership. Ultimately, the ambassadors became a stronger organization because the ambassadors decided how they would operate going forward. According to our then chair-elect, "The changing of our constitution and bylaws to create a more effective group has been a really interesting transition. I believe as we continue to grow and come up with new ideas, it will probably change even more to allow us to best represent the libraries."

While the ambassadors internally focused on negotiating their goals during the year, they also became integral to our outreach efforts. One significant contribution of the ambassadors is representing the libraries with prospective and current students at recruitment and orientation events. Librarians connect with (or reassure) parents, while ambassadors connect with (or reassure) students. Ambassadors relate with other students through shared majors or hometowns and easily segue into discussing library resources.

The connection is also felt by our donors and alumni, who express how much they enjoy meeting ambassadors at events. During our second year, we increased the presence of the ambassadors at the Friends of K-State Libraries Annual Gala, both in number attending and greater integration with the evening's events. The ambassadors' presence was welcomed by our university provost, who thanked them for attending during her remarks. Ambassador participation at events like these helps remind donors that their gifts have a very real impact.

Year Three: Enacting Change

The third year for the libraries' student ambassadors ushered in increased activity and leadership opportunities with the addition of committees. As voted on by the ambassadors, the eight standing committees were:
1. Graduate Students: represent graduate student concerns
2. Promotional: promote the awesomeness of the libraries, including services, resources, and library and ambassador events
3. Building: understand the physical building, from HVAC to furniture, and its effect on student use
4. Education: educate ambassadors about the libraries to be informed advocates
5. Events: plan events, including organizing and coordinating volunteers
6. Incoming Students: outreach to new students, working with campus offices like New Students Services
7. Membership: recruit new members; create social bonds within the ambassadors
8. Executive: the existing committee comprised of officers and advisors

Each committee would be ambassador-led with an assigned advisor for guidance. The advisors believed the ambassadors' increased impact on the libraries was worth their additional time commitment. The advisors selected committees in the summer based on the scope of each committee, our positions in the libraries, and personal interest. All advisors serve on the executive committee; the remaining committees were divided, with two advisors selecting two committees each and one advisor selecting three committees. It soon became apparent that serving as the advisor for three committees was not feasible, so we recruited a fourth advisor to our team. The libraries' new undergraduate experience librarian, Charissa Powell, joined the advisors and was matched with the Incoming Students committee.

Once the newly recruited ambassadors joined us, all ambassadors signed up for committees through open enrollment at a meeting. Our chair reminded everyone that each ambassador was required to participate in at least one committee. The advisors and officers hoped that self-selection would increase participation and sense of community through a shared purpose.

Each committee identified a chair, primarily by common consent, for whoever volunteered. Most ambassadors welcomed the opportunity to gain leadership experience by chairing a committee. However, some committees were primarily comprised of new members who were reluctant to assume a leadership role with limited experience. After assurances of support from advisors and committee members, new ambassadors agreed to lead, proving to be strong chairs. This demonstrates the flexibility needed when creating a new program: when the unexpected happens, make the best decision you can.

Highlights from the committees include: a 3-D printing workshop, a Shakespeare masquerade, and building community by recognizing members during monthly meetings and social events like bowling. One ambassador, following a basement to rooftop tour of our main library as a member of the Building and Facilities committee, presented about maintenance issues and related costs of running the library to her speech class. Afterward, classmates shared how important the libraries were to them and that they were more receptive to student fees based on her speech. We eagerly anticipate future ambassador-driven endeavors as the committees gain traction.

As advisors, we observed that inviting the ambassadors to take on larger roles each year, defining who they are and their impact, has increased the ambassadors' engagement with the libraries. Our ambassadors agree, with one stating:

> At first, it was difficult to see how the ambassadors were influencing the libraries because we were still trying to figure out what we wanted that influence to be. It wasn't until we formed the committees in our third year that I truly felt like we were making an impact on the libraries. No longer were the advisers coming to the meetings to tell us what was going on; we had each committee presenting different things that were happening around the libraries. Additionally, I truly felt like we were valuable when the advisers or the dean asked for our opinions and feedback. In this way, I felt valued as both a student and an ambassador. (Ambassador Interview)

Lessons Learned

With several years of experience establishing and helping the ambassadors evolve, we can share four lessons we have learned:

Lesson One: Establish a Clear Mission

As advisors, we rely heavily on the program's charge to find our balance between supporting and empowering our ambassadors. The ambassadors also recognize the extent to which a defined mission impacts their contributions:

> Our group has been successful because we were given the freedom to define our purposes. On a very broad scale, a successful group has clearly defined goals with a set structure on how to achieve those goals. In our specific program, we defined ourselves as a group that provides a voice for the students to the libraries and a voice for the libraries to the public. (Ambassador Interview)

Lesson Two: Trust your Ambassadors

Allow the ambassadors to assume responsibility and listen to their ideas, even if they conflict with yours. When librarians ask students for input, they have to be open to genuinely considering student ideas and implementing them, as feasible. This trust can increase an ambassador's engagement:

> I'm fairly involved on campus, but my experience with being an ambassador has been unique because I feel like our efforts are so integrated with the library. What we do actually has an impact, and that has been encouraging to me. (Ambassador Interview)

Lesson Three: Commit Yourself

A successful ambassador program requires time and energy from advisors and ambassadors to attend meetings, plan programs, and volunteer for events. Committed advisors, often working outside the typical workday, need support from library and university administration to run the program and to demonstrate that ambassadors' contributions are valued. When our dean attends meetings and welcomes ambassadors to donor events, she reinforces the importance of their contributions.

Lesson Four: Be Flexible

Learning what is best for your program requires experimentation and time. Ambassador commitment fluctuates under the weight of coursework, jobs, internships, study abroad, and life. Understand what is most important for the mission of the program, and allow for the ebb and flow of semesters, challenges, and opportunities.

Reflection

We have spent this chapter explaining the time, resources, and commitment needed to make a program like this work. After three years of running this program, the question becomes: Is it worth it? When many libraries and universities face budget challenges and staffing shortages, we must think strategically about how we spend our time. For us, the answer from both administration and advisors is a resounding, "Yes."

The largest benefit to the libraries is the improved connection with our student body. This is true for large, important decisions, like bringing a student fee proposal to our student government association, but also in more routine, daily library activities, like our communication and marketing efforts for our student audience. Individually, our ambassadors share their insider knowledge with friends and classmates. More broadly, the ambassadors are a conduit to future students, current students, and alumni alike. They embody the thousands of students the libraries impact every year, giving voice to the learning and communities that can develop.

Many academic librarians enjoy working with students, but our connections with students is often fleeting, lasting the duration of a reference interview or, in rare cases, a semester. One of the benefits the ambassadors identified about committees was getting to know the advisors better. Beyond our official roles, we advisors cherish the informal relationships we build with our ambassadors and were heartened to learn the ambassadors want librarians to know who they are.

At this point, it is too early to study the engagement of our ambassadors post-graduation; we hope they will be our advocates as alumni. While student employees are an important constituent for libraries—and we appreciate their feedback and insight—they are often constrained within an office or department. Therefore, the ambassador program allows us to engage students more widely. Our ambassadors enter the program with an affinity for the libraries, and their passion grows as they learn more about the libraries and librarians.

> Being able to see the impact I've made on the libraries
> gives me a sense of ownership in this library that I lacked
> before this program. I spend more time at the libraries
> now because I am more comfortable with the resources
> available to me and the atmosphere that we have helped
> shape. (Ambassador Interview)

The best part of being an advisor for the K-State Libraries Student Ambassadors is being a part of the extraordinary growth shown by the ambassadors. Witnessing their growth in confidence and knowing that we helped someone develop has been an incredible opportunity. We are proud of all of the ambassadors, current and past, who dedicated their time, and especially grateful to those who assumed formal or informal leadership, which was vital to the success of this program. The ambassadors are an integral part of the libraries' strategic plan, and their input is invaluable. We learn from each other and strive to improve the library experience for our community. If the previous years are any indication, the ambassadors and the advisors will grow as individuals and as a group, and contribute to improved services for the libraries' users.

Notes

1. Candace R. Benefiel, Wendi Arant and Elaine Gass, "A New Dialogue: A Student Advisory Committee in an Academic Library," *The Journal of Academic Librarianship* 25, no. 2 (1999): 111–113, doi:10.1016/S0099-1333(99)80008-1; Erin Dorney, "Students as Stakeholders: Library Advisory Boards and Privileging our Users," Library with the Lead Pipe, last modified February 6, 2013, http://www.inthelibrarywiththeleadpipe .org/2013/students-as-stakeholders-library-advisory-boards-and-privileging-our -users/.
2. Amy Deuink and Marianne Seiler, "Students as Library Advocates the Library Student Advisory Board at Pennsylvania State-Schuylkill," *College & Research Libraries News* 67, no. 1 (2006): 18–21.
3. Amy L. Deuink and Marianne Seiler, *The Library Student Advisory Board: Why Your Academic Library Needs it and How to Make it Work* (Jefferson, NC: McFarland & Company, Inc., 2009).

Bibliography

Benefiel, Candace R., Wendi Arant, and Elaine Gass. "A New Dialogue: A Student Advisory Committee in an Academic Library," *The Journal of Academic Librarianship* 25, no. 2 (1999): 111–113. doi:10.1016/S0099-1333(99)80008-1.

Deuink, Amy and Marianne Seller. "Students as Library Advocates the Library Student Advisory Board at Pennsylvania State-Schuylkill," *College & Research Libraries News* 67, no. 1 (2006): 18–21.

Deuink, Amy and Marianne Seller. *The Library Student Advisory Board: Why Your Academic Library Needs it and How to Make it Work* (Jefferson, NC: McFarland & Company, Inc., 2009).

Dorney, Erin. "Students as Stakeholders: Library Advisory Boards and Privileging our Users," In the Library with the Lead Pipe, last modified February 6, 2013, http://www .inthelibrarywiththeleadpipe.org/2013/students-as-stakeholders-library-advisory -boards-and-privileging-our-users/.

Part 6

STUDENTS AS LIBRARY DESIGNERS

CHAPTER 15

JUST ASK THEM!

Designing Services and Spaces on the Foundation of Student Feedback

Emily Daly, Joyce Chapman, and Thomas Crichlow

Building a Culture of Student-Centered Assessment

At Duke University Libraries, student contributions are vital to improving services and spaces. Since its creation in 2013, the libraries' Assessment and User Experience Department (AUX) has worked to increase students' involvement in assessing and enhancing library services and spaces. Charged with evaluating and improving all library users' experiences, AUX staff routinely seek input from students in an effort to effect user-centered change. In the past, Duke Libraries staff spent long hours helping students adapt to librarians' approaches to research, and data collected from users was often limited to anecdotal feedback and heavily influenced by staff members' personal opinions. Over the last several years, library staff have devised multiple methods to learn from students and adapt library tools and services to meet their evolving needs. In so doing, Duke University Li-

---

braries has transitioned from a culture in which staff made decisions based on instinct or isolated experience to a responsive culture with students' opinions and feedback at its center.

Since assessment and user experience were formalized into the work of designated staff members and a department, we have been able to take a coordinated and holistic approach to assessment. Assessment efforts were previously ad-hoc, lacking in coordination and consistency, limited in methods and tools, and dependent on both the skill sets and time of staff with other duties. Several years later, we find we are able to plan comprehensively for assessment across multiple library units and departments. Further, we are able to utilize more varied and robust methods for gathering information from and about students on topics ranging from spaces and furniture to the impact of research consultations on student learning. One important aspect of this user-centered approach to improving library services, interfaces, and spaces is triangulating methods: While we greatly value what can be learned from each data source, we never rely on a single data collection method to make important decisions for the libraries. Combining information from multiple data points enhances our understanding of how and why students interact with library staff, services, and spaces.

In this chapter, we will present a series of short case studies that illustrate methods we have found effective for seeking students' input and ensuring that student voices help shape library services and decision-making. We will discuss: the benefits of our approach to student-centered assessment; what we have learned from the studies we have conducted over the last three years, including the advantages and drawbacks of each method; and how we intend to sustain student-led innovation in the libraries.

The case studies highlight techniques for involving students in enhancing existing spaces and resources, and developing innovative services:

- Guerrilla usability testing,[1] referred to as "on-the-fly" usability testing at Duke Libraries, in which students are recruited at random as they enter the library to complete brief tasks using the library website or physical service points, and then provide suggestions for improving web interface or services
- Online surveys advertised through website banners, blog posts, or direct email that give students the opportunity to answer questions about library services and spaces

- Focus groups and visioning workshops, during which students are invited to meet with staff and other students to share their experiences using Duke Libraries
- Observational studies, in which staff unobtrusively watch how students use library spaces during a predetermined period of time
- Student advisory board meetings, at which students who have applied for board membership contribute ideas and feedback on a range of issues over one or more academic years[*]
- Student assistant positions, which allow paid undergraduates or graduate students earning course credit to contribute directly to efforts to design and administer user studies and assist in implementing user-centered changes to web interfaces and services.

Case Studies

Customizing Spaces and Furniture

At Duke Libraries, staff and administrators frequently look to students to guide decisions related to furniture and space design. Recent planning for a new Research Commons[†] involved students from the start. Staff engaged faculty, graduate students, and undergraduates in a visioning workshop intended to provide direction as we determined the purpose, function, and aesthetic of the libraries' Research Commons. Thanks to deeply engaged student advisory board members, we were able to continue to seek student feedback over the course of the three-year-long project. Because we intended our Research Commons to be particularly geared toward the needs of graduate students, we asked our Graduate and Professional Student Advisory Board for feedback on blueprints at multiple points during the design process. We also incorporated questions related to our designs and goals for the space into graduate student focus groups we conducted following a university-wide user satisfaction survey. From the survey and follow-up focus groups, we learned that students expect library staff to help them

---

[*] More information about the libraries' Undergraduate Advisory Board and Graduate & Professional Student Advisory Board is available at https://library.duke.edu/about/advisory-boards.

[†] The libraries' Ruppert Commons for Research, Technology, and Collaboration, branded as "The Edge," opened on the first floor of the main library in January 2015. More information is available at https://library.duke.edu/edge.

find, analyze, and visualize data, so our Research Commons features a Data & Visualization Services Lab. While library staff had already envisioned incorporating such a lab into the new space, seeking user feedback affirmed the decision. As library staff finalized floor plans and selected finishes and furnishings, we repeatedly sought input from student advisory board members. For instance, we looked to our undergraduate board members to help name a set of small, open booths in a way that would convey their purpose to students. They named the spaces "Meet Ups." Additionally, staff drafted a set of policies to govern use of short-term lockers in the space. Fortunately, we requested feedback from advisory board members, who were quick to tell us the policies would not meet students' needs. In response, staff extended time limits for the lockers and developed policies that made the lockers more convenient for students to use. As we have done with many aspects of services and policies in our Research Commons and throughout the libraries, we requested additional feedback from students after they actually began using the lockers to ensure the policies they helped develop worked well in practice.

In order to make decisions about library spaces, we have found it valuable to observe students at work. Depending on what we need to know in order to redesign a space effectively, we observe students' behavior and use of furniture and equipment at different points during the semester and at multiple times during the day and night. We engage student assistants in these projects in an effort to involve students as much as possible, and their participation makes it possible to collect observational data on the weekends and as late as 11:00 p.m.

In the 2014–2015 academic year, we conducted an observational assessment to understand more fully how students use—or choose not to use—study spaces and various pieces of furniture at the main campus library. The study provided library staff and administrators with evidence that students using the main library are far more likely to study independently than in groups and choose individual study carrels and small tables instead of oversized "comfy" chairs. As a result, we have opted not to replace or reupholster all worn oversized chairs and instead invest in individual seating and study carrels. The study also revealed that students develop makeshift standing stations out of map cases and other flat surfaces, an observation we responded to by purchasing ten standing desks.

Observational studies are most effective in helping us learn "what" students use, not "why" they choose a particular type of furniture or area in which to study, or what else they might choose if given the option. To gain this information, we often seek input from student advisory board members or focus group participants. At multiple points, we have used low-cost, low-tech methods, such as asking students to draw their ideal study spaces or brainstorm enhancements they would make to library spaces if given the option. We then pair these findings with data collected from other studies. For example, from our observational studies, student surveys, and additional interviews, we have learned that students are keenly interested in spaces where they can stand to study and prefer places where they can work quietly and independently. As funds become available to purchase new furniture for study spaces, we will invest in as many individual study carrels, tables intended for independent study, and options for standing while studying as possible.

Creating a Device Lending Program

As the numbers of devices that students routinely bring to the library has increased, so too have their requests that more devices be made available to check out from the library. In response to this feedback, library staff had considered lending devices and technology a number of times and had worked with Duke's student government to identify equipment and funding. However, library administrators were concerned about managing and replacing heavily-used equipment and supplying a sufficient variety of devices to meet users' needs—potentially a considerable financial and logistical burden.

To gather further data on student interest in a device-lending program, AUX staff sought additional feedback from students in the libraries' 2013 biannual satisfaction survey. Following the survey, we held ten focus groups with graduate and undergraduate students to discuss technology lending and other survey topics in greater depth. We then elicited further feedback on a potential lending program through student advisory boards, asking students whether such a service would be useful, what types of items students would want to borrow, and what policies around technology lending (such as fines and time limits) should look like. The findings were clear: Students value having access to technology (laptop and phone chargers in particular) while they study and expect the library to provide this service.

We also spoke with local peers, such as North Carolina State University Libraries, where staff had successfully implemented device-lending programs that students used extensively. After soliciting significant feedback from Duke students and learning about students' perceptions and behavior at peer libraries, we were able to successfully advocate for a device-lending service with Duke's library administration. AUX staff worked closely with student advisory board members and student government leaders to identify devices and funding, and while we advertised the program's launch through official library channels, we relied heavily on students to spread the word: For instance, an undergraduate blogged about the new service, and her blog post was picked up by a number of non-library student Facebook groups, citing the new loaner program as an important addition.

Since the start of the program in April 2015, we have collaborated with campus IT staff and student government members to add new devices and models to our pools of chargers, and we expanded the lending service to a second branch library. We have successfully surmounted the original concerns related to lending devices. While we have lost a small number of devices, student government members have been eager to supplement the pool with new models and replacement devices. And with significant help from these invested undergraduates, we have been able to identify devices that meet the majority of students' needs.

Modifying Room Reservation Policies and System to Meet Students' Expectations

The libraries' Research Commons includes nine project rooms that can be reserved by groups working on research projects on a recurring basis for weeks or months at a time. After seeking input from students, we outfitted project spaces with display screens, writeable walls, and lockable cabinets. Individuals or groups can also reserve rooms on a non-recurring basis for up to three hours at a time when rooms are not in use.

When the Research Commons first opened, the policies governing use of the nine project rooms and the steps required to reserve them differed dramatically from those in place for the rest of the libraries' heavily used group study rooms. Project rooms could be reserved for non-recurring use only from an iPad located just outside each room or from a touchscreen kiosk located in the Research Commons. This policy required users to visit the Research Commons in person to make a reservation, a practice students found burdensome and confusing since they were able to book group study rooms in other parts of the library entirely online.

After hearing from students that they found this in-person reservation process frustrating, AUX staff conducted a usability test in the lobby of the main library, randomly asking six students to show us how they would attempt to reserve a project room from start to finish. After they completed the task, students answered follow-up questions about their experience reserving a room and the reservation policy itself. Students we talked to made it clear that the process staff had developed was unintuitive, cumbersome, and needlessly time-consuming. As a result, we transitioned these spaces to the online system that students use to book all other group study rooms in the library.[*] Iterative assessment is important to iterative improvement, and in the semester following our initial usability study, we conducted a repeat usability test. Once again, we observed students reserve a project room, this time with the modified policies and online reservation system in place. This group of test participants indicated that the changes in policy were a significant improvement and suggested additional improvements to the reservation system's online interface (i.e., optimize the room reservation pages and system for mobile devices, since they are likely to use their phones to book spaces, add a "sign out" function to the touchscreen kiosk in the Research Commons to assure students their information is secure), which were subsequently implemented.

Students demonstrated that we were wrong in our assumptions of how they wanted to reserve and use project rooms and showed us we had made it needlessly difficult to reserve project rooms in a space we hoped would be used heavily by students. After observing their behavior and talking with both test participants and student advisory board members about their experiences in the Research Commons, we were able to make changes that helped us better promote new spaces to our target population and enable students to reserve rooms quickly and easily in ways that fit their schedules and expectations.

Designing a More Intuitive Search Results Interface

The Duke Libraries homepage[2] serves as the main entry point to resources that are distributed across multiple silos, such as the catalog, articles, and research databases. For many years, students, faculty, and staff who needed

---

[*] Students use http://library.duke.edu/using/room-reservations to learn about and reserve group study and project rooms.

to access these resources were challenged by a multi-tabbed search box that forced them to choose among four or more distinct pathways, each providing access to only a subset of the libraries' vast resources.

After observing frustrated and confused students attempt to make sense of our search box in numerous usability tests and focus groups, AUX staff members collaborated with colleagues throughout the libraries to develop a unified search results page, commonly referred to as a Bento Box approach.[3] This approach allows library users to search multiple silos from a single search box prominently displayed on the library homepage and then see all results on a single page, organized into sections according to format or type of resource. Our goal was to make it easier, even intuitive, for users to discover library resources; however, we knew we risked overwhelming users by combining results from a number of sources. To help guide us toward presenting search results in a way that was as easy to understand as possible, we sought extensive input from students through conversations in advisory board meetings, interviews with library student assistants, online surveys, and usability tests piloted and conducted with assistance from undergraduate and graduate students.

Because this change represented a dramatic shift in how we presented library resources, we knew it was important to gather input from students at every stage of development. We discussed paper and online prototypes of a unified search results page in semi-structured interviews and modified usability tests with student advisory board members, using their input to help guide decisions about how to present information on the results page. We then sought additional feedback on prototypes through one-on-one interviews with student assistants who routinely help users locate resources at the main library's service desk.

Over the course of this project, we conducted five usability tests so we could observe students interacting with the search interface, both while it was in development and after it was launched. Because these studies spanned a broad timeframe, we were able to test the assumptions we made as we constructed early prototypes and then assess the effectiveness of the live unified search results interface. These on-the-fly usability test sessions averaged five student participants each, and could be completed in around ninety minutes. Working from a table set up near the main library entrance, we randomly asked students entering the building—some frequent library users, others coming only to attend class or go to the library's coffee shop—to participate in a test in exchange for a snack or beverage from the coffee shop. AUX practicum students and undergraduate and graduate student assistants helped us design, pilot, and administer usability tests. These students helped us refine questions and tasks before each study, providing valuable insights into how their peers might engage with the search results interface and relate to the usability test methodology and script.

After we launched the unified search results page, we continued to seek feedback from students through other avenues. We had multiple discussions with advisory board members about how they used the search tool and results interface, and we conducted a short online survey that asked students what they liked best and least about the new search interface. Survey results, combined with web analytics of the search interface, affirmed some of our earlier decisions and supported findings from on-the-fly testing. Findings from these studies informed many of the iterative changes to the page, such as a streamlined presentation of search results and a "Top Result" that highlights resources and terms frequently searched for by students.

The frequency with which we sought input from undergraduates and graduate students, and the variety of methods we used, meant that students' voices and their approaches to research were a near constant presence shaping this project. Students were eager to assist throughout development, and library staff continue to value students' opinions as we make ongoing improvements to library search interfaces.

Improving Students' Experiences with Research Consultations

It is increasingly common for AUX staff to collaborate with staff in other departments to evaluate services aimed at meeting students' needs. For instance, AUX staff worked with Research and Instructional Services staff to assess the impact of research consultations on student learning and to develop best practices for future consultations. We began by speaking with student advisory board members about their experiences with research consultations and learned that many did not know they could schedule appointments with subject librarians; others became aware of the service late in their time at Duke and wished they had taken advantage of it earlier. With significant help from students, we developed and tested two anonymous surveys: one to be distributed to students immediately upon completion of a research consultation, and a second to be sent at the end of the semester to everyone who participated in a research consultation during the previous semester. Student advisory board members helped us word survey questions using language they understood and identified with. They were also instrumental in determining the ideal timeframe and incentive for the end-of-semester survey. Their advice likely contributed to the survey's high response rate.

Our goals for the two surveys were twofold: We hoped to understand how students learn about and perceive the consultation service, and we wanted to know the impact individual meetings with librarians have on student learning. The immediate survey took only a couple of minutes to complete. It identified whether this was the first time the student had taken part in a research consultation, whether they had ever seen a librarian in any of their classes to teach them about library research, how they found out research consultations were possible, and students' overall satisfaction level with the experience. In the end-of-semester survey, we assessed the impact of research consultations on student learning. We asked whether or not the sessions helped students feel more confident to do research for their papers or projects; what they learned from the sessions; what, if anything, students did differently as a result of the sessions; and how the process of requesting or scheduling a meeting could be improved.

We shared anonymous aggregated results from both surveys with librarians who conduct research consultations and worked with these subject specialists to respond to our findings. For instance, survey results indicated that students find the online form for scheduling a consultation with a librarian cumbersome, so we encouraged all subject librarians to use an online scheduling tool* that simplifies the scheduling process. We then explored ways to highlight the consultation service and new scheduling process on the libraries' website. Survey results also revealed that some students were unsure of what to expect when they scheduled an appointment with a librarian. As a result of this feedback, more librarians are now communicating with students in advance to ask preliminary questions and set expectations for their meeting. After discussing what we learned from student advisory board members and survey respondents with subject spe-

---

* We use the LibCal "My Scheduler" Tool, http://springshare.com/libcal/appt.html. See http://library.duke.edu/about/directory/staff/7241 for an example of a librarian profile that includes a link to schedule an appointment.

cialists, we distributed guidelines for conducting research consultations that are intended to make the experience more streamlined, consistent, and effective for students.

Sustaining Student-Led Innovation

Duke University Libraries has gradually but assuredly transitioned from an institution with no formalized comprehensive assessment program, and a culture that relied on anecdotal information, to an institution with a department dedicated to performing assessment, regularly gathering student feedback, and responding to users' needs. This change in approach has resulted in an increased capacity to plan comprehensively for library assessment and integrate student feedback, data analysis, and reporting into our work. We have found that this approach generates enthusiasm among students for new services and spaces in the libraries, and fosters a culture in which staff routinely seek students' feedback as they consider new initiatives or improve existing services. By relying on formal mechanisms and regular feedback channels to gather input from students, we have brought the undergraduate and graduate student body into the assessment lifecycle in a way that results in meaningful change.

We have learned a great deal in our efforts to solicit feedback from students and fold their suggestions into enhancing existing services and developing new programs. Years ago, there was a misconception at Duke Libraries that it was difficult to gather and use student feedback to guide decisions about library services and spaces, and staff instead prioritized faculty input. In recent years, we have effectively demonstrated that the barrier to soliciting input from students is lower than originally thought. Instead of being reactive to student needs, we are now proactive. We do not make wholesale changes to spaces, services, or the libraries website without first talking to students or observing student behavior.

There are advantages and drawbacks to each of the methods featured in our case studies. Guerrilla usability testing, or "on-the-fly" testing as we have come to call it in Duke Libraries, is fairly easy and requires relatively little time. By conducting short, focused tests and recruiting participants as they enter the library rather than scheduling sessions in advance, we are able to observe six to ten students use library interfaces or resources and then talk with them about their experiences. We are typically able to accomplish this work in under two hours and then translate what we watch our student participants do into recommendations for meaningful change. After we implement changes, we request additional feedback from students to ensure we have addressed their initial concerns. Drawbacks to usability testing are that test sessions typically reach fewer than ten students at a time. We attempt to overcome this shortcoming by conducting tests on a monthly basis. To simplify the testing process, we conduct all tests in the library, which means our participant groups are limited to those students who enter the building to attend class, visit the coffee shop, or use library services during times when we happen to be conducting usability sessions.

While usability tests are short, include only one student at a time, and target a particular task or service, focus groups provide an opportunity to talk to a small group of students simultaneously about a range of issues. In focus groups, we are able to delve deeply into topics, follow up on students' responses to questions, and gain insights from students who naturally build off their peers' comments in the group setting. Focus groups participants are always pre-scheduled, which means we are with students for a longer period of time, often about an hour. Like usability testing, focus groups reach a small percentage of our target population. Another drawback is that focus groups require more of our time, both to coordinate and for analysis and follow-up. It requires a considerable amount of effort to transcribe and analyze qualitative feedback from ten or more students speaking for an hour on numerous topics. Finally, because we are requesting more of students' time in exchange for this rich, qualitative feedback, we often feel compelled to provide an incentive. We have been successful, however, in recruiting focus group participants with no more than coffee and cookies, which helps keep costs relatively low.

Surveys are likely the easiest way to solicit feedback from the largest number of students. Unfortunately, it is extremely challenging to design survey questions that students understand fully and can respond to quickly with no mediation or follow-up conversation. For this reason, it can be difficult to interpret the meaning of survey findings. Additionally, students receive numerous survey invitations and tend to ignore those that do not relate directly to them, so we have found it necessary to offer an incentive in order to get responses from non-library users, thereby increasing costs. Surveys do, however, serve as a way to quickly and easily gather feedback from students who use the library and those who may not. We often use surveys as a starting point for other studies. Follow-up focus groups, interviews, or usability studies can provide opportunities to delve more deeply into the topics survey participants hint at or comment on in their responses.

Similar to usability studies, observational studies are entirely uninfluenced by students' opinions about what they do. Rather than asking students to describe their experiences or preferences—accounts that can sometimes be unreliable—we simply watch what they do in their natural environments. Observational studies require no incentives or related expenditures and are relatively easy to coordinate, as they do not require active participation from the students we observe. It can, however, be time intensive and challenging to collect data, especially if the goal is to get snapshots of what users do over the course of a full day. Depending on the tool used to collect observational data, it can be time consuming to analyze findings; we have surmounted this potential challenge by using Suma* to collect, analyze, and visualize data.

At Duke Libraries, we have been able to establish a dedicated AUX department with three staff members responsible for conducting user studies and making student-centered improvements to library spaces, services, and resources. We realize, however, that many libraries have limited resources for assessment and user experience initiatives and few, if any, staff to lead such efforts. Staff in such libraries might consider recruiting undergraduate or graduate students in library and information science or related fields. Recruiting practicum students interested in earning course credit or gaining experience observing user behavior and evaluating and enhancing services expands professional staff members' reach. Further, we have found that including student assistants in our departmental work infuses an important perspective and insights that only undergraduate and graduate students removed from the daily operations of the library can provide.

In addition to looking to our student assistants for direction, we rely heavily and frequently on members of our student advisory boards. In fact, these boards were born out of library staff members' needs for relatively low-cost, low-effort methods to check in periodically with students or to solicit students' feedback on a particular service or aspect of library op-

---

*Suma is an open-source software project developed by North Carolina State University libraries that enables staff to conduct observational studies on a tablet and analyze and visualize findings through a web-based reporting interface. See more at http://library .duke.edu/suma/analysis/reports/#/about.

erations. These groups of approximately fifteen students from a variety of majors and backgrounds meet at least three times per semester and are instrumental in guiding decisions about new services and spaces. We ask our advisory board members for feedback on a range of issues, from designing web interfaces and furnishing spaces in the library to helping us decide whether or not to pursue a new program. We frequently ask advisory board members to seek input from their friends and colleagues in an effort to hear from as many students as possible, and we regularly solicit input from members through email when we cannot wait until a meeting to make a decision. Members of our advisory boards repeatedly report feeling invested in these groups and grateful that the library requests and responds to their feedback. Many stay on the boards for the duration of their terms at Duke. Likewise, library administrators frequently request feedback from these groups before making decisions, and countless services and spaces—from names of study areas and types of furniture to locations of printers—reflect students' priorities and values.

We have learned that it is critical to solicit feedback from student assistants and members of the libraries' student advisory boards to provide direction early in the process of developing a new service or user study. Students are eager to weigh in on whether library staff should pursue a new service or expenditure, or whether staff time and financial resources would have greater impact elsewhere. For instance, Research and Instructional Services librarians had long considered developing a peer research support service for students. We shared the concept with our student advisory boards and assistants and heard that students would not find value in such a service. Rather than spend time developing a new program students told us they would not likely use, we abandoned the idea and focused instead on enhancing our research consultation service, which students indicated was more important to them than peer research support. By creating the advisory boards, we have opened a two-way channel of communication. Not only do we go to students for advice, students now have a more direct way to approach us with concerns and ideas—and they feel more comfortable doing so. We have come to see our advisory board members as ambassadors for the libraries, and they routinely tell their peers that library staff are open to student feedback and willing to make changes that reflect students' evolving needs.

Even with staff dedicated to seeking students' input in a systematic and programmatic way, we remain ever mindful of our goals: to gather as much feedback from as many students as possible on an ongoing basis and to make improvements to meet students' expressed needs. Whenever possible, we reduce or eliminate time and resources spent managing the logistics of a complex study in an effort to get significant feedback as quickly and easily as possible. For instance, we stopped performing traditional usability testing (i.e., pre-scheduled, lengthy sessions in a usability lab) and replaced it with a less resource-intensive methodology. This modified method allows us to focus our efforts on talking to and observing students engage with library interfaces, as we are no longer spending time and energy recruiting students through fliers and email and then scheduling hour-long usability sessions. We also find that reducing barriers such as formal usability labs and recording software helps put students at ease. And if students are comfortable, they are more likely to share insights that help us understand and respond to their needs more fully.

We have also discovered that it is essential to engage our colleagues in soliciting students' opinions and gathering information about their needs and behaviors. It is not possible to build or sustain a student-centered culture without buy-in and active participation from staff throughout the libraries. Our colleagues now routinely consider students' opinions and behaviors before embarking on new projects. They are keenly interested in collecting observational data, conducting usability tests, or leading focus groups with students who heavily use—or choose not to use—library resources.

The techniques and projects described above have generated significant enthusiasm among students for new services and spaces, and have helped foster a culture in which staff continuously seek feedback and work to improve all aspects of students' experiences with the libraries. Further, these methods have helped library staff make data-informed decisions before investing time and resources in developing new spaces, services, and online interfaces, resulting in innovative services that truly meet the needs of students and help them see Duke University Libraries as a vibrant and relevant center of research and learning.

Notes

1.   David Peter Simon, "The Art of Guerrilla Usability Testing," UX Booth, last modified July 2, 2013, http://www.uxbooth.com/articles/the-art-of-guerrilla-usability-testing.

2. "Duke University Libraries," Duke University Libraries, last modified May 11, 2016, http://library.duke.edu/.
3. Cory Lown, Tito Sierra, and Josh Boyer, "How Users Search the Library from a Single Search Box," *College & Research Libraries* 74, no. 3 (2013): 227–241, doi: 10.5860/crl-321.

Bibliography

Duke University Libraries. "Duke University Libraries." Last modified March 30, 2016. http://library.duke.edu/.

Lown, Cory, Tito Sierra, and Josh Boyer. "How Users Search the Library from a Single Search Box," College & Research Libraries 74 (May 2013): 227–241. doi:10.5860/crl-321.

Simon, David Peter. "The Art of Guerrilla Usability Testing." UX Booth. Last modified July 2, 2013. http://www.uxbooth.com/articles/the-art-of-guerrilla-usability-testing.

CHAPTER 16*

PIZZA FOR YOUR THOUGHTS:
Building a Vibrant Dialogue with Students through Informal Focus Groups

Kenneth J. Burhanna

Introduction

In fall 2012, three Kent State University librarians met with a group of eight undergraduate students in a conference room and shared a lunch of pizza and soda. They talked about what students liked and disliked about the libraries. Students shared their concerns. For example, some worried about security when leaving the University Library late at night. Students suggested new service designs: for example, why not have a help desk located at the library entrance? Students left the discussion more knowledgeable about the libraries and with a sense that the libraries valued their voices. Librarians left the discussion energized by the students' ideas and insights. They had discovered a valuable approach to learning about the needs and perceptions of students. Kent State University Libraries (KSUL) had held its first Pizza for Your Thoughts (PFYT) session, thus beginning an informal focus group program aimed at gathering feedback from students while teaching, promoting, and building social capital for the Libraries. This chapter will describe the PFYT program, including its genesis, management, and impact on library services and operations. Recommendations will also be shared for others considering similar programs.

Background and Literature Review

Kent State University is a large public university of more than 41,000 students at nine campuses located throughout Northeast Ohio. The fall 2015 enrollment at the Kent campus, where the program under consideration has been held, was 29,477, with undergraduates comprising about 80 percent. KSUL's PFYT program was motivated by a desire to begin a dialogue with students. They turned to an idea from Julia Zimmerman, dean of Florida State University Libraries, who experimented with pizza-incentivized feedback sessions earlier in her career, and shared the idea with Kent State University Libraries' dean Jim Bracken. When contacted in the fall of 2015 about the genesis of PFYT, Dean Zimmerman shared that pizza for your thoughts "…was my first (startling) realization that until we talked to students directly, creating a relaxed atmosphere in which they felt comfortable opening up, we really didn't know what was going on with them or how to best serve them."

"Pizza for Your Thoughts" is not a new concept. Many have turned to pizza as a classic incentive for young adult and student participants. A quick Internet search can find many examples of branded PFYT programs. Two higher education examples include PFYT sessions by the Elihu Burritt Library at Central Connecticut State University[1] (seeking feedback on their website) and the University of Missouri-Kansas City's Department of Sociology Club[2] (generating dialogue on current events and their sociological implications).

The use of focus groups to solicit in-depth, qualitative data about users' perceptions has become a popular methodology for librarians, among many other types of researchers.[3] Focus groups or focus group interviews offer advantages that may match the objectives of library leaders and be appropriate for library settings. Morgan and Krueger identify five key advantages.[4] The focus group method:

1. Provides a nonthreatening context for discussions between decision-makers (those in power) and library users (perceived to have less power).

2. Helps to close the gap between professionals (librarians) and their target audience (students in this case).
3. Is useful in exploring complex behavior and motivations (i.e., why students use certain library services as opposed to others).
4. Helps inform the degree of consensus on specific topics (i.e., library weekend hours).
5. Creates meaningful dialogue and builds respect among participants.

These advantages work to empower participant students, building trust and confidence in the library organization. This is particularly helpful in the case of PFYT, as the program aims to do more than generate feedback. It also seeks to educate, promote, and build social capital. In practical terms, focus groups are usually more efficient than other qualitative approaches, as feedback can be generated from multiple participants at once.[5] They are also cheap and quick.[6]

Focus group methods present some challenges, too. Focus groups require a moderator with some level of skill.[7] They are not a good setting for the exploration of sensitive issues.[8] They also tend to produce conformity, which raises concerns about consensus determinations generated through focus group discussions.[9] Consequently, focus group feedback and analysis provide data points and topics of interest, which may merit additional exploration and should not usually be treated as definitive evidence that one action, policy, or program should be implemented or changed.

Informal focus groups, sometimes called field or natural focus groups, differ from formal focus groups in several important ways, but ultimately these differences can be thought of as defining a continuum of degree by which focus groups can be highly informal, highly formal, or somewhere in between.[10] Figure 16.1 below depicts this continuum.

Highly Informal Focus Group	Highly Formal Focus Group
Timing not predetermined	Timing carefully planned
Setting in natural environment	Setting planned and controlled
Group size not predetermined	Group size is controlled, limited
Respondents self-select	Respondents pre-selected
Few predetermined questions	Most questions predetermined
May or may not use incentives	Incentives always used
Researcher may have prior relationship with participants	Researcher has no relationship with participants

Figure 16.1. Informal–Formal Focus Group continuum.

The literature has little to say about informal focus groups, but it is likely that most focus group methods discussed in scholarly papers lean toward the formal side of the continuum. It is possible that informal focus groups are absent from the literature due to their informal nature, meaning that the results of these explorations are used anecdotally and are not chronicled by researchers. KSUL's PFYT program is closer to the informal side of the continuum. While the timing of the sessions is predetermined, most other elements are informal.

Another approach that libraries have taken to create a dialogue with students are library student advisory boards.[11] Student advisory boards can be effective sources of feedback and input on libraries, but they differ in ways that make the organization less objective and often more political. Student advisory boards are student groups formally connected to their libraries. For this reason, they can have their own agendas and begin to "create" their own views on the library in relation to what they want to accomplish. Student advisory boards sometimes implement services or raise money. KSUL desired a more nimble, informal approach to speaking with students. The feedback from student advisory boards may also offer less variety. Student advisory board rosters change once a year or less in general. PFYT's self-selected participation offers new perspectives with each session.

Program Description

KSUL did not plan the first PFYT as an ongoing program, but all of the components of the program were evident in that first session. These include target audience, marketing, timing, location, incentives, facilitation, note taking, and staffing. In the following sections, each of these program components will be discussed in more detail.

Target Audience
PFYT has targeted students since its start. Figure 16.2 displays the cumulative participation numbers for PFYT, including the distribution by student status. Not surprisingly, the majority of participants are undergraduates. On occasion, KSUL has targeted specific students. Early on, PFYT sessions were held in three branch libraries, targeting the student users of those locations. Also, KSUL has collaborated with Graduate Studies to hold two sessions for graduate students.

	Participants
Undergraduates	353
Graduates	42
Faculty/Staff (external to library)	3
Total Participants	398

Figure 16.2. Pizza for Your Thoughts cumulative participation.

Marketing

KSUL began marketing PFYT by making a public address announcement, followed by a few librarians walking the lobby and halls, encouraging students to join them for free pizza. Later, display ads on the website and listings on the libraries' online event calendar were used. One of the most effective strategies for marketing has been to partner with other units on campus and ask them to recruit their students for PFYT, as KSUL did with Graduate Studies. Over time, word-of-mouth has also helped: as students have participated, they have told their friends about the program. PFYT has also been promoted regularly at other KSUL student events.

Timing and Location

Timing of sessions has not changed in any substantial way since the start of the program. Though KSUL has discussed offering evening or morning sessions, we have yet to do so. All PFYT sessions have occurred at noon, usually on Wednesdays. Location, however, has changed a great deal. Figure 16.3 lists all PFYT sessions by date, topic, and location. Three main location types have been used for the program: conference rooms, open seating areas (i.e., Wick Poetry Corner), and classrooms. KSUL has experimented with location in order to identify one that is easy-to-find, comfortable, and offers privacy.

Incentives

Clearly, food has been used as the main incentive for participants. By the second session, KSUL had settled on a standard menu of pizza, salad, soda, and water. The bill per session has averaged $170. Early on, a second incentive was added in the form of FLASHperks—a program for Kent State students that rewards them for attending and participating in campus events.

Date	Location	Topic
Sep 2012	Conference Room	Open
Oct 2012	Map Library	Map Library
Nov 2012	Performing Arts Library	PAL
Jan 2013	Poetry Corner	Library Seating
Mar 2013	Architecture Library	Arch Library
Apr 2013	Poetry Corner	Open
Sep 2013	Poetry Corner	Open
Oct 2013	Classroom	Reference Website
Nov 2013	Poetry Corner	Student Success
Feb 2014	Poetry Corner	Special Collections
Apr 2014	4th Floor UL	Discovery Layer
Sep 2014	Poetry Corner	Open
Oct 2014	Poetry Corner	Open
Nov 2014	Poetry Corner	Open
Jan 2015	Conference Room	Open
Jan 2015	Conference Room	Open
Feb 2015	Poetry Corner	Open
Mar 2015	Poetry Corner	Open
Apr 2015	Poetry Corner	Open
Sep 2015	Classroom	Open
Oct 2015	Classroom	Open
Nov 2015	Classroom	Open

Figure 16.3. Pizza for Your Thoughts sessions by date, location, and topic.

Facilitation

Dean Bracken has served as lead facilitator in most of the sessions. An assistant dean and the user experience librarian have usually served as additional co-facilitators. Facilitation has proved to be one of the most important and challenging aspects of PFYT. Because the program has multiple objectives—to generate feedback, educate students, promote the libraries, and build trust—facilitators must wear multiple hats. For example, a facilitator must be able to switch gears from instructing (answering a student question about subject librarians) to promoting (Meet with a Librarian service) back to soliciting feedback without presenting leading questions. KSUL facilitators have found it helpful to remind themselves that students are supposed to speak more than they do.

Facilitation also depends on the session topic. As Figure 16.3 shows, some PFYT sessions have focused on specific topics, such as feedback on a new discovery layer tool, while other sessions have been open. Even in sessions focused on topics, facilitators followed a very informal structure in leading sessions. Typically, all sessions followed this structure:

1. Welcome
2. Rapport setting / small talk
3. Student introductions (if group smaller than twelve)
4. Facilitator states purpose of session
5. Facilitator begins with open-ended questions
6. Dialogue emerges naturally
7 Students are given opportunity to ask questions
8. Wrap up and thank you.

Note Taking and Staffing

Initially, facilitators took notes during the sessions, but this proved unwieldy. By the third session, the dean's assistant had taken over these responsibilities. The notes are shared with library staff through email. The dean's assistant also takes care of scheduling the sessions, reserving the space, ordering the food, and managing student workers, who help with set up and cleanup activities. Over time, the staffing commitment has become streamlined as the program has become a regular event. Recently, members of the libraries' statistical consulting unit have begun attending PFYT sessions to take additional notes. This has added a new layer of detail to analysis, helping to draw out themes and recommend areas for program improvement.[12]

Observations, Results, and Informed Actions

Observations

Participation in the PFYT program has been strong, averaging about nineteen students per session. Figure 16.4 shows PFYT participation by session. Early sessions had very low attendance, and then later, as more students became aware of the program, sessions had as many as forty-one attendees. KSUL librarians have found the most manageable group size to be twenty or fewer.

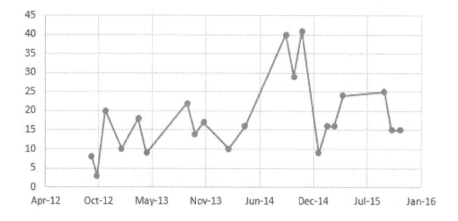

Figure 16.4. Pizza for Your Thoughts participation by session.

In general, PFYT draws a new set of students for each session, but some "regular" attendees have emerged. Facilitators routinely acknowledge these returning participants and remind them that in return for lunch KSUL expects them to share their views. These regular participants have proved to be beneficial, as they start conversations and help other students feel at ease. "Grab and dash" participants have also emerged. These students take food and attempt to leave the session location. Early on these students were not stopped, but in recent sessions, facilitators remind students upon arrival that the food is for PFYT participants. This reminder along with a controlled location have begun to limit this type of participant.

Results

Though the PFYT data is largely anecdotal and often contradictory, it represents an engaged dialogue full of questions, suggestions, praise and complaints. What follows is a summary of this data organized around five guiding questions.

1. What Brings Students to the Library?

Facilitators ask this question several different ways throughout the sessions. Why are you here today? Why do you come to the library? What brings you to the library? Figure 16.5 lists responses to this question that have appeared more than once. What is notable about these responses is that they are extremely diverse. They are listed in Figure 16.5 in alphabetical order, but printing, tutoring, and studying were the reasons most often given for coming to the library. These findings confirm the libraries' role as student success hub, providing access to a variety of services from the libraries (collections, reserves, reference) and other partners (the Information Services' help desk, Academic Success Center tutoring, and the English Department's Writing Commons).

Responses with Multiple Occurrences (Alphabetical Order)
Books
Big tables
Classes (Some classes are held in University Library)
Coffee
Computers
Group study areas
Late night hours
Myself (I love libraries)
Proximity to multiple forms of help
Pizza for Your Thoughts sessions
Printing
Private/Quiet study
Reserves services
Research
Research help
Specialized software / Student Multimedia Studio
Tech help
Tutoring
Whiteboards
Writing Commons/Writing tutoring

Figure 16.5. What Brings Students to the Library?

2. *What Students Don't Know?*

This question focuses on student awareness of library services and resources. Discussions around this question have been empowering in two ways. First, the discussion provides an educational and promotional opportunity. For every student who doesn't know about a service or resource, often another student does, and then a conversation across participants sometimes occurs when students teach each other. This is also an opportunity for library staff to teach and promote on the spot, which happens often during sessions. Second, the answers inform service, programming, and library promotional efforts. Figure 16.6 lists responses to this question that have appeared more than once. In particular, KSUL librarians have noted the students' lack of awareness about subject librarians and have begun to experiment with new engagement approaches, such as a personal librarian program.

Responses with Multiple Occurrences (Alphabetical Order)
3D printing
Book
Branch libraries
Campus book delivery
Generally how to use the library
Interlibrary loan
Laptop checkout
Library events
Research consultations / Meet with a Librarian
Reserve services
Special Collections
Subject librarians
Textbooks on reserve
Video camera checkout

Figure 16.6. What Students Don't Know?

3. What Students Don't Like?

Students show little hesitation in sharing complaints. Likely this indicates that the sessions have provided an open and safe venue to be critical. Figure 16.6 lists the complaints that have been mentioned multiple times. Among these, three complaints have been heard most often: printing, access to power, and library cleanliness. Kent State University charges for printing in the libraries and computer labs. This raises concerns about cost, access, and instructional design. Lack of access to power outlets has been a repeated complaint. The University Library was built in 1970, and the lack of sufficient power is among its several shortcomings. Students have expressed concerns about Library cleanliness many times, and in response, KSUL has added garbage cans, made cleaning wipes available, and hired additional daytime housekeeping services.

Responses with Multiple Occurrences (Alphabetical Order)	Informed Action?
Book delivery: it's too slow	
Cleanliness: bathrooms, computers, tables, hallways, floors are dirty	Yes
Computers: not enough of them	Yes
Elevators: too slow and noisy	
Group study: need more rooms	
Library hours: longer on Saturday, earlier on Sunday	
Library orientation: needs improved for new students	Yes
Power outlets: not enough of them	
Printing: costs too much	Yes
Printing: it's not wireless	Yes
Printing: unclear instructions	Yes
Private study: need more rooms	
Quiet study: it's not quiet	Yes
Research assistance: not enough help available	
Tutoring: not offered for enough courses	
Tutoring: hours too limited on weekends	

Figure 16.7. What Students Don't Like?

4. What Students Like?

Students also share what they like about the libraries, and PFYT facilitators have been happy to learn that students have found a lot to like. One student summed it up this way: "Everything is pretty rock and roll in the library!" Figure 16.8 lists the most common compliments. Most gratifying is that several of them reference actions the libraries have taken that have been informed by earlier PFYT feedback. This is also indicated in Figure 16.8. These compliments let KSUL know that PFYT is a productive program and communicates to colleagues what is working well in the libraries.

Responses with Multiple Occurrences (Alphabetical Order)	Informed by PFYT Feedback?
Big tables	
Charging stations	Yes
Disinfecting wipes	Yes
Exercise bikes	Yes
Fab Fourth / Fourth floor of University Library	Yes
Hand sanitizing stations	
Laptop checkout	Yes

Library tutorials	
Kent Reads / library lecture series	
Quiet study spaces and rooms	
Reserve services	
Scan to email for free	
Sense of safety in the building	
Sense of camaraderie while studying	
Spill kits / caddies with cleaning supplies on library floors	Yes
Stress free zone events during finals weeks	
Student Multimedia Studio	
Water fountains	
Walkstation / Treadmill	Yes
Writing Commons / Writing tutoring	

Figure 16.8. What Students Like?

5. What Students Suggest?

Every PFYT session provides an opportunity for students to make suggestions. This has been the richest area of feedback. The sessions have produced hundreds of suggestions. A general content analysis of these suggestions shows that they fall into seven areas: equipment, events, food, instructors, promotion, resources, and textbooks. Figure 16.9 shows some of the more interesting student suggestions organized by topics. Despite the volume of suggestions, KSUL has considered and adopted several of them. The suggestions related to equipment, for example, have proved to be fairly affordable and easy to implement. Figure 16.8 also indicates which sessions have informed KSUL decision making.

Theme	Suggestion	Informed Action?
Equipment/ Facilities	Add storage lockers	Yes
	Add exercise equipment	Yes
	Provide handheld whiteboards	Yes
	Provide laptops for checkout	Yes
	Increase number of garbage cans	Yes
	Make cleaning wipes available	Yes

Theme	Suggestion	Informed Action?
Events/ Programs	Hold a sleepover in the library	Yes
	Offer yoga during Stress Free events	
	Offer free massages during Stress Free	
	Have a movie night in the library	
	Hold a gaming night in the library	
	Hold a Nerf gun battle in the library	
	Show sports events in the library	Yes
Food/ Beverage	Provide coffee after midnight	Yes
	Provide microwaves	Yes
	Accept food plan in the library	
	Put real food in vending machines, not just candy	
Instructors	Ask them to list subject librarians on their syllabi	
	Ask them to accept online assignments	
Promotion	Provide bigger, better signage in library lobby.	Yes
	Create large sign on outside of library	
	Work with resident assistants (RAs) to help promote the library	
	Invest in social media	Yes
Resources	Add service point in the lobby entrances	Yes
	Provide free printing in return for library event participation	
	Create library mobile app for basic functions and alerting	
	Have subject librarians listed on student online accounts (called FLASHLINE)	
	Create a nap area with blankets to be checked out	
Textbooks	Allow students to donate textbooks to the library	
	Create a textbook exchange program	
	In general buy more textbooks	Yes

Figure 16.9. What Students Suggest?

Informed Actions

As Figures 16.7, 16.8, and 16.9 indicate, feedback and suggestions from PFYT have informed several library decisions. In most cases, these actions should be considered guided actions, as KSUL has not acted on these points of feedback in isolation, but has taken them into account along with other factors and contextual issues as part of their decision-making process. In an effort to be illustrative, rather than exhaustive, three guided actions are briefly discussed below to add depth to how PFYT feedback and dialogues have informed KSUL.

Ask Me Desk

When KSUL began holding PFYT sessions in the fall of 2012, they had already been experimenting with providing service for students in the lobby of the University Library right when they entered the building. Student workers armed with an iPad were positioned during busy times in the lobby. This experiment was a lukewarm success, as entering students couldn't understand why the students with an iPad were there. This approach was eventually discarded, but the idea of a highly visible service point was still being discussed, now as an "Ask Me Desk." With this is mind, Dean Bracken asked students at early PFYT sessions about their experiences upon entering the building and where they went for help. Students universally supported the idea of a designated desk for questions, visible as soon as they entered. One student stated, "Librarians should be the first thing you see when you walk through the doors, not the escalator (an escalator is centrally located in the lobby). You don't immediately see someone to ask a question (as it is now)." The PFYT facilitator followed by asking if improved signs would help? A student said, "One person was more helpful than a bunch of signs."

These conversations fired new internal conversations about an Ask Me Desk, and by the following fall such a desk was in place and being staffed forty hours a week. The Ask Me Desk has proved to be a great success, not only serving its purpose as an easily accessible service point, but has also brought visibility to the libraries. The university president and other cabinet-level administrators walk through the lobby frequently and have expressed gratitude and fondness for the new service point.

Discovery Layer

A PFYT session was dedicated to exploring assumptions around the implementation of a discovery layer service at KSUL in spring 2014. The discovery layer working team facilitated the meeting. They projected a functioning prototype of the interface for students to review and had a conversation with them about searching for library resources. The discussion was fruitful. Students in attendance generally preferred a single interface for search, as opposed to visiting multiple interfaces. They immediately connected the single-interface concept with Google. Most said that they normally went to Google first to see what they found before turning to the library. More advanced students indicated that they would still search specific databases, but that the discovery interface was helpful for starting a search. The discover layer working team took the session's feedback into consideration and moved forward toward the successful completion of their project. The session confirmed what many believed, and changed the disposition of some team members, previously opposed to a discovery search interface.

Library Cleanliness

Early PFYT sessions produced a great deal of feedback related to the lack of cleanliness in the University Library. The bathrooms, the stairways, the table tops, and the computer keyboards were described as being dirty or shabby. Students implored KSUL to provide more garbage cans. One student summed it up, saying, "The library is beautiful, but it is dirty." KSUL had struggled for years to put in place sufficient housekeeping services to keep the University Library clean. It wasn't that they didn't value this quality to the degree that students did. It was a matter of finding the right solution. During a discussion about library cleanliness, a student suddenly said, "If you put out wipes, I'll just cleanup for myself."

"Would that work?" asked the facilitator. The students all agreed. Within a matter of days KSUL had placed containers of disinfectant wipes and more garbage receptacles throughout the building. KSUL also began to send small patrols of student workers out on daily cleanup duty. They added a daytime student housekeeper. Later, based on feedback from a new building observation program, spill kits were placed on each floor under signage asking students to help keep the library clean. Spill kits include wipes, paper towels, and cleaning spray. Because students communicated how important clean facilities were to them, and were willing to contribute themselves, they inspired library leadership to think creatively and to invest resources.

Recommendations

Based on their experiences with the PFYT program, KSUL librarians have recommendations for others who wish to engage students in feedback discussions. What follows are thirteen suggestions for avoiding problems that KSUL experienced or for building on the PFYT approach.

1. **Develop a set of ground rules.** Though PFYT is an informal program, formal ground rules should be shared with participants in writing at the start of sessions. KSUL shared ground rules verbally without a script. This resulted in inconsistent ground rules for participants. Suggested ground rules include the following: *We value your candor and ideas. Sharing your name is optional and not required. Please raise your hand if you have something to say. You may stand to get more food at any time. This is an informal, relaxed session. You may leave at any point. Above all we thank you for your time.*

2. **Develop guidelines for facilitators.** One of KSUL's challenges has been how to facilitate a balanced dialogue. Facilitators admit at times to asking leading questions or talking more than listening. A list of guidelines that can be reviewed before each PFYT session can help avoid these pitfalls. A good set of facilitator guidelines should remind facilitators to: speak to inquire and educate; set their assumptions aside; invite those not speaking to share; ask open-ended questions; limit comments to a few minutes (don't let one voice dominate the conversation); maintain a patient pace (students are eating and talking); use leading questions to start a dialogue, not finish one; thank students for their participation.

3. **Use a pre-session questionnaire.** KSUL experimented with questionnaires in some PFYT sessions to gather additional data from participants. Questionnaires should be designed to align with discussion questions. In some cases, the questionnaire and subsequent session discussion were not related, which confused participants. The questionnaire should preface the discussion, gather general demographics, and help get the participants thinking about the discussion to follow.[13]

4. **Create a template to standardize data collection.** The template should record date, time, location, names of staff attendees, student demographics from questionnaires, plus the notes and ques-

tionnaire responses themselves. Care should be taken to format data and transcripts so that they can easily be analyzed with software like SPSS (quantitatively) and NVivo (qualitatively).[14] Lacking a template, KSUL data collection was inconsistent.

5. **Take care in selecting a location.** The best location is easily found by participants, offers comfortable seating and tables, and provides a modicum of privacy. KSUL found that an active-learning classroom provided the best balance of these qualities. The classroom door also provided great benefit, as it was easy to control group size by monitoring a single door.

6. **Keep your participant group size at twenty or fewer.** KSUL had PFYT sessions with as many as forty-one students. This was too large. Groups larger than twenty become unproductive, as many students will not have an opportunity to talk, the food will go quickly, and time will be spent on managing the size of the group. The most effective way to manage group size has been to select a location that comfortably holds the ideal number of participants and has a door that can be used to control entry after capacity has been met.

7. **Check with food vendors for donations.** KSUL had the good fortune of having a local pizza shop donate pizzas for many of the sessions in return for sharing their promotional materials. You might work with campus dining services to explore options for food donations in return for student feedback.

8. **Consider working with vendors for potential session topics.** KSUL invited a furniture vendor to one PFYT session that focused on new seating options. The vendor brought several sample chairs. Students tried them out and provided feedback. This approach could be tried with new information resources, interfaces, and other new technologies.

9. **Engage library staff in sessions.** A powerful outcome of PFYT has been how it helped develop metacognition about the libraries for library staff. It was pointed out earlier in this chapter that focus groups can help close the gap between users and professionals. The notes from PFYT sessions are shared throughout KSUL and staff are encouraged to review and discuss them. Even more powerful has been the opportunity for staff to sit in and sometimes partic-

ipate in PFYT sessions. This allows them to test assumptions and hear from users about what they think and do. It also encourages staff to revise how they speak about and describe the library, as the student in front of them says something like, "When I hear the word circulation, all I think about is the system within the human body that moves blood."

10. **Prepare for staff pushback.** While PFYT can engage staff and help them think about the library in new ways, some staff will likely not engage and push back at the idea of "naive" students weighing in on library resources and services. Patience is suggested in these cases. Staff with this point of view are likely over-estimating the role PFYT feedback plays in library decision-making. Care can also be taken in how PFYT is communicated to staff. The informal nature of the program should be stressed, and staff should be reminded that PFYT feedback *contributes* to the libraries' thinking and does not *direct* that thinking. Program facilitators should reach out to those who push back, offer to answer their questions and invite them to attend future PFYT sessions.

11. **Collaborate for student recruitment.** KSUL had success in collaborating with Graduate Studies to recruit students for PFYT sessions. This approach could be taken with student groups, specific majors, or with international students.

12. **Consider targeting faculty, staff, or community members with similar programs.** KSUL has tried a version of PFYT with faculty called "Coffee with the Libraries," with limited success. But the general premise of coupling refreshments with a friendly conversation can make connections and gain insights from a variety of constituencies. Variations on the PFYT approach could include event-specific conversations. For example, on the morning of homecoming, KSUL offers cider, coffee, and doughnuts in the lobby of the University Library. Each person or family that walks through and enjoys refreshments presents a new opportunity for an informal conversation, a friendly impression, and additional feedback about the libraries.

13. **Consider related research studies.** First consider seeking Institutional Review Board (IRB) approval of sessions in order to collect identifiable data. To this point, KSUL has not captured identifiable

data, aside from asking informally for student status. With IRB approval in place, a detailed demographics section could be added to the session questionnaires. Second, consider the possibility of follow-up studies with PFYT participants to answer questions like: What does PFYT teach students? How does it raise awareness for the libraries? Does PFYT help build student trust in the libraries?

As has been mentioned more than once, PFYT is an informal program. Its data is highly subjective and anecdotal. Session structure has been varied and inconsistent. The facilitators have not followed formal guidelines, and, admittedly, at times have asked leading questions. While the researcher might view these as limitations, the practitioner should consider them novelty drivers, ensuring that the program remains fresh and original. No two PFTY sessions are the same. The value of PFYT is not found in the reliability or validity of its findings, but in the dialogue that it builds, and the reflection and subsequent actions that result. The PFYT program represents a growing dialogue. KSUL plans to continue PFYT into the foreseeable future with hopes of continuing this valuable lunchtime dialogue.

Notes

1. Sharon Clapp, "Pizza for Your Thoughts," *Burritt Library Blog, Central Connecticut State University*, April 22, 2015, http://library.ccsu.edu/wp/2015/04/22/pizza-for-your -thoughts/.
2. "Pizza for Your Thoughts?" *Department of Sociology Blog, University of Missouri-Kansas City*, April 3, 2015, http://info.umkc.edu/sociology/2015/04/02/pizza-for-your -thoughts-friday-april-3-2015/.
3. Graham R. Walden, "Informing Library Research with Focus Groups," *Library Management* 35, no.8/9 (2014):558, doi:10.1108/LM-02-2014-0023; Melissa L. Becher and Janice L. Flug, "Using Student Focus Groups to Inform Library Planning and Marketing," *College & Undergraduate Libraries* 12, no. 1 (2005): 3–5, doi: 10.1300/ J106v12n01-01; Gwyneth H. Crowley et al., "User Perceptions of the Library's Web Pages: A Focus Group Study at Texas A&M University," *The Journal of Academic Librarianship* 28, (2002): 205–206, doi: 10.1016/S0099.
4. David L. Morgan and Richard A. Krueger, "When to Use Focus Groups and Why," in *Successful Focus Groups: Advancing the State of the Art*, ed. David L. Morgan (Newbury Park, CA: Sage Publications, 1993), 15–18.
5. James H. Frey and Andrea Fontana, "The Group Interview in Social Research," in *Successful Focus Groups: Advancing the State of the Art*, ed. David L. Morgan (Newbury Park, CA: Sage Publications, 1993): 32.
6. Morgan and Krueger, "When to Use Focus Groups and Why," 4.
7. Ibid., 5.
8. Ibid., 6.

9. Ibid., 7–8.
10. Frey and Fontana, "The Group Interview in Social Research," 33–34.
11. Amy L. Deuink and Marianne Seiler, "Introduction" in *The Library Student Advisory Board* (Jefferson, NC: McFarland & Company, 2009): 5–6.
12. Kristin Yeager, Meghan Novisky, and Subir Goyal, "Pizza for Your Thoughts Summary, Fall 2015 Semester," Internal report, Kent State University Libraries, December 18, 2015): 1–7.
13. Yeager, Novisky, and Goyal, "Pizza for Your Thoughts Summary," 7.
14. Ibid.

Bibliography

Becher, Melissa L. and Janice L. Flug. "Using Student Focus Groups to Inform Library Planning and Marketing." *College & Undergraduate Libraries* 12, no. 1 (June 2005): 1–18. doi: 10.1300/J106v12n01-01.

Crowley, Gwyneth H., Rob Leffel, Diana Ramirez, Judith L. Hart, and Tommy S. Armstrong II. "User Perceptions of the Library's Web Pages: A Focus Group Study at Texas A&M University." *The Journal of Academic Librarianship* 28, (2002): 205–210. doi: 10.1016S0099-1333(02)00284-7.

Deuink, Amy L. and Marianne Seiler. "Introduction." In *The Library Student Advisory Board*. Jefferson, NC: McFarland & Company, 2009.

Frey, James H., and Andrea Fontana. "The Group Interview in Social Research." In *Successful Focus Groups: Advancing the State of the Art*, edited by David L. Morgan, 20–34. Newbury Park, CA: Sage Publications, 1993.

Morgan, David L., and Richard A. Krueger. "When to Use Focus Groups and Why." In *Successful Focus Groups: Advancing the State of the Art*, edited by David L. Morgan, 3–19. Newbury Park, CA: Sage Publications, 1993.Walden, Graham R. "Informing Library Research with Focus Groups." *Library Management* 35, no. 8/9 (2014): 558. doi:10.1108/LM-02-2014-0023.

Yeager, Kristin, Meghan Novisky, and Subir Goyal. "Pizza for Your Thoughts Summary, Fall 2015 Semester." Internal report, Kent State University Libraries, December 18, 2015.